HOW THE PILL CHANGES EVERYTHING

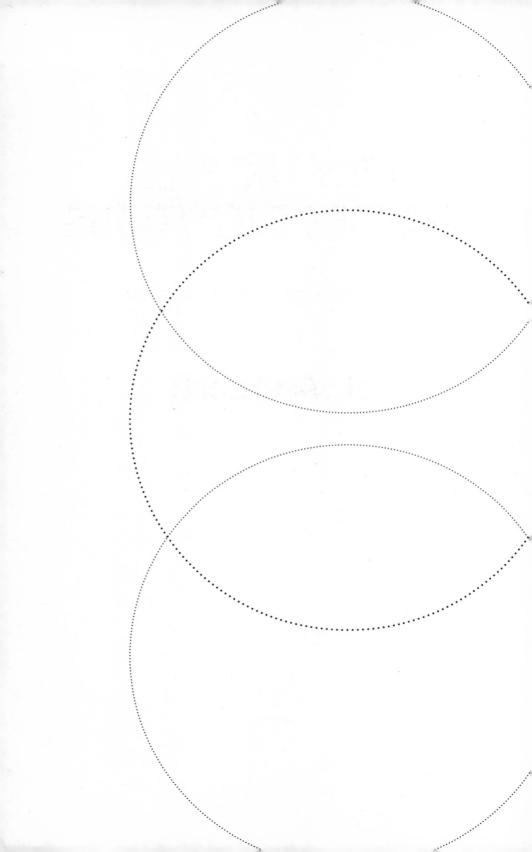

HOW THE PILL CHANGES EVERYTHING

Your Brain on Birth Control

DR SARAH E. HILL

First published in the United States in 2019 by Avery, an imprint of
Penguin Random House LLC

First published in Great Britain in 2019 by Orion Spring
an imprint of The Orion Publishing Group Ltd
Carmelite House, 50 Victoria Embankment
London EC4Y 0DZ

An Hachette UK Company

5 7 9 10 8 6

A CIP catalogue record for this book is
available from the British Library.

ISBN (Trade Paperback) 978 1 4091 7883 5
ISBN (eBook) 978 1 4091 7885 9

Printed and bound in Great Britain by Clays Ltd, Elcograf S.p.A

www.orionbooks.co.uk

FOR **YOU**

CONTENTS

Part III—The Big Picture

HOW THE PILL CHANGES EVERYTHING

INTRODUCTION

Let me start this off by saying that I don't have an agenda.

Well, maybe that's disingenuous. Nobody writes a book without an agenda. So I guess I probably have one, but it might not be the one you thought I had when you picked up a book about your brain and the birth control pill. This isn't the kind of book where I tell you a bunch of horrible, alarming facts about the pill and try to convince you that the pill has messed up your brain in at least 763 different ways, none of which are reversible. It's also not going to be the kind of book where I tell you that you shouldn't be on the pill or strongly hint that if you stay on it, you'll pay for this ill-advised life choice by developing cancer, experiencing long-term memory loss, or growing a tail.

This isn't going to be one of those books.

I spent more than a decade of my life on the pill, and I'm pretty sure that I'm better off for having been on it. During that time, I was able to graduate summa cum laude from college (nerd!) and go on to get a PhD from one of the most competitive psychology programs in the country (double nerd!). Although not everyone would want to spend their late teens and early twenties subjecting themselves to this sort of educational masochism, I did. And the pill helped me do these things without having to worry about the possibility of getting benched because of a pregnancy I wasn't ready for. By freeing me from the reproductive consequences of sex, the pill played a huge role in helping me earn the highest degree in my field, build a productive research lab, and have my two children once I felt ready. I am hugely grateful for the opportunity to do all these things, and I'm pretty sure that I would have had a much harder time with all of them if it hadn't been for the pill. I'm not writing this book to try to talk you out of taking the same pill that granted me the opportunity to be in the position to write a book in the first place. This isn't that book.

But this isn't going to be the other kind of book you might expect it to be, either. I'm not going to recount for you a one-sided love story about women and the pill riding off into the sunset and living happily ever after, which is the other agenda you might expect from a book like this. Although the pill has done a number of amazing things for women, as you will soon see, these wonderful things come at a cost. Some of the costs are pretty significant, too. And the thing that's troubling about them is that most women have no idea that they're paying them.

I know I sure didn't.

You see, rather than being something that happens *to* you, your hormones are a key part of what makes you, you. You quite literally *are* your hormones. And when you change your hormones—which is what hormonal contraceptives do—you change the version of yourself that your brain creates. Because of this, the pill's reach goes far beyond the small number of targeted effects we take it for. It affects everything. And there's a growing body of research in psychology and neuroscience that shows this to be true. You just haven't been told about it until now. And once you learn everything I've learned, I think you'll agree that there's a good chance that we'll look back at our era one hundred years from now and be shocked that we were so cavalier with women's hormones.

Although the science looking at how the pill changes women is still in its infancy, we know enough to help you make informed decisions. First, you'll need to understand a few things about how your brain works and the role your hormones play in making you who you are. Then you'll need to understand what the research says about how all this changes when you're on the pill. The former has been the focus of my research for more than fifteen years as an evolutionary psychologist who studies women and health. The latter is something that I discovered only recently, after a series of three unrelated events led me to begin my scientific journey into the world of women's brains on the birth control pill. In many ways, this journey has turned out to be the story of my young-adult life.

It may be your story, too.

THE THREE UNRELATED EVENTS

Like most good adventures, my journey into the world of the brain on birth control began in an unremarkable way, without realization that something important was about to happen. It all started when I went off the pill, a decision I made in a non-grand fashion. I knew that I was done having children, so my husband and I opted for a more permanent solution to pregnancy prevention. Since he was man enough to take the lead on that one, I was able to ditch the pill without thinking too much of it.

Now, to give you a bit of background, at this point I'd been on the pill pretty consistently for a little more than a decade. I'd gone off it here and there, but never for very long. I went off it to get pregnant, and I stayed off it for a year after each pregnancy to breastfeed. However, I can hardly count these experiences as being a representative sample of a normal psychological state for myself, since they were either very brief (pre-pregnancy) or clouded by a disorienting cocktail of sleep deprivation and post-pregnancy hormones (breastfeeding). Nonetheless, I wasn't expecting my world to change in any noticeable way based on my decision to go off the pill. I thought its consequences wouldn't extend beyond my ability to release an egg every month.

This turned out to be a miscalculation.

A couple of months after going off the pill, I realized that I felt . . . *different*. I didn't notice it while it was happening, but one day I realized that my life had recently felt brighter and more interesting. Like I had walked out of a two-dimensional, black-and-white movie into a full-color, three-dimensional, *meaning*-filled reality. I started exercising again and cooking—things that I used to take a lot of pleasure in but had kind of forgotten about. I had more energy. I noticed attractive men. I cared about how I looked in a way that I hadn't in a long time. I just felt . . . alive. Like, fully, vividly, awesomely, humanly alive. This didn't happen all at once. I didn't realize that any of these changes were happening until after they had happened. I just one day realized that I felt awake from an almost ten-year nap I hadn't known I was taking.

As I reflected on all these changes in myself, I did the thing that women have learned to do in such situations: I wrote them off as being "all in my head."* I figured that going off the pill probably had something to do with it, but it seemed too sci-fi to think that my birth control pills would make me feel like I'd had a personality transplant. I figured that this was just another one of those weird things that happens to me, but doesn't happen to anyone else. Or that maybe it was a by-product of reaching my thirties or the result of my getting more exercise. I filed my experiences away in the "weird sh** that happens to Sarah when she starts or stops a medication" drawer in my brain and moved on with my life.

This was event number one.†

Flash forward a year or so, and you will find me standing in an elevator with a good friend of mine at a psychology conference. We were busy catching up and talking about research when she asked me whether I'd read a cool new paper that had come out about the pill and women's romantic and sexual relationships. I hadn't read it, so she proceeded to tell

....

* Which is a pretty stupid statement when you think about it. Your brain is in your head, and it is the command center for *everything* else in your body. So, of course, everything is in your head.

† Now, the scientist in me feels obliged to tell you that I have no way of knowing for certain that these changes I experienced were caused by going off the pill (I didn't conduct an experiment on myself). But—as you'll see from your reading—there's every reason to believe that the pill may have had something to do with it.

me that it showed some interesting differences in the relationship satisfaction and divorce rate between pill-taking and non-pill-taking women. We'll talk a lot more about this study in chapter 5, but here's the punch line: Being on the pill seems to influence the types of men that women get involved with, their satisfaction with their partners, and even their likelihood of getting divorced. As we continued out of the elevator, we chatted about the results, speculated about whether these findings explained the relationship dynamics of different couples we knew (nerd gossip—it's a thing), and then shared our own experiences being on and off the pill.

This paper, which I read when I got home, totally blew my mind. Seeing evidence that small changes in individual women's hormones have consequences for something as macro as the divorce rate was like brain Velcro to me. I couldn't stop thinking about it. I've always been taken by research showing the law of unintended consequences playing out in complex behavioral systems, and the idea that individual women's hormones might have cascading effects on cultural patterns in the world was just too provocative to ignore. This paper is now required reading in one of my classes and has inspired new research in my own lab.

This was event number two.

The last of the three unrelated events happened to me at a different psychology conference yet another year later (I do other things with my time—I swear). In this case, I was at a research talk given by a research collaborator of mine, Dr. Bruce Ellis, on the effects of childhood adversity on the stress response. Bruce's talk was interesting for a variety of reasons that I won't get into here (I have learned after years of putting people to sleep at dinner parties that *interesting* is a highly subjective term), but I heard one thing in particular that made my brain stop in its tracks: Women on the birth control pill—unlike every other healthy human being on earth—are missing a key feature of their stress response.

We'll talk a lot more about this and why it's a big deal in chapter 7. For now, you just need to know that this is a pretty wild thing to find out *isn't* happening in an otherwise healthy person, and it can have some important implications for things like learning and memory, as well as anxiety and depression.

Now, for whatever reason, learning about this hit me like a lightning bolt. My mind was instantly flooded by realization after realization that made all these seemingly disconnected pieces snap together in my brain.

Birth control pills are hormones. There are hormone receptors everywhere in the body. The brain is flush with hormone receptors. Female sex hormones influence sex, attraction, stress, hunger, eating patterns, emotion regulation, friendships, aggression, mood, learning, and so many other things. Of course the pill changed me. Of course it influences relationship satisfaction and the divorce rate. Of course it influences the stress response. The pill contains hormones, so it changes who you are. The pill changes . . . everything.

I'd be lying if I didn't confess to you that I am hugely embarrassed this hadn't occurred to me up until this point. Despite building a career researching motivation, attraction, and, yes, even the effect of women's hormones on behavior, I had a huge blind spot when it came to the hormonal contraceptives I took for more than a decade of my life. It never occurred to me that the pill would change me. Given that this didn't occur to me as a psychologist, I am guessing there is a fair chance it probably never occurred to you, either. If you're anything like me, the only thing you probably spent that much time worrying about with respect to your birth control pills is the possibility that they might cause weight gain. Or a stroke. But again, if you're like me, the weight gain is definitely the more alarming of these two side effects . . . Well, as alarming as something can feel when you're missing half your stress response.

Once I returned home from this conference, I began to research whether there might be an explanation for the way I felt when I went off the pill. I wanted to see whether the experiences I had might be documented in the scientific literature or shared by other women. The results of this research revealed to me that I was not alone and that my experiences were not unique. Psychologists and neuroscientists have been publishing research on this stuff for years. But I had no idea, and I'm guessing that you didn't either. There is virtually no information available to most women about what the pill does to the brain. The only information out there is buried deep in the pages of scientific journals. And, in addition to being all but completely inaccessible to those who don't work in universities (subscriptions to these journals are super-expensive), these articles are often filled with jargon and aren't always a whole lot of fun to read (the brain doesn't always like to learn about itself).

I'm writing this book to put all this information in one place for you and to make it as easy to understand as possible. I'm also hoping to teach you a few cool things about the way that women's brains work and offer you some thoughts to consider about the pill, health, and life. Some of this will come from the results of research done in my own laboratory. Some of it will come from research done in the laboratories of other scientists whose work I trust and respect. I'll also share stories from my own life and the lives of other women who have shared their stories with me. Each of us deserves to know as much as possible about the medications we put into our bodies, even when the effects in question aren't life-threatening (the focus of most medical research). Some of what I will tell you will shock you. Some of it will simply verify things you've suspected for a long time but figured were all in your head.

Here is just some of the territory we're going to cover:

- Although many of us think of hormones as something that "happen" to us, that isn't quite right. You *are* your hormones. They help to form your very identity, the beliefs that you have about yourself, and your behaviors. So going on and off the pill can change your very sense of who you are. It can prompt a change in identity—one that's seemingly common but that scientists haven't fully explored yet.

- The pill changes the brain. Brain scans of women who are on the pill show structural and functional differences when compared with those of women who are off the pill.

- Women on the birth control pill don't have the cortisol spike in response to stress that every other healthy human does. Researchers have been regularly documenting this effect since the 1990s. And it's shocking. As we'll discuss, cortisol plays an instrumental role in telling our body that something meaningful is going on—and not just bad stuff. It tells us when something exciting is going on, too.

- Being on the pill might influence who women choose for dates and mates, and may have a meaningful impact on their relationship satisfaction and the likelihood that their relationships will survive.

- The pill may have important implications for women's social mobility, men's achievement motivation, marriage patterns, economic growth, and the divorce rate. Data shows that women's sexual standards and men's achievement levels operate in lockstep, meaning that the pill might also have side effects on *other people's behavior*. How's that for an unusual side effect?

In addition to teaching you new things about hormones, women, and how they both change on the pill, I will give you an inside look into science and what it means to do research on women. A major lesson in this book is that we need better lab practices to help ensure that researchers take the time to study women (this problem is pervasive in research on humans, nonhuman animals, and even *cells!*).* Female subjects and even female cell lines (which are the very first targets of study for new drugs and research into the development of diseases like cancer) remain under-

....

* A well-known exception to this trend is described in the terrific but disturbing *New York Times* best-seller *The Immortal Life of Henrietta Lacks* by Rebecca Skloot (Crown, 2010). This book recounts the striking tale of a poor African American woman whose cervical cancer cells were taken from her eight months before her death in 1951. This was done without her knowledge, consent, or compensation. These cells (called HeLa cells, after the first two letters of their originator's first and last names) were used to create the world's first and most commonly used "immortalized" cell line for scientific research. Nonetheless, the majority of cells used for research are male rather than female.

represented and understudied in biomedical research despite reforms made to increase their inclusion. So we need to make sure that science continues to advocate for the inclusion of women in all research studies exploring issues that affect both men and women.

I close this book with a letter to my daughter, which I hope will help her—as well as you—make an informed decision about birth control options. I will consider all the information presented in the preceding chapters and discuss the many questions that it raises. Are we better off on the pill? Should we consider finding alternative means of safely freeing women from the reproductive consequences of their sexual behavior? Although there are no clear-cut answers (and the answer will be different for each woman, depending on her individual goals and circumstances), I am hoping to start a dialogue—a dialogue between women and their doctors, women and their partners, women and their friends, and women and their daughters. One of the most amazing things about writing this book was the number of conversations it has started. These conversations usually begin, "This might be TMI, but . . ." or "I hope that this isn't an overshare, but . . ." The women then proceed to share stories that they thought were "all in [their] head." I hope that this book will be the starting point for many new such conversations. And here's something to help you get started: *This might be TMI, but . . .*

A FEW NOTES ON HOW I'VE ORGANIZED THINGS

I've divided this book into three sections. The first section ("You Are Biology") is all about what it means to be a woman, biologically speaking. I will tell you about your brain, your hormones, and why the process of evolution by natural selection has made us different from men in the first place. These chapters are designed to give you an understanding of how you work and why you work that way. Although you may wonder why I'm telling you all this stuff in a book about the birth control pill, it's absolutely essential. We have been far too cavalier with our hormones, and I can't help thinking that we would be a lot more careful with ourselves if we understood how we work and why we work that way. You need to know how your brain works, you need to know how your hormones influence your brain, and you need to know how all that changes on the pill. I lay the groundwork for this understanding in the first section, and I think you will find that it's some of the most fascinating stuff you've ever learned. Women are even more interesting than you could have possibly imagined.

The second section ("This Is Your Brain on Drugs") is all about how the pill works and what we know about how it affects women's brains and lives. I will tell you about the different types of hormones in the pill and about how the pill changes your sexual and mating psychology, your stress response, your mood, and a bunch of other stuff that goes on in your brain. This is the stuff that psychologists have known about for decades, in some cases, but that you probably haven't heard about until now. I will walk you through what we know and tell you what still needs to be learned. After you read this section of the book, you will be armed with all the information you need to make an informed decision about whether the pill is right for you.

The last section ("The Big Picture") covers some meta-issues with the birth control pill. First, we'll talk about how women's behavioral changes on the pill can have cascading consequences on the behavior of others and are changing the face of marriage, pregnancy, and the workplace. Then we'll discuss why you haven't known about any of this until now. This ends up being a very complicated issue. Part of the answer is political (people tend to get uncomfortable talking about "women" and "hormones" in the same sentence), part of it is practical (the research is challenging to do well, and women are difficult to study), and part of it is because we are all motivated to believe that birth control, as an issue, is solved. Regardless of the reasons, we need to continue to push science to learn more about women and the issues that are important to them.

FOR THOSE OF YOU WHO DON'T COLOR INSIDE THE LINES

Most of the research I discuss in this book is focused exclusively on the experiences of heterosexual cisgender women, because they are typically the people who go on the birth control pill. Although some lesbian women, as well as transgendered women *and* men, go on the pill for reasons other than pregnancy prevention, research hasn't quite caught up with this yet.

If you are a reader who doesn't happen to fall into the very narrow category of humans that researchers typically study when it comes to the pill, this doesn't mean your experiences don't matter. They do. And I hope you are still able to learn about yourself based on the research I present. All of us are more alike than we are different. And this is true even for those of us who have spent most of our lives being made to feel different from everyone else. We're all human, and a lot of our experiences are shared. So even if the research in the following pages doesn't perfectly describe you, please know there is a place for you in its results. Research suggests that the mating psychology of gay and transgendered women isn't all that different from that of their heterosexual cisgendered peers. And in cases where you think that meaningful differences may have been overlooked by the research establishment, push for better science. Your story matters. I hope you are able to see parts of your own story in the pages of this book.

To all of you, I write this book to put you in a position of power. To arm you with the results of the latest science on the pill so that you can make an informed decision about what you want to do and who you want to be. Although the science is still new and there is a lot to be learned, it is unacceptable for you to stay in the dark any longer. We know too much for you to know so little.

Now let's get started. We have a lot to talk about.

PART I—
YOU ARE
BIOLOGY

CHAPTER 1: WHAT IS A WOMAN?

Although there are a whole bunch of different ways that a person could answer a question like this one (we could talk about gender identity or social roles or any of the other numerous forces that make you who you are), we're going to look at what evolutionary biology has to say about it. Because it turns out that we can learn a lot about women by understanding the things that our brains were designed to do.

You see, each one of us is the result of an unbroken chain of successful survival and reproduction that has gone on now—uninterrupted—for millions of years. If even *one* of your ancestors had failed to survive long enough to reproduce, or simply failed to reproduce, you wouldn't be here.

This is a pretty remarkable thing to think about.

As women, we have inherited from our successful female ancestors traits that allowed them—generation after generation, and *without pause*—to make good decisions about everything ranging from whether to approach a snake (no!) to whether to have a clandestine love affair with the hot guy from a neighboring tribe (maybe!). Traits that promote successful survival and reproduction get passed down from one generation to the next. Traits that don't promote survival and reproduction don't. It's that simple. This process of inheritance is called natural selection. And it turns out to be a very powerful explanatory tool when it comes to understanding what it means to be a woman and to have a female brain.

YOU ARE YOUR GAMETES

To understand what it means to be a woman and to have a woman's brain, we first need to define what it means to be female. And in the eyes of evolutionary biology, this is something that's defined by the size of your gametes (a.k.a. your sex cells). If you have a limited supply of large, calorically expensive gametes, you are a female and we call your sex cells "eggs." If you have an unlimited supply of small, metabolically inexpensive gametes, you are a male and we call your sex cells "sperm." And although this designation may sound overly simplistic (and potentially even a little crass), it's at the very heart of almost all reliably occurring sex differences observed in creatures great and small, including human beings.

And it's actually incredibly fascinating stuff.

For instance, being the sex with the larger, more expensive sex cells means that women—*before they even meet the future fathers of their children*—have *already* invested more in any babies that they may have than their future baby-daddies-to-be have. And in humans (and many other species), this investment asymmetry only grows larger once an egg gets fertilized. We are mammals, after all. And for female mammals, reproduction is costly. So having larger sex cells oftentimes means setting the stage for costly reproduction.

And costly it is. Women hoping to reproduce have to be willing to share their bodies with another human being for nine months. This is no small request. It's energetically costly. It's uncomfortable. And it's a logistical nightmare for a woman's immune and circulatory systems. Further, despite the wonder that is modern medicine, complications from pregnancy and childbirth continue to kill several hundred women around the world *daily*.

But there's more!

You see, there's also lactation. And even though this activity is no longer required for successful reproduction to occur, it was something of a nonnegotiable in our evolutionary past. Women had to lactate to feed their infants, and lactation is also pretty costly. In addition to requiring women to secure an additional six hundred or so calories each day to offset the metabolic expense of milk production, it is also time consuming and would have made things like food acquisition difficult for ancestral women. Although I have never personally attempted to forage for food while having a suckling infant stuck to my chest, I can't imagine that it would exactly help.

The takeaway here? Women's minimum level of investment in reproduction is much greater than men's. *Much*. And this means that women— over the course of our evolutionary history—have been confronted with a number of adaptive challenges that are specific to being the internally gestating, greater-investing sex. Ultimately, this is why men and women are different. Evolution by selection has shaped women's and men's psychology differently because sometimes the types of traits that best promote survival and reproduction differ, depending on whether they are present in a male or female body. Similar evolutionary challenges create similar brains. Different evolutionary challenges create different brains.

To illustrate this point, I want you to consider the prospect of having sex with a stranger. And I want you to consider this from the vantage point of someone living during the time of our ancient ancestors. Imagine living on the African savanna without all the luxuries of modern living, including birth control.

First, let's imagine this scenario as a man.

This scenario (keeping in mind men's inexpensive gametes and low minimum investment in reproduction) is a pretty sweet deal. Even if the stranger isn't all that good-looking or fun to be around, if she's interested in sex and nothing more, the costs are very low for men if they wish to oblige. In fact, this type of sexual scenario is actually a pretty big "get" in terms of being an opportunity to pass down genes at almost no cost. This is precisely the type of trait that selection tends to favor. Traits that promote gene transmission get passed down to children, who then possess those traits. And then they pass them on to their children, who pass them on to theirs. And when this process of inheriting traits that promote reproduction goes on for millions of years, you can expect that the trait will begin to characterize the species (or at least one sex in that species). Modern men's mating psychology should be characterized by a penchant for sexual opportunism, because their ancestors would have passed down more copies of their genes than their more sexually restricted contemporaries.

But what about women? With our rare, expensive gametes and minimum nine-month investments, how should we respond?

Not like men, that's for sure.

To start with, because a woman's own body is the limiting factor in terms of her ability to reproduce, women can't increase access to gene-transmission opportunities simply by finding new partners. No matter how many men a woman has sex with over the course of a week, she can produce only—at most—a single pregnancy. For this reason, women who desire sexual novelty, per se, in their choice of partners won't pass down more copies of their genes than women who prefer to take a one-partner-at-a-time approach to mating. This isn't to say that there aren't benefits to be gained by women from short-term mating. There are (and I'll tell you about some of them in chapter 3). It just means that increasing access to reproductive opportunities is not among them. A woman's opportunities for reproduction are limited to the number of children her own body can produce and not by her access to men.

So, casual sex hasn't been as beneficial to women's reproductive output as it has been to men's. This alone would be enough to prevent selection from favoring sexual opportunism in women. However, in this case, the fate of this trait as an evolutionary nonstarter has been further ensured by the fact that it has also been historically very costly for women. And this is, again, because of the whole pregnancy thing.

Although women nowadays can pretty much have it all—careers, relationships, casual sex without pregnancy—our female ancestors weren't quite so lucky. When they were having sex, there was always the chance that the sex that they were having was going to result in a pregnancy. And this is a bfd,* since the children of single mothers, historically, haven't fared very well. These children are more likely to die from every recordable cause of mortality than are children whose dads stick around to help provide food, care, and protection. Although contemporary laws, contraception methods, and social programs for children and their mothers have helped close these gaps somewhat for contemporary women, we've inherited our mating psychology from women who didn't have these options.

Given these differences, we should expect to find that women are coyer and less sexually opportunistic than men. We should also find that women tend to prefer a more prolonged courtship period than do men and are less interested in sexual novelty for novelty's sake than are men.

And you know what? That's exactly what the research finds.

Most women are less sexually opportunistic than most men. Hundreds of studies have now found this to be true. For example, in one of the most-talked-about experiments of its kind, researchers had attractive male and female actors take turns standing in a quad on a college campus in Florida. They were then instructed by the researchers to approach random members of the opposite sex and say in a casual tone, "I've been noticing you around campus. I find you very attractive." The experimenter would then follow this with one of three requests (randomly assigned across encounters): "Would you go out with me tonight?" "Would you

....
* bfd: big f***ing deal.

come over to my apartment tonight?" or (the not very subtle) "Would you go to bed with me tonight?"

You can see the results below.

Fifty percent of both men and women agreed to the date.

After that, though, things differed pretty dramatically depending on whether the request was being made to someone who had a male or a female brain.

For women, fewer than 10 percent agreed to go back to the man's apartment. And none of the women agreed to sex. Not one.

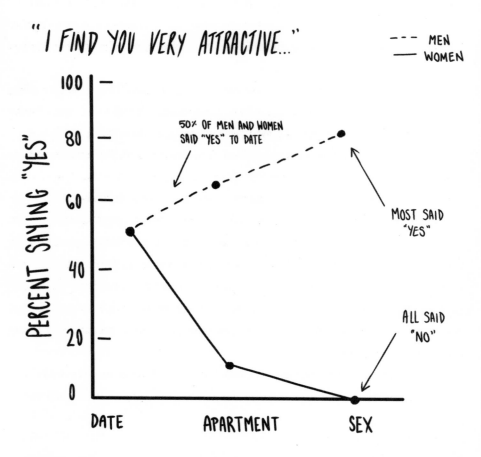

Men's and women's responses to opposite-sex strangers asking if they would like to (a) go on a date, (b) go back to the stranger's apartment, or (c) have sex with them.

At this point, you might be thinking to yourself, "Of course no one said yes to sex. Who would do that? Only a total lunatic would request sex from a stranger, so—of course—no one would say yes to such a bizarre, apropos-of-nothing sexual invitation."

Except 80 percent of men did.*

Bizarre or not bizarre, men weren't about to look a sex-bearing gift horse in the mouth. Most men are more sexually opportunistic than most women because sex has historically been very costly for women and far less costly for men. In fact, for men, it has come with the possibility of being able to transmit genes into the next generation without too many follow-up costs. Being a female means that sex is costly, and our psychology reflects those costs. Our psychology has been shaped by the myriad female-specific adaptive challenges that come along with being the sex who is obligated to invest more.

Now, before we break into a hymn of the oppressed, it's worth noting that a number of unique adaptive challenges also come along with being male. Take, for example, the issue of paternity uncertainty.

Women, being the internal gestators of offspring that they are, always know that any child they have is theirs. Like, *theirs*, theirs. This means that—over the long span of evolutionary time—women would have always benefited from investing heavily in their children. After all, such an investment would help promote the ultimate success of her genes, since she is certain that every child that she is a bona fide genetic relative. This certainty in relatedness between a mother and her children has made heavy parental investment a no-brainer for women. This is why we invest so heavily in our children, even if they show no overt indicators of being one of our relatives.

For men, it's a little more complicated. Since they aren't the ones who gestate babies, they can't know for certain that any child they have is

---

* An interesting sex difference occurs when you tell men and women about these results. When you tell women about them, they say, surprised, "Eighty percent of men said yes?!?!" When you tell men about them, they say (with equal surprise), "Twenty percent of men said no?!?!"

theirs (or "theirs," as the case may be). This poses an adaptive challenge to them that women don't have to confront when making choices about parental investment. This is known as the problem of paternity uncertainty. And even though you might think it's not a real problem that men have to worry about, a recent meta-analysis (which is a study of other studies—sort of a super-study) tells us otherwise. Although the average rate of non-paternity (which is what we call it when men think that they're the father of a child that actually isn't theirs) for men who report feeling highly certain about being the biological fathers of their children is somewhere between 2 and 4 percent, for men who feel relatively less certain about their relatedness to their children, the rate is closer to 30 percent.

Ouch.

Because of this, men tend to be more discriminating than women in terms of how much they invest in their kids, investing more in those whom they feel are more certainly theirs and less in those for whom relatedness is more dubious. For example, in one study, researchers had external judges evaluate the facial resemblance of children to each of their parents. They also had the parents rate their perceived similarity to their child and report their psychological and emotional closeness to their children.

What they found was that mothers' facial resemblance to their children did not predict their emotional closeness to their children *at all* (see the bars on the right of the figure opposite). For the dads? As you can see from the bars on the left, it mattered. A lot. Dads who report feeling the most emotional closeness with their children tend to resemble their children more than those who report low emotional closeness to their children. Several studies have now demonstrated that men's parenting psychology is highly sensitive to cues bearing on the likelihood that their children are genetically related to them. Women's parenting psychology, on the other hand, is not. Men and women have each confronted some survival and reproductive challenges that are unique to their biological sex, and their brains are different from one another as a result.

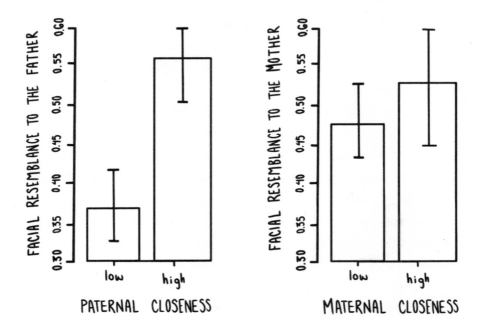

Facial resemblance was measured by quantifying the proportion of correct parent–child matches made by a sample of outside evaluators. Women's facial resemblance to their children has no impact on their emotional closeness to their children. Men's facial resemblance does.

NOTHING IN WOMEN MAKES SENSE EXCEPT IN THE LIGHT OF EVOLUTION

Now, I must point out that research like this describes patterns that are observed across large samples of men and women. It might not necessarily describe *you*. It also doesn't imply that casual sex is some sort of an evolutionary aberration for women. This is far from the truth. In fact, much of the research in my own lab has focused on the various contexts that promote sexual opportunism and sexual risk-taking in women.*

....

* For example, we have looked at the way that women's developmental experiences with their fathers and their vulnerability to illnesses influence their sexual risk-taking behaviors. It turns out that both father absence during early life and being vulnerable to getting sick favor riskier sexual behavior in women.

Instead, this is all simply to say that women's psychology is different from men's in some ways—*on average*—because the demands of childbearing and child care have made it necessary for our female ancestors to solve some adaptive problems that didn't need to be solved by men. The way that we respond to men, children, snakes, spiders, mating opportunities, chocolate cake, and the face of our best friend each reflect solutions to adaptive challenges that confronted our ancestors. And in cases where the survival and reproductive challenges confronted by men and women have been the same, our brains are the same. And in cases where the survival and reproductive challenges confronted by men and women have differed (usually because of the differences in the size of our sex cells), our brains differ. Men have inherited traits that helped promote survival and reproduction when found in male bodies. Women have inherited traits that helped promote survival and reproduction when found in female bodies.

All of this means that we can learn a lot about what it means to be a woman by understanding the survival and reproductive challenges that our female ancestors had to solve to get us where we are today. And the nature of these challenges is influenced in key ways by our reproductive biology. Whether we like it or not, our brains have been built by the process of evolution by natural selection to be different from men's brains because we have babies and men don't. And although it might be more convenient to dismiss this difference than to embrace it, it has a cascading impact on numerous aspects of our psychology, including those that govern mating, parenting, food intake, our relationships with relatives, our relationships with non-relatives, our willingness to escalate in competitions, and whether we're likely to behave aggressively when provoked. Being a woman means having a brain that sees sex as very consequential and trying to outearn our peers as less so. It means being more discriminating about sex partners but less physically aggressive. It means having more autoimmune disease but less hypertension. You have inherited the traits that make you the person you are today because countless generations of women before you were able to successfully survive and reproduce. And they did so without pause or misstep. To be a woman is to be an evolutionary success story. Each of us has in us the inherited wisdom of our female ancestors. It's in our bodies, it's in our brains, and it's in our hormones.

WHY YOU SHOULD BE OKAY WITH THIS AS A FEMINIST

At this point, I know that some of you might be bristling in response to my attempt to reduce you to your uterus. I can appreciate your objections if this is the perception you have. I happen to have both a uterus and an advanced degree, and I think that the latter is far more interesting and meaningful in terms of making me who I am than the former. There's a lot more to me than my uterus, and I'll bet that there's a lot more to you than yours, too.

The good news is that this perception couldn't be further from the truth.

Sure, you are biology. And your uterus and greater minimum levels of required parental investment are all part of that. But you can choose to do with that biology whatever the hell you want. You're a woman, after all. And one with millions of years of inherited wisdom on your shoulders. And knowing how you work can only help you make better, smarter decisions about how to get where you want to be. And if that's not a pro-woman, feminist position, I don't know what is.

Acknowledging that men and women are different from each other and understanding that these differences, ultimately, can get boiled down to differences in the minimum amount of investment required for reproduction does not (I repeat, *does not*) imply that (a) all women *should* have children, (b) *all* women *want* to have children, or (c) any other offensive idea that includes some combination of these two "rules." Women are different from men because of differences in our reproductive biology, but that doesn't mean that all women will make the same choices our ancestors did.

We don't have to.

We have birth control.

And when you think about it, isn't the "pure socialization" explanation for our differences from men far worse for women than the biological explanations that I am asking you to consider? I can't think of many things that trivialize women's femaleness more than the idea that we're different from men because we have mindlessly adopted the cultural mores and social norms thrust on us by society, the media, and our well-meaning but old-fashioned parents. I am not sure how this perspective on sex differences can get the stamp of approval from feminism when it puts women in a much more submissive position than does the biological perspective. The "women as a cultural construction" perspective describes women as passive receptacle of social roles imposed on us by men. The evolutionary biological perspective describes women as being the benefactors of millions of years of inherited wisdom from our female ancestors.

How is the former position better or more empowering to women than the latter?

Anyone who tells you that biology is inconsistent with feminism doesn't know what they are talking about. To make informed choices about your body and about your health, you need to become an expert in YOU and the biological processes that go on in your body. And this means understanding why we have been designed by evolution by selection to have the brains we have and the hormones we have. We can't fully understand our minds, brains, and behaviors unless we understand the processes that designed us. To bastardize my favorite quote of all time by the evolutionary biologist Theodosius Dobzhansky ("Nothing in biology makes sense except in the light of evolution"): Nothing about women makes sense except in the light of evolution. And if you don't believe me now, I think that this next story might do the trick. It's the story about your period. And it is a story that's so wild that it deserves its own subhead.

THE WILD STORY OF YOUR PERIOD

Before I get to the good stuff, let me give you a little reminder about what your period is. Your period is the shedding of the endometrial lining that your body builds up each month in preparation for pregnancy. The endometrium is where the fertilized egg implants itself. When no egg is fertilized, the lining of the endometrium is broken down and exits the body in the monthly nuisance that is having your period.

Now, it might seem like the monthly shedding of a built-up endometrial lining is just a by-product of being a mammal. Mammals internally gestate, which means that they have wombs, which means that it would be totally reasonable to assume that all mammals build up an endometrial lining that is shed each month when conception doesn't occur.

The thing is, they don't.

The overwhelming majority of mammalian females out there don't menstruate. Only a small handful of species do, which tells us that having a period is not a necessary evil that comes along with internal gestation.

So, why do we have a period?

Well, one possibility considered by scientists is that it is just "one of those things" that natural selection has maintained simply because it popped up as a side effect of some other trait and wasn't costly enough to be selected against. Although this might be possible, it's not very plausible. Menstruation is *not* uncostly.

First, there are the metabolic costs. Nothing in life—not even an unused endometrial lining—is free. Using bodily resources to build up a new endometrium each month takes energy that could be used for other building projects in the body, like cell repair, neurogenesis, immune function, and other stuff that our body might want or need. This is why most other internal-gestating females simply reabsorb their endometrial lining. This type of bodily recycling program minimizes the expense of creating a new endometrial lining each month.

But we don't do that. We shed them. And this is sort of a weird thing to do, since it's really wasteful to shed all those cells every time an egg doesn't implant itself.* Although metabolic costs aren't a big deal in our modern, food-rich environment (in fact, many of us might welcome some extra metabolic costs from time to time), for the majority of our evolutionary history, they were. Because our species has spent most of its time living off the land, so to speak, our bodies are optimized to survive in environments where access to food was less certain and less available than it is currently. This means we have been designed by selection to be metabolically thrifty, making the wasteful shedding of the endometrium something that needs to be explained.

And if this weren't costly enough, there's the mess of it all. Blood is messy and it makes you a beacon to predators. It doesn't take a degree in biology to recognize that attracting predators isn't exactly positive when it comes to promoting a woman's survival or reproductive success. And let's not forget to mention that women often feel pretty crappy during their periods. Menstrual symptoms cause more than one hundred million lost work hours annually for U.S. women. And for some, these cramps are so debilitating that they aren't able to do much beyond curse Mother Nature and reach for the Advil (which didn't exist in our evolutionary past, meaning that our poor female ancestors had it even worse than we do).

So is menstruation really cost-free? I would say no.

Which brings us back to where we started. Women have periods and most other mammals don't. And periods are costly in lots of different ways that have consequences for survival and (ultimately) reproductive success.

So why do we have them?

It turns out that the answer is a little macabre but super-interesting.

....

* It is important to note, though, that modern women menstruate a lot more frequently than women did in the evolutionary past because we aren't constantly pregnant or lactating (thank you, birth control). Research on hunter-gatherer women living in conditions that best approximate the type of conditions that our ancestors likely inhabited shows that they have five times fewer menstrual cycles than modern women. This means that the average contemporary woman is wasting a lot more endometrial linings than our ancestors did. Nonetheless, the idea that we would shed them at all—at a rate five times that of our ancestors—requires explanation.

To start with, let me tell you that everything you think you know about pregnancy is probably wrong. Well, not everything. But some of the things are. In particular, your beliefs about pregnancy as being a beautiful, loving, altruistic exchange between a mother and her developing embryo. That part is all wrong. Although pregnancy may look sweet, blissful, altruistic, and loving on the outside, a mother's womb is actually a battleground where wars are waged between a mother's best evolutionary interests and those of a fertilized egg.

You see, a mother and a fertilized egg don't have completely overlapping interests when it comes to implantation. Although women have 50 percent of their genes in common with any embryo that's inside their bodies, they have 100 percent of their genes in common with themselves. This last part might sound like one of the stupidest things you've ever heard, but it's actually really profound. Mothers—because they are twice as related to themselves as they are to any fertilized egg that tries to implant—don't always see eye to eye with that fertilized egg about whether he or she is worth the requisite nine-month investment that follows implantation. Given the substantial time and resource investment involved in pregnancy, mothers shouldn't be willing to tie up their reproductive resources in developing a fertilized egg that doesn't have a good chance at surviving into adulthood. Women's bodies should therefore be discriminating about which fertilized eggs they invest in and which they do not.*

....

* Please don't take any of what I am saying out of the biological context in which I am presenting it. I can see how someone might assume that I am suggesting that having a baby who has any sort of developmental atypicality is "bad" or "unnatural." Please know that I would never imply such a thing. Any baby born into this world has made the cut. And it's also important for me to mention that if you have had the experience of having an embryo that didn't make the cut (i.e., if you have suffered a miscarriage), it wasn't your fault. You didn't "choose" that. I am giving you an explanation for why women's reproductive systems work as they do. This is not a prescription for how things should be. Just because biology favors a trait doesn't make the trait "good" or "desirable." Both of my babies were born preterm and spent time in the neonatal intensive care unit. I wouldn't be a mother if it weren't for modern medicine intervening and saving them from what would have been "natural" in our evolutionary past (death). What is and what should be are two different

Now, this sort of choosiness is obviously not an ideal situation for a fertilized egg (particularly if it has some funky mutations that make it unlikely to survive into adulthood). In the eyes of the fertilized egg (which is twice as related to itself as it is to the mom), it should be granted the opportunity to try to make it in the world, regardless of whether survival might be a long shot. After all, this is its one chance at life. And we are programmed for survival. Because of this, the fertilized egg should be willing to give up without a fight only if the cost to the mom would be so great that it would make her significantly less able to reproduce in the future (which is also good for the fertilized egg, since the fertilized egg will share 50 percent of its genes with his or her future brothers and sisters). Barring such extreme cases, though, the fertilized egg should try pretty much any trick that it might have up its sleeve to take up residence in the mom's uterus and tap into her bloodstream so that it can begin to grow.

So what the hell does this have to do with the endometrium, you ask? Everything.

Although many of us think of the endometrial lining as being this warm, snuggly blanket that lovingly embraces a fertilized egg, that's totally not at all how it works. The endometrium is actually a perilous testing ground for a fertilized egg, and it *prevents* rather than encourages implantation. The cells of the human endometrium create a cell-packed, fortress-like wall on the inside of the uterus that the fertilized egg must burrow through if it hopes to implant and find a blood source to provide it with the energy it needs to grow. And rather than shepherding the egg through the implantation process, its densely packed cells make it *more* challenging for the fertilized egg to tap into mom's blood supply there than almost anywhere else in the body. How do we know that? Well, scientists have tried to implant mouse embryos in a bunch of other loca-

....

things, and it's useful to keep them separated. We can appreciate how we work without using that as a guide for how to live our lives and the design of the societies we live in.

tions on the body, expecting them to wither away and die since they were deprived of the endometrial lining to nourish and sustain them. Much to their surprise, what they found was exactly the opposite. Not only did these embryos not die; they flourished. These little despots mercilessly burrowed their way through the tissues wherever they were implanted, destroying everything in their wake as they rummaged around for arteries to tap into to fuel their continued growth and expansion. The endometrium is actually one of the hardest places to grow an embryo, since the environment is downright inhospitable to a newly fertilized egg.

So much for that loving embrace.

Now, there are good evolutionary reasons for this. At least as far as the would-be mom is concerned. First off, this challenging environment provides a first test of viability for the fertilized egg. If the fertilized egg doesn't have the moxie required to burrow its way through this fortress, it might not have what it takes to survive in the real world. Those that aren't able to make this first round of cuts don't implant, and the mom never even knows that there was a fertilized egg there to begin with. Mom sheds her endometrium so that this likely unviable fertilized egg doesn't try to stick around and implant itself without having first gained mom's seal of approval. Approximately 32 percent of fertilized eggs are believed to meet this fate.

For those that manage to burrow their way through this inhospitable landscape, a second round of screening occurs, based on the amount of human chorionic gonadotropin, or hCG, released. The hormone hCG is released by an implanted embryo to prevent the mom's body from triggering the biological cascade that initiates menstruation.* Healthier embryos

....

* This is the same hormone that makes women feel sick early in pregnancy, which also serves an important adaptive function. Research suggests that pregnancy sickness may function to help prevent the mom from ingesting teratogens, which are chemicals and compounds that have deleterious effects on embryo development (particularly in the early stages, when the building blocks for the nervous system are being laid out). Things like broccoli, meat, eggs, and other strongly flavored and bitter-tasting foods are rich in these

produce more hCG, and less healthy embryos produce less hCG. So if an embryo isn't producing enough hCG to pass mom's standards for investment (which itself varies depending on how favorable conditions are for reproduction), mom's body will cut her losses by triggering the biological cascade that causes the shedding of the endometrial lining, embryo and all. An additional 24 percent of fertilized eggs are believed to meet this fate. The tissues of the endometrium protect the mom from having her circulatory system tapped into by embryos that she hasn't yet decided to accept. And with around half the fertilized eggs not making the cut before most women even know they are pregnant, this is a mechanism that gets put to use more frequently than you might guess.

Humans have periods because shedding the endometrial lining allows women to be choosy about investment in pregnancy. And the reason we do this and most other species don't is that the costs of investing in the wrong pregnancy are higher for human females than for those of other species. In addition to having much larger upfront costs than required of females of most species (nine months of pregnancy is nothing to sneeze at), childbirth is much more dangerous for human females than for females of other species. The unfortunate combination of women's narrow hips and babies' giant heads makes birth a tricky endeavor. Women's bodies are smart to be choosy about pregnancy. And the shedding of the endometrial lining is part of this wisdom.*

Understanding women requires understanding the biological principles that make us who we are. And understanding how we work gives us more power and more control over our lives, not less. And it helps lay the groundwork for understanding how something so small and seemingly unimportant as women's sex hormones can affect *everything about who a woman is*. Reproduction is the engine that drives the process of evolution

....

sorts of compounds, which is why most women don't want to eat them during the first twelve to fourteen weeks of pregnancy.

* Although some other theories are out there about the function of the monthly shedding of the endometrium, this is the one that has the most convincing evidence to date.

by selection. This means that everything about us is built on a foundation of gene transmission. Even things you'd never guess had anything to do with sex or reproduction—like the functioning of your stress response and immune system, as well as your appetite and interest in trying new things—exist in their current form because they helped optimize gene transmission. This means that sex—and your sex hormones—are a core part of who you are.

CHAPTER 2: YOU ARE YOUR HORMONES

Your hormones are about as misunderstood a group of chemical signals as you'll ever meet in your life. The way that hormones influence women's psychology and behavior is something that has been simultaneously trivialized, mischaracterized, and bastardized by people who—most of the time—have no idea what they're talking about. So I'm going to tell you about what your hormones are and what they do so that you can forget about all those misconceptions and learn to appreciate all the amazing things these misunderstood messengers do to make you, you.

Before we get too deeply into this, though, I want to ask you to take a few moments to try to wrap your head around the idea that you are a biological entity. And not just in a "you have inherited the psychological wisdom of your successful female ancestors" evolutionary-big-picture kind of way, but also in a "your mind is a product of the goings-on in your brain"* gears-and-sprockets kind of way. This is harder than you might think, because the human mind has a really hard time believing that it is the product of what the physical brain is doing. Even people who study

....
* If you believe that we have a soul that is separate from the body and that is the essence of a person (rather than biology), I want you to know that I totally respect that. Everything in this book is still relevant to you and is too important to ignore. I like to think that people can make room for biology in any belief system that they hold. Hopefully, this is true for you, too.

the brain for a living have a hard time holding that thought in their heads for very long. My own brain conveniently forgets this little autobiographical detail the moment I stop forcing myself to think about it. It's so fundamentally at odds with what it feels like to be a living, breathing person, with a social life and restaurant preferences, that our brain has a hard time believing it to be true. But it is. Biology is at the heart of everything that we do, that we feel, and that we *are*.

Even reading this book is the result of biological activities going on in your brain right now. The words on this page and the ideas that I am asking you to entertain are causing your brain cells to add new connections and prune away others. And if I hooked you up to a super-duper, finely tuned brain scanner (the likes of which has yet to be invented, but hope springs eternal), we would see that your brain has physically changed in response to learning about itself. The experience of being you is a biological phenomenon created by the activities of physical structures in the body.

And this is true of every little quirky detail about ourselves that makes us feel like us. Our personality. Our likes and dislikes. Our emotions and capacity to experience love. Every piece of information you have ever learned and every ridiculous, random thought you have ever entertained owes itself to electrical and chemical signals being released and transduced in your brain. If I were to ask you—right now—to imagine yourself doing the hokey-pokey with a trained chimpanzee at a birthday party for Justin Bieber, your brain would instantly pull from all the neural circuitry that you have dedicated to childhood party games, old-world primates, and teenage heartthrobs to create a mental picture of man and ape coming together to put their right foot in, their right foot out, their right foot in, and so on. And although I'll bet that you've never even considered the possibility that you had any neural circuitry dedicated to any of these things, if you can think about them, you do.

You are utterly, heartbreakingly biological.

While this detail is something that we tend to forget with amazing ease, it's critical when it comes to thinking clearly about the pill. This is because, when it comes down to what makes you, you, the two things that matter most are (1) your nervous system (and its chemical messengers, the neurotransmitters) and (2) your endocrine system (and its chemical messengers, the hormones). Although most people are quick to acknowledge the role of their nervous system in making them who they are (the brain is part of the nervous system, after all), they tend to downplay the role of their hormones. There's a tendency to externalize them and think of them as something that *happens* to us (as if our essence is a hormone-free version of ourselves)* instead of being part of who we are. But, just like our neurotransmitters and the synaptic firing patterns in our brain, hormones are a key part of what creates the experience of feeling like ourselves. And this means that something like the pill—which changes a woman's sex hormone profile—can change the person a woman has come to think of as being her self.

HORMONES 101

So let's start with the basics and talk about what hormones are. Hormones are signaling molecules that get synthesized in one part of your body and are then released into the bloodstream and picked up by any cells in the body that have matching hormone receptors. Because they are diffused in the bloodstream, hormones can travel great distances,

....

* I am not sure where the tendency to externalize our hormones comes from, but I think that major biological shake-ups like puberty and pregnancy might have something to do with it. Take puberty, for example. It's like here you are: Person A. And then sex hormones arrive on the scene, and you suddenly become hairy, moody, and prone to breakouts. And you still feel like Person A, but you feel like Person A under the influence of hormones. Because these hormonally mediated changes are relatively easy to identify— and it wouldn't do any of us any good to have a major identity crisis every time our hormones tried something new—many of us tend to think about our hormones as being more like an overlay on who we are rather than being a part of us.

reaching receptor sites that are far away from wherever they're made.* This sort of diffuse release system allows them to act on lots of different body systems at once, making them an efficient means of communicating messages that need to be heard by lots of different parts of the body at the same time. They're a little like a loudspeaker that way. They broadcast instructions for lots of different cells in the body to hear, and those cells in the body that are supposed to listen (those that have receptors for those hormones) do what they're supposed to do as a result of the message.

The primary job of hormones is to keep all our bodily systems on the same page about what the body should be doing at any given moment in time. Although this is something that most of us take for granted, imagine for a moment how much of a mess you'd be in if half your body thought it was preparing for sleep while the other half thought it was running from a bear. Worse yet, imagine that this was all going on when you were actually getting ready to have sex. It would be a total disaster. Without hormones broadcasting instructions to help keep our bodies functioning in an integrated and coordinated manner, we would soon succumb to death by physiological cacophony. And if you think I'm just being dramatic, here is a non-exhaustive list of some of the activities our hormones have been coordinating lately: digestion, metabolism, sensory perception, sleep, respiration, lactation, stress, growth, development, sex, childbirth, menstrual cycle, mood, and anything that you've ever done in a bathroom with the door closed. Although we tend to recognize the actions of our hormones only when something's gone awry (a misbehaving thyroid or an ill-timed pimple), they're essential for survival.

And you thought *you* were underappreciated.

....

* Hormones get to where they need to go based on the presence of specialized receptors on the membrane and in the cytoplasm or nucleus of cells throughout the body. They work in a key-in-lock kind of way, with hormones being like tiny keys floating around in the bloodstream, opening only the doors with the matching keyholes. This is how you get targeted action by hormones, despite the fact that they are released diffusely in the bloodstream.

Your hormones coordinate pretty much everything that your body does. And it's not just the stuff that happens from the neck down. Your hormones also coordinate the activities that go on in the brain. Although it might seem a little bass-ackward that the brain uses hormones to influence its *own* activities, this sort of biological hack job is the type of thing that evolution by selection specializes in: solutions to problems that are cobbled together based on hardware that already exists.

You can think about the relationship between the body, the brain, and the hormones as being kind of like the relationship between an airplane (body), a pilot (brain), and computerized flight-plan software (hormones). If the pilot wants to go to Rome, she'll run the plane's Rome software. If she'd like to go to Paris, she will run the Paris software. And so on. Each software program lets each of the plane's parts (e.g., the wing flaps, the rudder, etc.), as well as the pilot herself, know what to do to get the plane headed in the right direction. The Rome software gets the pilot and the plane working together to make it to Rome. The Paris software gets the pilot and plane working together to make it to Paris. Hormones tell the body and brain what software is being run so that everyone is on the same page about what they should be doing and where they should be heading.

Even if it ends up being Cleveland.*

And these instructions aren't just for little tweaks and minor modifications. The impact of hormones on the version of ourselves that our body creates is sometimes huge. To give you an example of this, I'm going to tell you about a crazy species of fish that has three genders. And I am doing this both because it illustrates how fundamentally different we can be under the influence of different sets of hormones and because it's too cool not to share.

....
* We tease the ones we love.

THE FISH WITH THREE GENDERS

Although it might seem odd to talk about fish in a book about the birth control pill, this fish is worth talking about in the context of any topic. I'd find a way to squeeze it into a book about the great dramas of the Elizabethan era if I had to. It's particularly interesting in the context of our discussion here, though, because it really does have three genders. And the reason it has three genders has everything to do with sex hormones.

The fish in question is the plainfin midshipman (*Porichthys notatus*), which is an extremely ugly but fascinating nocturnal fish native to the Pacific Ocean. The reason it has three genders is that there are two types of males, rather than just one. And these two types of males are so fundamentally different from each other in how they look and act that biologists couldn't in good conscience classify them as being the same thing. They're just too different.

The first type of male is called (ever creatively) the Type I male. These are the burly, sexy Lotharios of the midshipmen world. They are eight times larger than females and produce loud, throaty grunts that the female midshipmen find irresistible. In spring and summer, these males set up shop close to shore, building nests sheltered among the rocks. They then belt out their throaty hums throughout the night to attract females to come lay their eggs in their nests.

The Type II male, on the other hand, is much smaller than the Type I male. His appearance and behavior more closely resemble those of a female than those of a Type I male. The only real way to tell Type II males apart from the females is by the presence of their reproductive organs, which are *seven times larger* than those of the Type I males.

Yes, I said seven times larger.

Now, before we get too carried away, it is worth noting that these fish reproduce by having a female's eggs fertilized *outside* her body. A female lays her unfertilized eggs in the nest of a Type I male and then goes about her business, often leaving the eggs unattended, feeling secure in the knowledge that her eggs will incubate safely in this territory defended by the large, sexy Type I male.

This doesn't leave a whole lot of options for the Type II males. They are too small to croon to the females or to defend territories of their own, so they have to resort to a sneaky strategy if they hope to reproduce. This is where their small size comes in handy. Because they're the same size as females, they can sneak into the territories defended by the Type I males by pretending to be a female midshipman (which presumably involves some clever sleight of fin to distract the guarding male from seeing the enormous genitals) and then fertilize any unattended eggs. This is why their reproductive organs are so large. That one sneak attack may be the only shot they get at reproduction, so they'd better have a whole lot of sperm to up their chances of getting a few of those eggs fertilized.

Although both types of males are born with the same genes, in Type I males one set of hormonally mediated switches gets turned on, and in Type II males a different set of hormonally mediated switches gets turned on.* And the result of this switching is that these two types of males look, act, and experience the world in completely different ways. All because of the activities of their hormones. The different hormones their brains were exposed to during development caused their brains to be put together differently. And the different levels of hormones their bodies are exposed to in adulthood cause them to respond differently to their environment. Their hormones play a key role in who they are.

And the same is true for you.

Whether you are a fish, frog, bird, chimpanzee, or person, your hormones play a profound role in everything that your body does. Because there are hormone receptor sites on virtually every cell you have—

....

* Although biologists are still working out the details of what's turning these switches on and off, it probably has something to do with cues indicating what pathway will best promote reproductive success, given the male's genetic and external environment.

including billions of cells in your brain—the impact of your hormones on what you think, how you feel, and what you do is nothing short of pervasive.

BUT MOSTLY, YOU ARE YOUR SEX HORMONES

Although all the hormones in your body do important things, it's hard to imagine any that have a more powerful or potent an influence on the activities of the brain (or the rest of your body, for that matter) than your sex hormones. This makes good sense when we consider the process that designed us. We have inherited from our ancestors a brain that puts all things related to gene transmission on the top of the biological to-do list, with sex bolded and underlined as priority number one.

For women, the predominant sex hormones are estrogen and progesterone. And the one that tends to get most of the attention is estrogen.* And this is for good reason: Estrogen is the hormone that's responsible for most of the things that we think about when we think about what makes women, women. For example, it's responsible for the development and maintenance of things like breasts and hourglass body shapes, as well as the development and regulation of the reproductive system. Estrogen is also instrumental in getting your body ready for the possibility of pregnancy each month, as well as motivating behaviors that make pregnancy

....

* Although there are three major types of naturally occurring estrogen in women—estrone, 17-beta estradiol, and estriol—I am going to limit my discussion of estrogen to 17-beta estradiol (a.k.a. estradiol). Estradiol is the main estrogen in reproductive-age women and is the estrogen that people are usually talking about when they say, "Estrogen . . ." So from here on out, when I say *estrogen*, know that I'm talking about 17-beta estradiol. I prefer to call it by its street name because it's simpler and decreases the likelihood that you will accidentally start calling it 17-beta estradiol in public (a behavior that will subject you to more eye-rolling and sighing than any of us should ever endure).

possible.* We'll talk a lot more about the nature of the psychological and behavioral changes that occur in women when estrogen is dominant in chapter 3. For now, it's worth noting that women generally feel a little more flirtatious and spunky during the estrogen-dominant half of their cycle than they do later on.

The other of women's major sex hormones is progesterone. Whereas estrogen is the flirtatious sex kitten of women's hormones, progesterone is more of the mom-jeans, Earth Mother hormone. This hormone helps coordinate all the nesting-related activities that help prepare the body for the possibility of embryo implantation, and helps close off the cervix to any germs or sperm(s)† that might try to make their way in after conception has occurred. When progesterone is on the scene, women tend to feel hungrier, sleepier, and more relaxed than they do at other points in the cycle. It makes women feel like doing the kinds of things that help get their bodies ready for the possibility of needing to grow another human being in the not-too-distant future.

Now, as you might expect from a brain that is wired for sex, sex hormone receptors are on virtually all the major structures of the brain. Think about what this means for a minute, because it's actually kind of profound. When cells in the body are equipped with hormone receptors, it means that they're programmed to do different things depending on whether that hormone is present or not. This means that your brain—that super-powerful CEO of your nervous system that is in charge of all the things about you that make you, you—has been programmed to act differently depending on the sex hormones being released in the body.

This is pretty deep stuff.

The version of yourself that your brain is creating *right now* is different from the version of yourself that would be created in the presence of a different set of sex hormones. Consider, for example, this excerpt from an

....
* Yes, I am talking about sex.
† I couldn't help myself.

interview with a man whose body—because of a medical condition—stopped producing the primary male sex hormone, testosterone. He lived without testosterone for four months before doctors caught the source of the problem.

> Everything that I identify as being me, my ambition, my interest in things, my sense of humor, the inflection in my voice, the quality of my speech even, changed in the time that I was without a lot of the hormone. There were things that I find offensive about my own personality that were disconnected then. And it was nice to be without them—envy, the desire to judge myself. I approached people with a humility that I had never displayed before.
>
> . . . So, yes, the introduction of testosterone returned everything.
>
> . . . When you have no testosterone, you have no desire. And when you have no desire, you don't have any content in your mind. You don't think about anything. People who are deprived of testosterone don't become Spock-like and incredibly rational. They become nonsensical, because they're unable to distinguish between what is and isn't interesting, and what is worth noting and what isn't.
>
> . . . I grew up in a culture, like all of us, that divides the soul from the body, and that that is your singleness. That is your uniqueness. And nothing can touch that. And then I go through this experience where I have small amounts of a bodily chemical removed and then reintroduced, and it changes everything I know as myself. And it violates the sanctity of that understanding, that understanding that who you are exists independent of any other forces in the universe. And that's humbling. And it's terrifying.

Your sex hormones play a role in creating the version of yourself that you have come to know as you. And this is obviously *huge* in the context of the pill. Most women who take the pill do so for a very targeted effect (preventing pregnancy) or for a small handful of other targeted effects (e.g., having clearer skin, knowing the exact day when you are going to start your period). However, targeted effects just aren't possible when taking a hormone. *Especially* a sex hormone. So, although you'll get the *desired* effect, the effects are not *targeted*. The hormones in the birth control pill are picked up by all the cells in the body that have sex hormone receptors. This means that they simultaneously influence the activities of billions of cells in your body at once, echoing throughout the body from head to toe. Particularly in the brain. As you will see in the chapters that follow, your sex hormones influence how you think, how you feel, how you see the world, how you behave, how you look, how you smell, the excitability of your brain cells, what your immune system does, how much you eat, and just about anything else you can possibly imagine.

WHY YOU SHOULD ALSO BE OKAY WITH *THIS* AS A FEMINIST

I know that there are probably at least a handful of you who are reading this and feeling a little squeamish about the idea that women's hormones—which change across the cycle—play a vital role in what they think, feel, and do. I can see how all this might sound like part one in a two-part argument proposing that women shouldn't be able to hold important jobs, own land, or vote because their ever-changing hormones make them wholly unreliable and fickle.

But it's not like that.

To start with, although our hormones vary cyclically, they're not fickle. They're actually pretty predictable. If you tell me a woman's age and the first day of her last period, I can make a pretty good guess about what her primary sex hormones are doing at that time. You can see the effects of this rhythmicity yourself by keeping a journal of how you think and feel across your cycle. You'll notice, as I have, that there is a lot of consistency in terms of how you feel when one sex hormone is dominant and then how you feel when the other sex hormone is dominant. Women's hormones are cyclical, but not fickle or capricious.

Interestingly, the same *cannot* be said about men's primary sex hormone, testosterone. Testosterone actually *is* a little fickle and capricious. For example, testosterone changes in response to age, the time of day, getting married, having children, the presence of attractive women, the win or loss of a man's favorite political candidate, the win or loss of his favorite sports team, and (I'm not making this up) the presence of guns. And this is far from an exhaustive list. Men's testosterone changes all the time. If I were to try to make a comparably good guess about what was going on with men's primary sex hormones at a given moment, I would need to know, at a minimum, his age, marital status, whether he has children, and the time of day that he provided his sample, as well as a description of all his recent activities, including whether he'd seen any attractive women, watched sports, or encountered any weapons on his way to his testing.

Men and women both have hormones that change. And when they change, they change what we think, feel, and do. And this is actually a *good* thing. It makes us smarter, wiser, and *better* at doing all the things that are required of us for successful survival and reproduction. They allow our whole body to work together to reach each of our evolutionary destinations (e.g., finding a mate, having children, caring for children, bonding with loved ones, coping with stress, and so on), and to do so without missing a beat.

Take, for example, the cool thing that happens to men's testosterone levels when they get married and have kids.

As you are probably aware, one of testosterone's defining features is that it is a potent motivator of sexual behavior and, even more than that, its myriad antecedents (e.g., competition for status and investment in mate attraction). For example, men's relatively high levels of testosterone are responsible for men being more likely than women to do things like snowboard backward down Mount Everest to impress a potential sexual partner and thinking about sex so frequently that it becomes mental wallpaper. And this makes good evolutionary sense because, as we know, genes can't pass on themselves. Men with higher levels of sexual motivation would have worked harder to impress more women and, if successful, would have passed down more copies of their genes than men with lower levels of sexual motivation.

But with a caveat.

You see, contrary to what most men would like to believe, it's not always in their best interest to maximize testosterone production. This is because there's more to life than just sex. Even for men. Although men have benefited, evolutionarily, from being more sexually opportunistic than women, men are also wired for pair-bonding and child care. Our very needy, highly dependent offspring have required this. Men have played a critical role in promoting the survival and ultimate reproductive success of their highly dependent children (as well as their children's mother), making it unwise for men to have their foot on the testosterone gas pedal all the time. High testosterone and all that it entails (being highly attuned to cues of sexual interest from other women and fantasizing nonstop about the next-door neighbor), although good for some things, can be downright counterproductive in the context of long-term pair-bonding and child care.

Thankfully, natural selection has a workaround for this.

Men's brains order the testes to turn down the volume on testosterone production when they get in long-term relationships. And they tell them to turn down the volume even further when they have young children to care for. It doesn't turn down the volume so low that men suddenly become pushovers—that would never do when they have a family to protect and mouths to feed. Instead, it just dials back the testosterone to decrease men's interest in exciting new sexual opportunities to enough of a degree to make room for domestic activities like changing diapers and reading *Goodnight Moon*.

For example, in one study of more than six hundred men, researchers measured men's testosterone levels twice. The first measures were taken when most of the men were single and childless (Time 1). The second measures were taken four and a half years later, when most of the men had started to settle down and have children (Time 2).

The first thing they found was that men who had higher testosterone at Time 1 were more likely to be married and have children at Time 2. This is consistent with the whole "testosterone motivates mating effort" thing—the men who worked the hardest to get the girl(s) did. They also found that testosterone naturally decreased with age for everyone in the sample. This is also not surprising, since this is another of those things that testosterone is known to do. The interesting result from this study was that the men who had become fathers showed more than double the decline in testosterone than was observed in their childless counterparts. *More than double!* And men who spent more than three hours each day caring for children—doing things like feeding, bathing, and spending countless hours reading the complete works of Dr. Seuss— had the steepest decline of all.

Men's brains have been wired for child care. And their changing testosterone is instrumental in shifting them from mating mode to parenting mode. When it's time to switch from being Don Juan to being someone's dad, men's brains order less testosterone released as a means of telling the body that it's time to execute the dad software.

So both men and women have changing hormones, and we are both better off for it. These changes are part of the biological wisdom that we have inherited from our successful ancestors. There is absolutely no truth to the idea that women's hormones change and make them irrational but men's don't. Science says so. This idea is nothing more than a position of convenience that gets adopted by sexist dipsh**s who want to keep women from competing for the resources and positions that have long been monopolized by men.

As women, we need to move past the false double standards that tell us that women are "hormonal" but men are not, and talk freely and openly about our hormones. Although minimizing the impact of our biology in making us who we are is bad for everyone, it's especially bad for women.* We have gotten to a place in our culture where our hormones are treated with such blithe disregard that women are prescribed the pill—which fundamentally changes their hormonal profile—as the first line of defense in even the most minor of bodily annoyances, like skin breakouts and irregular periods. I don't mean to minimize how much it sucks to deal with either of these things, nor am I recommending that you go off the pill if you use it for these purposes (I'd never claim to know more about what is best for you than you yourself do). Instead, I say this to you because you deserve to make decisions about your health with your eyes wide open. As women, we have all had a huge blind spot when it comes to our birth control pills. Your sex hormones influence which version of yourself you are, which means that you need to know about who you are on it and who you are off it. Having this information can help you choose which version of yourself you want to be and understand the version you already are.

We'll turn to these ideas now.

....

* For example, I can't help thinking that people would take a lot better care of their bodies if they really embraced the idea that their body—of which their brain and hormones are a part—makes them who they are. Eating healthy, getting enough sleep, managing stress, and exercising are so, SO good for the brain. Doing these things changes what the brain does, making you the best version of yourself you can be. They aren't just good for your body from the neck down.

CHAPTER 3: YOU IN THE TIME OF FERTILITY

The idea that women's hormones influence which version of themselves they are is well illustrated by the ways that women's behaviors change in response to their changing hormones across the cycle. And these changes are far, *far* more interesting than the whole "women get moody before their periods" idea that has dominated conversations about women's hormones for the past hundred years. That crude and unflattering caricature obscures what is actually an amazingly well-designed system aimed at promoting conception and implantation. And as you'll see, these hormonal changes not only influence what women themselves think, feel, and do, but they also can influence *what other people think, feel, and do.* And if that's not cool, I don't know what is.

YOUR OVULATORY CYCLE (NOT YOUR MENSTRUAL CYCLE)

In case this is the first time you've heard it described this way, the monthly release of a mature egg that can be fertilized and develop into a tiny human is called ovulation. And although most people call women's monthly cycles their menstrual cycles, I think that this description is focused on the wrong thing. The release of an egg is the star of the show, not your period. So from here on out, we're going to refer to women's monthly cycles as their ovulatory cycles (which is the terminology used by the researchers who study it, anyway), and I think that you'll agree that it's about as finely tuned a piece of neuroendocrinology as you'll ever encounter.

Broadly speaking, women's cycles can be broken into two halves, each of which is dedicated to accomplishing one of the two tasks required of women's bodies for reproduction to occur. These two tasks are conception (coordinated by estrogen, which is dominant during the first half of the cycle) and implantation (coordinated by progesterone, which is dominant during the second half of the cycle).*

The conception phase of your cycle (which is called the follicular phase) starts on Day 1, when you get your period, and continues until an egg† is released at ovulation (which usually occurs somewhere around Day 10–14ish). Estrogen increases during this phase, peaking just prior to ovulation with the release of a mature egg (see the figure on the opposite page).

The implantation phase of the cycle (which is called the luteal phase) starts after ovulation, when a temporary endocrine structure called the corpus luteum is formed in the newly vacated egg follicle. Its job is to produce progesterone, which rises steadily across the second half of the cycle, generally peaking somewhere near Days 20–22.

Now, the ovulatory cycle is, in many respects, the perfect way to illustrate the degree to which changing our hormones changes what we

....

* This is a simplification, of course. If you are interested in the nitty-gritty details, I encourage you to check out the papers listed in the references for this chapter.
† Interestingly, although several follicles begin developing eggs each month, only the most dominantly developing follicle is allowed to fully mature an egg. The other, less robustly developing follicles are programmed to shrink and die, allowing the body to put its best egg forward at each cycle. It's like a mini natural-selection process goes on in a woman's body before conception even occurs. During this time, estrogen rises, preparing for the egg to be released and helping to build the endometrial lining of the uterus to prepare for the possibility of pregnancy. It also changes the texture of cervical mucus to make it a more hospitable environment to any sperm who happen to find themselves in the neighborhood.

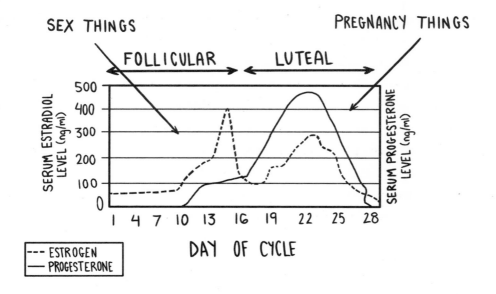

Women's hormonal changes across the ovulatory cycle.

think, feel, and do based on the activities each hormone is charged with coordinating. Because estrogen is in charge of coordinating the activities related to conception, we should find that during the time in the cycle when it is the dominant hormone, women are the versions of themselves that help facilitate this activity. And because progesterone is in charge of coordinating the activities related to implantation and pregnancy, we should find that during the time in the cycle when it is the dominant hormone, women are the versions of themselves that help facilitate these activities.

We'll spend the rest of this chapter talking about women's psychology and behavior during times in the cycle when estrogen is dominant. In particular, we'll focus on how the increasing levels of estrogen that occur when conception is possible influence what women think, feel, and do. This research nicely illustrates the way our hormones influence which version of ourselves we are at a particular moment in time. It also provides a snapshot of the hormonal road not taken by women on the pill.

As we'll talk about in more detail in chapter 4, one of the things that the pill does to keep women non-pregnant is prevent the hormonal cascade that prompts ovulation. However, in addition to preventing the maturation and release of an egg (the intended, targeted effect of the birth control pill), it also prevents women's bodies and brains from doing all the *other* things that they're supposed to do at times in the cycle when an egg is ready to be released. For some women, this might be a good thing. For others, maybe not. But there's really no way to know what the pill means for you without knowing who you are without it.

So, let's see what this version of you might look like.

SEX IN THE TIME OF FERTILITY

If you're one of the millions of American women who's had to suffer through an awkward middle school health class, there's a good chance that you've probably heard about all the stuff that estrogen does from the neck down to promote reproduction. A little pituitary hormone stimulation here and a little thickening of the endometrial lining there. However, a big piece of the puzzle that you probably haven't heard much about is just as essential to the process of reproduction as the release of an egg.

And that, my friends, is sex.

Although women nowadays can get pregnant without a male partner, this hasn't always been the case. For most of our evolutionary history, reproduction was done the old-fashioned way, with boy meeting girl, boy and girl falling in love, and boy and girl making babies through a pleasurable encounter that allowed male gametes an opportunity to find themselves in proximity of an egg. So, given that estrogen is in charge of the conception half of the cycle, in addition to finding that it does things like promoting the development of the uterine lining, we should also find that it influences women's psychology and behavior in ways that help facilitate conception.

Which it so totally does.

Let's start by talking about the effects of cycle phase on women's desire for sex. Since reproduction requires getting sperm within proximity of an egg, this means that it has required women to have some S-E-X. More specifically, this has required women to have S-E-X at a time in the cycle when it is likely to result in sperm being present at the same time as a released egg. And although the egg is very impatient (it would rather disintegrate than wait around unfertilized for more than twenty-four hours), sperm can stay alive for five-ish days in a woman's reproductive tract in the pursuit of an egg. This means that if conception is going to occur, women need to have sex within twenty-four hours of ovulation or up to five-ish days beforehand. Given that estrogen is charged with coordinating the body's conception-promoting behaviors, we should find that the estrogen surge that occurs near ovulation leads women to want more sex then than they do at times in the cycle when conception is not possible.

Which, it turns out, they do. Numerous studies have now shown that the periovulatory phase of the cycle (the five or so days prior to ovulation and on the day of ovulation itself) is marked by an increase in sexual desire—changes that are driven by increasing levels of estrogen during this time. For example, in one study, researchers found that changing levels of estrogen (measured from daily saliva samples taken from women across two cycles) were *positively* related to women's sexual desire across the cycle, whereas women's changing levels of progesterone had the opposite effect. These hormonally mediated patterns in sexual desire are also found in lesbian women and are even found in nonhuman primates. (I'll bet you never would have thought you shared *this* in common with a rhesus macaque.)

Now, from an evolutionary perspective, these changes in desire are only important inasmuch as they contribute to changes in sexual *behavior*. Getting on an airplane will not take you to Bora Bora unless the plane takes off. So we should also find that the periovulatory phase of the cycle is associated with an increase in actual sexual behavior.

And it is.

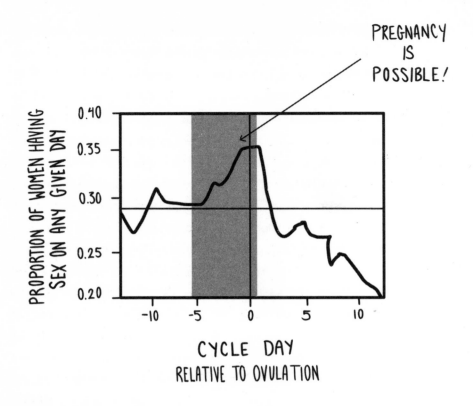

PREGNANCY IS POSSIBLE!

PROPORTION OF WOMEN HAVING SEX ON ANY GIVEN DAY

0.40
0.35
0.30
0.25
0.20

-10   -5   0   5   10

CYCLE DAY
RELATIVE TO OVULATION

Women's sexual desire is highest at times in the cycle when conception is possible.

For example, in one study of sixty-eight partnered women, researchers collected daily urine samples across multiple cycles to precisely pinpoint the timing of ovulation. The women were also required to keep daily diaries about their sexual behavior. The results of this study found a striking jump in women's sexual behavior near the fertile window in the cycle, followed by a sustained drop as cyclical fertility declined during the second half of the cycle, when progesterone is high (see the figure above). Numerous other studies have found similar results and have supported the idea that these effects emerge from changes in women's sexual motivations at the time when conception is possible.* This makes good

....

* Please note—and I will remind you of this periodically because it's easy to forget—this does not mean that women are necessarily *hoping* to get pregnant at this time. In fact, if

evolutionary sense. In addition to facilitating pair-bonding by promoting emotional closeness (which is another cool thing that sex does for us),* sex is a good way to get genes from one generation to the next. It makes good old-fashioned evolutionary sense that our hormones promote sexual behavior during times when conception is possible.

But let's take a step back. You see, sex is good and sex is fine. However, we both know that sex usually does a much better job at gene transmission when it is done with a partner than when it is done alone. Not that there's anything wrong with *that* (and you can bet that women are also probably more inclined to do that sort of thing near ovulation, too, with all that excess sexual desire floating around), but it's an evolutionary dead end if that's the only sex you're having. Because non-evolutionary dead-end sex has historically required women to have sex with a living, breathing man, researchers have hypothesized that the hormonal changes that occur near ovulation (high estrogen relative to progesterone) should also prompt women to bring their mate-attraction A game.

Consistent with this idea, research finds that women feel sexier, are more open to new experiences, and put more effort into their appearance at high fertility than at low fertility across the cycle. Women at high fertility also wear more makeup, wear sexier clothes, buy sexier clothes, and wear more red, which is a color known to make women appear particularly attractive and desirable to men. This research suggests that estrogen plays a fundamental role in motivating women's appearance-enhancement efforts,

....

you are anything like me, there have been plenty of times when you were having periovulatory sex and hoping desperately *not* to get pregnant. Unfortunately, the process of evolution doesn't care about our conception-related wishes. Instead, selection favored psychological, physiological, and behavioral traits that have promoted successful reproduction, whether we really wanted to reproduce or not. But don't blame Darwin; blame your grandma. We have inherited these traits from our female ancestors who reproduced enough to pass these traits on to us.

* In one particularly cool study, researchers looked at the role of sexual afterglow (which is an actual thing—it's that love haze that you experience after having sex) in facilitating emotional closeness in 214 newlywed couples. What they found was that the strength of sexual afterglow—that is, the lingering feelings of increased sexual satisfaction that continue after an act of sex—predicts marital satisfaction with these couples.

with these efforts peaking along with estrogen in the cycle. Estrogen—because it coordinates bodily activities that promote conception—makes women feel sexier and more interested in doing things to maximize their attractiveness to men. It also increases their interest in sex and makes them more likely to actually have it.

But not with just anyone.

Given the substantial investment women have to make in reproduction (remember the whole nine months plus the risk-of-untimely-death-from-childbirth thing we talked about in chapter 1), we shouldn't find that all their efforts are being directed toward the possibility of having sex with anyone who happens to have a Y chromosome. Instead, women should be exacting about the types of qualities they are looking for in their mates. In particular, we should find that estrogen increases women's interest in qualities possessed by men that have been associated with positive reproductive outcomes.

SEXY IS IN THE HORMONES
OF THE BEHOLDER

This is an idea that has a lot of layers to it, so I want to walk you through the theoretical background. It's first worth noting that women can get two types of evolutionary benefits from their choice of romantic and sexual partners. First, there are the benefits that influence a woman's own ability to survive and reproduce (i.e., her evolutionary fitness). These are called *direct* benefits and include things like love, care, affection, dinners out, deposits made into joint checking accounts, and a willingness to provide parental care to existing or future children. Because these types of benefits are most advantageous when they occur over time (you have a sexual fling with a fisherman and you eat fish for a day; you marry a fisherman and you eat fish for life), these qualities tend to be most beneficial in the context of long-term relationships.

But these benefits aren't the only game in town.

A woman can also increase her evolutionary fitness by choosing partners who have the potential to offer *indirect* fitness benefits. These are the genetic benefits that a woman can give her child simply by choosing to mate with a partner who has the type of genes that promote healthy, surviving offspring. And—as luck would have it(!)—the men who are most likely to give us these benefits are the men we're most attracted to anyway. That's right: Having your head turn at the sight of Mr. Square-Cut-Jaw-with-the-Awesome-Shoulders who you see at the gym actually serves a bona fide evolutionary function. It's a means of helping you get good genes for your future offspring.

And you thought you were just being shallow.

I know that it sounds too good to be true, but it's not. You see, there's actually nothing inherently sexy and desirable about sexy and desirable men. You just find them to be this way because your brain finds the qualities that they possess rewarding. Tall, symmetrical men with deep voices, ambition, and swagger cause our brain to produce beautiful fireworks that make us feel good because these qualities provide cues to things like health and developmental stability, which create more successful pregnancies and healthier children. And that's all that needs to happen for a mate preference to evolve. Your brain has inherited the tendency to find sexy men sexy because your female ancestors—by exhibiting this same preference—were able to pass down genes to enough surviving children to get you where you are today. Sexiness is in the brain of the beholder. And the brain becomes particularly attuned to these qualities when estrogen is high.

Which brings us back to fertility.

Given that the periovulatory phase of the cycle is when conception is possible, it would make good evolutionary sense for women to have a heightened preference for sexy men at this time. Sexy men mean good genes (those indirect fitness benefits), and good genes mean healthy children. And if these children are male, they also receive the added benefit of having a good shot at growing up to be sexy men, which we know will give them a reproductive advantage. Because they're sexy. And women like that. It's therefore totally reasonable to predict that women's mate preferences might shift at high fertility in a way that prioritizes sexiness over pretty much anything else that a man might have to offer at this time. Such a preference shift would increase the likelihood of getting good genes (genes that promote survival and reproduction in one's genetic lineage) at a time when conception is possible.

More than two decades of research has now found support for this hypothesis, called the ovulatory-shift hypothesis.* Women have heightened attunement to good-genes markers at high fertility and find the men who possess them to be sexier and more appealing. For example, women at high fertility prefer the scent of men who are socially dominant and have symmetrical faces. They also prefer more masculine male faces and deeper, more masculine male voices, and overall find socially dominant, confident men more attractive than they do at non-fertile points in

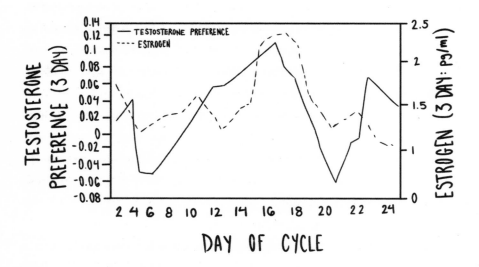

Women's levels of estrogen predict the levels of testosterone that they prefer in their partners (estrogen loves testosterone).

....

* Although other studies have failed to find these effects.

the cycle. In one particularly rigorous study of this type, researchers found that women's preference for facial masculinity (a marker of testosterone) in men operates almost in lockstep with their levels of estrogen over the cycle. Estrogen loves testosterone (see the figure on the previous page). And although these types of effects are generally most reliable and robust when women are considering who they want to have sex with (short-term mates), research also indicates that women who are married to men who possess these traits report higher marital satisfaction at high fertility than at low fertility.

In one particularly clever study looking at women's desire for sexy men at different times in their cycle, researchers observed women's interactions with men at two points: once at high fertility and once at low fertility. At each laboratory session, women interacted with two men. One was a confident, charismatic bad-boy type. The other was a reliable, caring Mr. Nice Guy type. Each woman interacted with the men one at a time over a video-chat system.* During each interaction, the man introduced himself, told the women a little about himself, and then asked the women questions about themselves. The women's responses and interactions with the men were recorded so that they could be coded for flirting behavior, and at the end of each session, the researchers had the women report their interest in each of the men they thought that they were interacting with.

The results of this study found that women reported greater interest in the sexy bad boy as a short-term sex partner at high fertility than they did at low fertility. They were also more flirtatious with the bad boy at this

....

* Well, that's what they were told, anyway. They were actually interacting with a prerecorded video of a man (done to keep things consistent across sessions), but the women had no idea. The video clips of the man were played in a carefully timed fashion such that the video man would ask questions and then the screen would fade to black while the women answered into a video camera. Once the women answered the question, the video of the man would reappear and he would ask another question. The women were told that the interaction would go on this way to try to minimize feelings of self-consciousness when answering questions. Psychology research is one part science, one part flimflam.

time. Fertility had no impact on women's interest in this guy as a long-term romantic partner, though, nor did it influence how desirable they found Mr. Nice Guy for any type of relationship. The takeaway here? Women are more interested in sex with sexy men at high fertility than they are at low fertility. This makes good evolutionary sense, as it would allow a woman to get access to high-quality genes for her offspring at times when sex is likely to lead to conception.

But does it?

The idea that women should be looking for short-term sex with charismatic bad boys at a time in the cycle when conception is most likely to occur—at first blush—may seem to contradict everything that we talked about in chapter 1. As you may recall, one reason that women tend to be less sexually opportunistic than men is that for the vast majority of our evolutionary history, children of single mothers haven't fared very well. Women pay attention to the size of a man's checking account and whether he interacts nicely with his nieces and nephews because ancestral women who paid attention to these types of things had more surviving descendants than those who didn't.

But this isn't necessarily at odds with this other research at all. Both types of preferences are part of women's mating psychology. Women want *everything*. Women want to be able to partner up with a man who has good-genes markers in excess *and* who's financially secure and interested in caring for children and helping clear the breakfast dishes.

Unfortunately, as most of us are painfully aware, the likelihood of finding all these qualities in one man is pretty low. There's a pesky tendency for sexy males of creatures great and small to shy away from commitment. For example, experiments with songbirds find that when you manipulate males' appearance to make them irresistibly sexy to females (think *Extreme Makeover: Songbird Edition*), the males respond to the subsequent increase in female attention by decreasing their investment in their existing mate and clutch of hatchlings. And when the opposite is done—and the males are manipulated to be *less* desirable to females—the males make up for their diminished sexiness by upping their parenting game and being more solicitous to their female partners. And although we can't do those sorts of manipulations in human males, research regularly finds that masculine, symmetrical, socially dominant men tend to behave similarly. Sexy men tend to exhibit less interest in babies and parenting, report more continued interest in extra-pair sexual opportunities when partnered, and have more relationship instability than do their less masculine, less symmetrical, and less socially dominant counterparts.

So, what's a girl to do if she wants it all?

Here's where things can get a little scandalous.

Mate choice usually requires that people make some trade-offs. And the research finds that the trade-offs women make depend largely on whether they are choosing a boyfriend/husband (a long-term partner) or a casual sex partner/hookup buddy (a short-term partner). When choosing a long-term dating or marriage partner, women usually prioritize traits that are associated with a guy's potential as a father, financial provider, and cooperation partner (direct fitness benefits). Paternal investment increases the survivability of children and also promotes their health, psychological well-being, and earning potential once they're adults. This is why women prioritize cues like kindness, loyalty, earning potential, ambition, and fathering potential when choosing long-term boyfriends and husbands. Although prioritizing these types of traits will often mean that women have to compromise somewhat when it comes to the sexy traits they also desire, choosing long-term partners who are willing and able to invest has historically been the way to best promote the survival success of their children.

When choosing short-term sex partners, on the other hand, women are able to make different trade-offs. Because short-term mating, by definition, won't involve a ton of investment, women can take all the chips that they would have invested in acquiring a partner who is an amazing person, a good earner, and loves children, and cash them all in for more sexiness than they would have been able to get if they were also looking for someone to stick around and care for children. This means that when women are choosing short-term sex partners, they can prioritize qualities like masculinity, social dominance, symmetry, and other qualities that suggest that this guy has the kinds of genes that will promote the success of their children (indirect fitness benefits).

The good news(!) is that—even in the face of the trade-offs that each of us must make when choosing partners—a woman can still get the best of both worlds for her offspring . . . she just might have to get each of these qualities from a different man. This means getting investment from one man (usually a primary partner who is loving, caring, and reliable) while getting sexy genes from someone else (typically unbeknownst to the primary partner). And if a woman were inclined to do such a thing in the totally unconscious pursuit of good genes for her offspring, what better time to do so than near ovulation?

Now, I know there's a good chance that some of you will find this whole idea appalling. Totally understandable. However, it's worth mentioning that the evolution of this type of conditional strategy is *inevitable* any time you have females who get both direct (resource investment) and indirect (genes) fitness benefits from their mates. For females of species that get only indirect benefits from mating—which is the case for the majority of sexually reproducing organisms out there, by the way—this isn't an issue, because they don't have to worry about investment. They don't need it. The only thing these females are choosing when they pick a mate is his genes. But for females of species that get both direct and indirect benefits from their partners, there will always be females who game the system by formally pairing with a good dad for his resource access and then getting sexy genes for their offspring from their hot neighbor.

Cheating, indeed.

Such a dual-mating strategy will generally get a female a better deal than what she would be able to get if she received both her direct and indirect fitness benefits from the same mate (although my husband will tell you that I am the exception to this rule). This isn't to say that for most females this is the best strategy. It is a tricky thing to pull off and is usually a pretty bad idea, since it comes along with a risk of abandonment, violence, and even death if you get caught. Instead, it is simply to say that women's mating psychology has built in its design the *capacity* for this type of strategy. We have this in our mental tool kit to be used in case of emergency. And even the most faithful and devoted of wives are not immune to exhibiting the types of psychological changes at high fertility that would promote a successful execution of such a mating strategy, if they were so inclined to act on it.

Which brings us to the darker side of the ovulatory-shift hypothesis. So the thing that I haven't yet told you about the effect of women's fertility status on their preference for sexiness is that this preference shift is oftentimes most pronounced in women who already have partners. Women in relationships—especially women in relationships with men who lack the qualities that are known to be markers of good genes—tend to exhibit a strong preference for sexy men at the point in their cycles when conception is possible. And this general pattern has been supported by nearly two decades of research.

For example, in one study, researchers asked women to pay attention to nine target passages taken from *National Geographic* and *National Wildlife* magazines. The passages were about things like geography, conservation, and various types of wild game. Not exactly titillating stuff. The women were instructed to repeat the target passages into a microphone attached to their headphones. The accuracy of their recordings was then coded for mistakes, missed words, and mumbling.

Here's the catch.

While women were listening to the passages about nature in one ear, they were hearing equally loud distractor messages in the other ear. Half the time, these distractor messages had flirtatious undertones (*I saw you across campus, and you looked so beautiful*), and the rest of the time they did not (*I was hoping you could tutor me in this class I have*). Researchers also looked at where women were in their ovulatory cycle. Was this a time in their cycle when conception was possible and estrogen high? Or was this a non-conceptive point in the cycle when estrogen was relatively low?

Consistent with the idea that women's mating psychology is attuned to cues that might facilitate a dual-mating strategy (if a woman were so inclined), partnered women were more preoccupied by the flirtatious distractions at high fertility than at low fertility. Single women, on the other hand, didn't show this effect. Other, similar research finds that partnered women—especially those partnered to men who are less attractive, less symmetrical, and less genetically compatible men—report experiencing a greater number of extra-pair sexual fantasies and more extra-pair attraction at times in their cycle when fertility is high compared with when fertility is low. Together, this research suggests that partnered women may exhibit psychological changes at high fertility to help facilitate a dual-mating strategy at times in the cycle when conception can occur. Although this isn't something most women do, the research suggests that women's mating psychology has been designed in such a way as to make this choice one that will offer her children better-quality genes than she might get from her primary partner.

In light of these types of effects, it's perhaps not all that surprising that women who have sexy boyfriends and husbands tend to be wary of ovulating women. Research finds that women are less willing to let their partners interact with ovulating women and perceive ovulating women as being less trustworthy than the same women when they are at a non-conceptive phase of the cycle. And all this goes on without women being consciously aware of the female rival's fertility status. Women just see a woman at high fertility, and something about her makes women feel uncomfortable about their partners interacting with her. And perhaps they are picking up on something that their partners might be picking up on, too . . . Which brings us to another cool thing about estrogen that you might not know: Our hormones at high fertility make us look, sound, and smell sexier than we do at low fertility.

CONCEALED OVULATION: FACT OR FICTION?

For a long time, it was assumed that women's fertility status across the cycle didn't matter all that much outside the realm of conception. This is because the majority of women—without being explicitly taught about the fluctuations in their cycles—don't even know it's happening. Human females don't generally advertise their fertility status by some conspicuous change in appearance, à la giant genital swellings in female baboons, or by going into heat like a dog or cat. And although many of our mammalian counterparts will have sex only during times in the cycle when conception is possible, human females have sex across the cycle. For these reasons—coupled with the fact that many women would be hard-pressed to tell you where they are in their own cycles—it was long believed that women's fertility status was totally concealed.

The past twenty years or so have shown that this idea, much like the idea that the sun revolves around Earth, sounds reasonable when you hear it but is not true. Ovulation may not be advertised by human females the way it is by female baboons, but men and women appear to be able to pick up on its subtle cues, leading to changes in how women are perceived at different stages of fertility.

Perhaps the most talked-about study looking at this phenomenon was done by Geoffrey Miller, a psychologist who's not afraid to stir things up in the name of science. Miller and his team of researchers wanted to explore whether men might find women more desirable at high fertility, and they wanted to study this in a naturalistic setting. To this end, the team of researchers moved their lab to the most unlikely of scenes for an act of science: a strip club. Now, before you let out a long, belabored sigh at the mere mention of such a study, hear me out. A strip club actually provides an interesting opportunity to see whether women's fertility status influences their sexiness to men in a quantifiable, nonreactive way. This is because men—without prompting by a researcher—naturally quantify their interest in different dancers by leaving a tip. Men tend to give higher tips to the dancers they prefer, allowing the researchers to test whether men find women more desirable at high fertility by looking at how much tip money the dancers earn across their cycles. Think what you will of strip clubs and the men who visit them, but this is a pretty ingenious method of data collection.

To test their hypothesis, the researchers had the dancers (half of whom were naturally cycling and half of whom were on the pill, which prevents ovulation by keeping hormones relatively stable across the cycle) record their tip earnings over the course of two months. The women also reported when their periods began and ended so the researchers could calculate where they were in their cycles.

The results of this study found that the dancers earned around $70 per hour when they were near ovulation. They earned around $35 per hour during their periods. And they earned around $50 per hour at other times, when fertility was waxing and waning. Women on the pill averaged around $37 per hour, with no peaks and valleys, like those observed by the naturally cycling women (see picture on the opposite page).

And although this study wasn't perfect, it was one of the first to test for—and find evidence of—men finding women more desirable at high fertility than at low fertility. Since then, several other studies, many of which have been much larger and more systematic, have found evidence for this general hypothesis. For example, in one study, researchers had two hundred men evaluate the attractiveness of women's body movements from video clips of their silhouettes dancing and walking at high and low fertility. Men found the movements made by women at high fertility to be significantly more attractive than those made at low fertility.

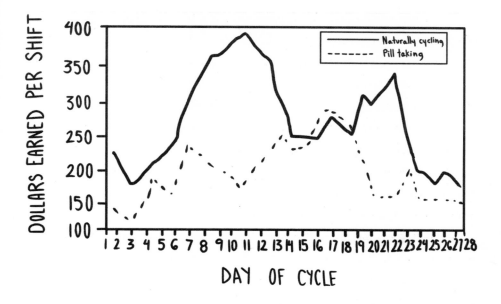

Female strippers who are not on the pill make the most money at times in the cycle when estrogen is highest.

Researchers also discovered that men and women find photographs of women's faces that were taken at the fertile phase of women's cycles as being more attractive than photos of the same women's faces taken at a non-fertile phase. Similar effects are found for vocal recordings, which men find more attractive at high fertility than at low. Other researchers find that estrogen, in addition to being associated with higher perceived attractiveness, also changes how feminine and healthy women appear. Women are perceived as being healthier and more feminine at the fertile phase of the cycle than at the non-fertile phase. And still other researchers find that women's faces and voices are considered less attractive at points in the cycle that are dominated by progesterone than those dominated by estrogen.

Together, this research suggests that women appear more attractive and desirable to men at times in their cycle when conception is possible. And this is way cool because most of us don't even know that it's going on. However, I think that some of the coolest research on how women's fertility status influences their attractiveness to men comes from studies looking at cues mediated by scent. It appears that women at high fertility smell better and sexier to men than those at low fertility, too. Several studies have found that women's natural body scents collected at high fertility (usually by way of collecting T-shirts worn by the women) are rated by men as being more desirable and pleasant than scents collected at low fertility. This relationship is not observed for women on the pill, who lack a cyclic estrogen surge. Others find that the scent of women's vaginal secretions are also perceived as being less intense and more pleasant at high fertility compared with those at low fertility, and that men's testosterone increases after smelling T-shirts worn by women near ovulation, but decreases when they smell T-shirts worn during the luteal phase.

In one particularly interesting study, researchers wanted to know whether smelling scents collected from women's armpits and vulvas* would influence men's release of sex and stress hormones (as we will talk about in chapter 7, stress hormones get released when something consequential is going on, whether good or bad). Because others have found that men experience a testosterone surge in response to the scent of ovulating women's T-shirts, these researchers hypothesized that they should find a similar pattern of results if men were to smell scents released from other areas in the body that contain a comparable number of specialized scent-producing glands. Hence, the vulva. The vulva contains as many scent-producing glands as the armpits do, and given their geographic location on the body, the scents produced in this region seem like reasonable informants about a woman's fertility status. Communicating fertility

....
* Which is the official term for women's external reproductive parts, FYI. Even though most of us just call the whole kit and caboodle a vagina—probably because the word *vulva* is so ugly—this is actually technically incorrect. The vagina is the tunnel where penises go in and babies come out. The stuff on the outside is a vulva. If you were so inclined to create a petition to change the name of this amazing structure, I'd be the first to sign it. In the meantime, we are stuck with *vulva*. Viva la vulva!

cues at this particular bodily junction could potentially benefit the female by offering an added incentive to her male consort to produce a high-quality ejaculate, as is observed in species like the Indian flying fox (*Pteropus giganteus*). This may seem like a crazy idea the first time you hear it, but I have been in science long enough to tell you that truth—in the realm of evolutionary biology, in particular—is much stranger and more interesting than fiction.

But I digress. To look at how men's hormones respond to the scent of women's armpits and vulvas at high and low fertility, the researchers had a group of women provide a sample of each once in the periovulatory phase (when conception is possible) and once late in the cycle (when it's not).

How did they do this, you ask?

Well, the researchers had women tape a cotton pad in their armpit overnight and wear an unscented panty liner for eight hours. They did this once at high fertility and once at low fertility. The women then turned in their samples, which the researchers simply stuck in the medicinal chamber of a nebulizer and then had men breathe in the scent(s) of a woman. The air they inhaled was either suffused with odors provided by a female donor or odors from a clean, unused cotton pad. The results of this study found that the sample odors provided by women in the fertile phase of their cycles increased men's levels of sex and stress hormones, with the strongest effect being found for the scents from the vulva. These men also reported being more interested in sex after smelling the high-fertility scents than after breathing in the control or low-fertility scents. Similarly, other researchers have found that smelling T-shirts worn by women at high fertility prompts men to spontaneously start thinking about sex (as if they needed prompting!), and that men interacting with an attractive female researcher at high fertility engaged in more behavioral mimicry—something that we do when we like someone and want them to like us back—than they did when interacting with her when she was at low fertility.

So is ovulation hidden? Probably not. The research tells us that women tend to be maximally attractive and desirable to men at times in the cycle when fertility is high (characterized by high estrogen relative to progesterone). Men have probably evolved attunement to these subtle cues of fertility status because their ancestors who picked up on these cues—and found the women possessing them more desirable—would have passed those abilities down to a greater number of descendants than would have those who were unable to pick up on these cues, or who picked up on them but were indifferent to them.* And although the link between increased attractiveness and fertility isn't something we are consciously aware of, we don't need to be conscious of it for it to do its job. Finding a woman desirable motivates sex, and that is all that is required for gene transmission to take place. No awareness necessary.

BEFORE WE GET TOO CARRIED AWAY . . .

Where you are in your cycle influences which version of yourself you are, but what exactly that version of you looks like (and how different it is from other versions of yourself) varies from woman to woman. The research suggests that, for many women, their high-fertility (estrogen-dominant) self tends to be sexier, flirtier, and more tuned in to hot men in the vicinity than their progesterone-dominant self. But just because that's what the research finds doesn't mean that this is necessarily true for you. Keep track of how you feel across a couple of cycles, noticing whether how you feel is based on the version of you that your hormones are helping to create. For some women, the version of themselves that is created during the estrogen-dominant half of the cycle—particularly near ovulation when estrogen rises sharply—is fun and energized. For others, this version of themselves is too easily distracted. Only you can know what

....
* Although the verdict is still out about whether these cues are strong enough to make them diagnostic of a woman's fertility status when used in real-world mate-choice settings.

your hormones mean for you. And as you learn about how your different hormones make you feel, if there are parts you don't like, you can change them! A lot of research shows that being aware of undesirable behavioral tendencies makes you better able to change your behaviors in ways that you want.

And if that doesn't work?

There's always the birth control pill.

The pill, as you'll see next, changes your hormones to create a different version of yourself. And it's a version of yourself that's lacking all the psychological, physiological, and behavioral changes that occur at high fertility.

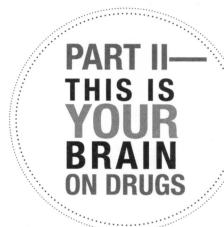

PART II—
THIS IS
YOUR
BRAIN
ON DRUGS

CHAPTER 4: HORMONES ON REPLAY

To understand what the pill does, we first need to talk about how it works. Although the birth control pill works its magic on your body in a couple of different ways, the most significant thing it does is prevent ovulation. No egg, no fertilization, no conception, no baby. Total genius.

Now, to get to the genius, we first have to talk about some technical stuff. And it's sufficiently technical that it can be kind of tedious to learn about (I'm human, too, after all). Stick with me, though, because understanding how everything works will help you understand some of the big question marks out there when it comes to the pill: things like "What are all these hormones I just swallowed telling my body to do—or not do?" and "Why do I feel crazy on the same pill that my best friend loves?" and "What's up with all of these bat-sh**-crazy side effects?" This is important stuff to know, so I've done my best to make it all as uncomplicated as possible. And if that fails? Well, I've included some pictures. And worth a thousand words or not, that might help get us through some of the tricky parts.

So . . .

Women's ovulatory cycles are coordinated through a communication pathway in the body known as the HPG axis (or hypothalamic-pituitary-gonadal axis, if you have a penchant for pedantry). The HPG axis is made up of the brain,* the pituitary gland, and your ovaries. It's illustrated for you on the next page. As with most things, your brain calls the shots with the HPG axis, but it does most of its work indirectly through the pituitary gland. The brain and the pituitary work together to coordinate the activities of the ovaries, which are the end point in this three-step communication pathway. Brain, pituitary, ovaries. Lather, rinse, repeat.

Now, as you might recall, the first day of your cycle is the day that you start your period. This is when the sex hormone crash that occurs at the end of a non-conceptive cycle causes your unused endometrium to bid your uterus a fond adieu. It also alerts the brain and pituitary to the fact that you are decidedly non-pregnant and that it's time to get cracking on another round of egg maturation and shoring up the uterine lining to start the whole process over again.

The way this process gets initiated is a little like the game "telephone" that we all used to play in elementary school—the one where you have to pass a message along to a whole bunch of people in a series of whispers. You whisper a message to James, who whispers the message to Carson, who whispers it to Logan, and so on.† Only in the HPG-axis version of this game, the chemical message that is passed along is *meant* to change. When the brain needs to kick-start a new ovulatory cycle, it releases a hormone called GnRH (gonadotropin-releasing hormone), which gets picked up by your pituitary gland. When the pituitary hears the brain whisper, "GnRH," it passes its version of this message on to the ovaries through the release of follicle-stimulating hormone (FSH) and luteinizing hormone (LH). See my picture on the opposite page. These two

....

* Specifically, it's the brain's hypothalamus, but we're just going to call it the brain. It's easier, it's less formal, and it will reduce the number of typos I have to correct.

† Which, when you think about it, is a really f***ed up thing to have kids play in school. It's just asking for trouble. Every time (*EVERY* time!) that we played this in school, it ended in tears or detention because the kid at the end of the chain would announce that the message had turned into "Julie is wearing a training bra," "Kelly got her period," or "Jon made out with his sister." What the hell is the point of this game, anyway?

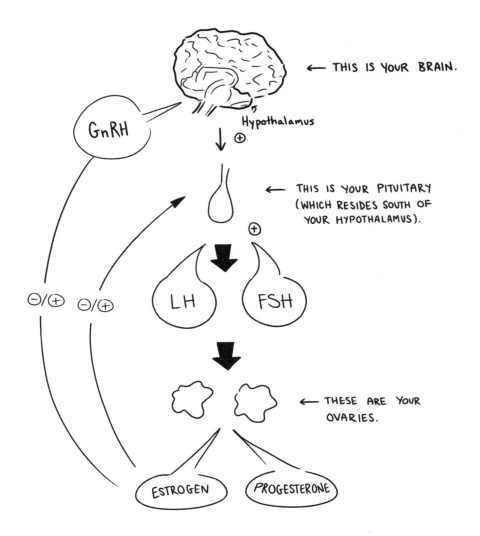

Your HPG axis and the hormonal cascade that prompts ovulation.

pituitary hormones are then responsible for stimulating the ovaries to start maturing egg follicles, which then causes estrogen to be released. And after ovulation occurs, the ruptured egg follicle creates the corpus luteum, which causes progesterone to be released.

The HPG axis regulates all these activities using a series of feedback loops. To this end, each of the HPG axis's major players (brain, pituitary, ovaries) have special receptor sites that monitor hormone levels in the body. Measuring these hormones tells them each where they are in the cycle and what they need to do next.

For example, when the brain and pituitary detect that both progesterone and estrogen levels in the body are low, this tells them that the body is not pregnant and it's time to start initiating hormone release to prompt egg development so that the body can try, try again. When estrogen rises sharply but progesterone is low, this tells the brain and pituitary that an egg is mature and ready for release, which prompts a surge of LH, thereby triggering ovulation. And when *both* estrogen and progesterone are relatively high and stable, this tells the brain and pituitary to chill out on the pituitary hormone release because the body is waiting to see whether all that hard work from the first half of the cycle will come to fruition in an implanting embryo.

The hormone crash that occurs on Day 1 of your cycle initiates a whole flurry of hormonal signaling from the brain and pituitary to help coordinate the activities surrounding the release and possible fertilization of an egg. However, once an egg is released (Day 12ish), the brain and pituitary can pretty much put their feet up and watch *The Bachelor*, because their hard work is done for a while. This is because the body is waiting to see whether anything materializes from the last round of egg development. So when hormone levels are low, the brain and pituitary have to do a bunch of stuff to initiate the possibility of conception (egg maturation and all that). But when hormone levels are high, the brain and pituitary can sit back until the next round of egg development.

The latter is the point in the cycle that is mimicked by the pill.

Rather than having dynamically changing hormones across the cycle like naturally cycling women do, pill-taking women get the *same* hormonal message delivered every day. The pill is able to cleverly work its magic by making the brain think that it is perpetually in a cycle phase in which FSH and LH aren't necessary. And when FSH and LH aren't being released in quantity, this prevents ovulation. And not ovulating means not getting pregnant. And not getting pregnant means sex whenever you want it. Just like men have been doing for years. By making small changes in their hormonal profile, pill-taking women's bodies prevent *themselves* from getting pregnant by not releasing an egg. Pregnancy prevention by hormonal déjà vu all over again. And *again*. Every. Single. Day. Which, whether you are a fan of the pill or not, you've got to admit, is pretty f***ing clever.

WHAT IS HORMONAL DÉJÀ VU?

With most pills, hormonal déjà vu is created via a daily dose of synthetic estrogen and progestin (a synthetic progesterone).* The dosage of hormones has been designed to be "read" by the brain as being roughly analogous to the progesterone-dominant second half of the cycle.

Now, you might be tempted to conclude that understanding women on the pill is simply a matter of understanding what women's brains usually do during the second half of the cycle. If this were true, we could anticipate that the brains and bodies of pill-taking women should do some of the same types of things that women's bodies do when they are in the luteal phase of the cycle.

And there may be some truth to this general idea.

But it's the kind of truth that has a big caveat. And the reason for this caveat is that no one really knows what the precise hormonal message relayed to women's bodies and brains by the pill *is*.

So, we know for certain that the brain and pituitary respond to the artificial hormones used in the birth control pill to the extent that they inhibit the release of FSH and LH. And we also know that these hormonal signals are picked up by the reproductive organs to the extent that

....
* Progestin-only pills manage to trick the brain using only artificial progesterone. These can work effectively because the high levels of progesterone that occur during the luteal phase are really the biggest moneymaker in terms of inhibiting pregnancy. They are usually paired with estrogen, though, since women generally prefer the way they feel on pills with both hormones.

they maintain the endometrium (preventing the breakthrough bleeding that occurs when hormones are too low). However, as of this writing, the full extent to which the artificial hormones in the birth control pill influence every other cell in the body that has hormone receptors for progesterone and estrogen—and whether they make these other bodily systems also act as if they are in the second half of the cycle when progesterone is dominant—isn't all that well understood. And this is something that we need to learn more about, because there's good reason to expect that the hormonal message the pill delivers—although similar enough to the "luteal phase" message to prevent ovulation—isn't perfectly equivalent to the same message when delivered by the body's own hormones. And part of the reason for this is that the hormones are made from different stuff.

For example, although the artificial estrogen (ethinyl estradiol) used in the pill is synthesized from actual estrogen, the majority of synthetic progestins out there are made from testosterone.*

Yes, testosterone.

Because the structural properties of progesterone molecules make them difficult to manipulate for use in medication, the progestins in birth control are actually made from something else. And in most of the pills out there, that something else is testosterone. Now, these testosterone molecules have been tinkered with in a way that makes them look like progesterone to your progesterone receptors (thus preventing the hormonal cascade that culminates in the release of an egg). However, they're not a perfect match. They don't bind to progesterone receptors quite as perfectly as real-deal progesterone does, and—proving that old habits die

....

* Like, the stuff in anabolic steroids, testosterone (T). But before you freak out about this, it's important to note that estradiol—which is synthesized in your own body—is also manufactured from testosterone using an enzyme called aromatase. So it's not totally cuckoo-crazy to have something in a female body that started out as T. However, the biosynthesis that transforms testosterone into estradiol fully converts these molecules into non-T-binding molecules. The same cannot be said for artificial progestins.

hard, even for hormones—they also have a pesky tendency to bind to testosterone receptors, too. This means they make women a little more testosterone-a-rific than women would normally be during the second half of their cycles. We're not talking about the type of thing that's going to secure you a place in your boyfriend's fantasy football league or get you eliminated from competing in the Olympics, but your pill might have masculinizing effects that you never bargained for. More on this in a minute.

So, what does all of this mean? Well, the precise hormonal message that is being read from the synthetic hormones in the pill doesn't necessarily mimic a naturally occurring hormonal message in the body. The fact that synthetic progestins bind to things other than progesterone receptors (for example, testosterone receptors) means that the hormonal message delivered by the pill will be at least somewhat different from the hormonal message typically conveyed by actual luteal-phase hormones. It is a useful starting point to predict that pill-taking women will exhibit biological and behavior tendencies that are more similar to those of non-pill-taking women in the luteal (waiting-for-implantation) phase of the cycle than at high fertility. However, the two hormonal messages aren't equivalent.

The good news is that you don't have to wait for science to figure out all the details to be able to make educated decisions about what the pill might mean for you. We know enough about the hormones in the pill and how the pill changes women for you to make informed choices about your health. For now, we'll talk about some of the hormonal differences in the various types of pills out there. Because it turns out that there are a lot of pills. And different pills do different things. Which is good stuff to know when you are trying to decide what the best option is for you.

PILLS, PILLS, AND MORE PILLS

The majority of birth control pills are combination pills that contain artificial estrogen and a progestin (an artificial version of progesterone). And although most pills out there use the same artificial estrogen (ethinyl estradiol, again, synthesized from estrogen), about ten different versions of artificial progestins are in use. These different types of progestins are grouped into four different "generations," based on the molecules from which they were derived and when they first appeared on the market (see the table below). You can check which kind is in your birth control by looking at the giant table at the end of this chapter.

Different Generations of Progestins

GENERATION	NOTES
First	Derived from testosterone (T). These are highly "progestational," meaning good at preventing the HPG cascade and preventing ovulation.
Second	Derived from testosterone (T). These are known to increase a person's risk of experiencing T-related side effects such as decreasing good cholesterol (HDL), increasing weight gain, and causing acne and hair growth in places you don't want hair. These effects are usually offset by the estrogen in these pills, but some women still experience these types of T-rific side effects.

Third	Derived from testosterone (T). However, the T molecules in this generation of progestins have been manipulated in a way that decreases the pesky T-related side effects (weight gain, acne, hairiness). These come with a higher risk of blood clots than second-generation pills do.
Fourth: Dienogest	A fourth-generation progestin derived from testosterone (T). However, unlike the others, this actually blocks T receptors, making it so T can't be "read" by the cells in your body. So even though it's made from T, it's anti-androgenic. This means fewer breakouts and less weight gain. This generation of progestin (including drospirenone, described below) is also really good for people who have problems with bleeding between periods.
Fourth: Drospirenone	Also a fourth-generation progestin, this is the only one that is not made out of testosterone; it's derived from a diuretic called spironolactone. Of all the progestins, this one has the most potent anti-androgen effects. It often promotes clearer skin and can promote initial weight loss because it exerts effects that can decrease water retention caused by estrogen.

The first three generations of progestins and one of the two fourth-generation progestins are synthesized from testosterone. Although these progestins act like actual progesterone in some respects (they bind to progesterone receptors, which prevents the HPG hormone cascade that culminates in the release of an egg), generations one through three also bind to testosterone receptors. As you might recall from chapter 2, when something binds to a specific hormone receptor, it makes the cell do whatever it's supposed to do when the given hormone is present. This means that pills using progestins derived from testosterone can have masculinizing effects on women, prompting things like breakouts, weight gain, and hair growth in places that you probably don't want hair. Some research suggests they may have some masculinizing effects on the brain, too, doing things like decreasing verbal fluency and increasing performance on mental rotation tasks. And if you're a black lemur (*Eulemur macaco*)—a sexually dimorphic primate, with brown-furred females and black-furred males—they make your fur turn black. Which is totally embarrassing. Even for a lemur.

First- and second-generation progestins are the most androgenic, which means that they're the ones with the most testosterone-a-rific side effects. Third-generation progestins have been modified to have fewer masculinizing side effects, but they are still made out of testosterone, and they still stimulate testosterone receptors; they just do less of it. These progestins are sufficiently non-masculinizing that many women don't notice any unwanted side effects. However, if you are among the lucky few(!) who are supersensitive to testosterone, fourth-generation pills may be your best bet, because fourth-generation progestins are not only non-masculinizing, they're actually anti-masculinizing. Their chemical structure blocks the effects of testosterone in the body. Unfortunately, blocking testosterone comes with costs of its own (they've been known to be libido killers), but some women might see this cost as being worth it to avoid unwanted hair growth and breakouts.

So what the hell are you supposed to do with all this information?

Well, I'm hoping that you use it to learn more about your options. As I mentioned, I've also provided a big table at the end of this chapter with more than forty of the most popular brands of hormonal contraceptives currently on the market. For each, I have listed the amount of artificial estrogen (ethinyl estradiol) as well as the type, amount, and generation of progestin it contains. Although you'll need to work with your doctor to find out which—if any—of these pills is the best place to start, I hope the info will help you troubleshoot this oftentimes confusing process of trial and error and determine what does and does not work for your body.

For example, if you're on a pill that you're not crazy about, look it up in the table to see (a) what generation of progestin it uses, and (b) what doses of estrogen and progestin it uses. My recommendation is that you first try to troubleshoot the progestin. If you are on a pill that uses a third-generation progestin, for example, and you don't like it, ask your doctor about trying one that uses a second- or fourth-generation progestin to see if you prefer how it makes you feel. Give it a couple of cycles before you make up your mind, and consider keeping a journal during this time. Note any changes in how you feel in terms of your mood, appetite, energy, sleep, libido, and any other life dimension that you think might be relevant to your decision (some additional things to look for may become apparent in later chapters). Once you find a progestin that your body responds to, you can work with your doctor to try to minimize some of the minor annoyances, like bleeding between periods, by playing around with different dosages of estrogen and progestin.

Finding the right pill can take some time and will require a little patience. It can be well worth the trouble, though, to find one that you like. Not having to worry about getting pregnant at an inopportune time is the ultimate equalizer and a huge deal for women. It just might not be easy. One thing that will become increasingly clear as we move through this book is that the way women's bodies respond to different formulations of hormones (or even different manufacturers' versions of the exact same synthetic hormones) can vary hugely. Each woman's body is different and will respond differently to adding artificial estrogens and progestins into the mix. For some women, these can increase estrogen or progesterone levels from where they were prior to taking the pill. For other women, they will decrease them. And the ways that these hormones influence everything else going on in the body and the brain will differ in ways that are specific to each woman.

To give you a quick example, I'll tell you about the experience that a friend of mine recently had when she tried switching from one type of pill to another. Now, I won't mention specific brands here, but I will tell you that the pill she switched to is the exact same pill that I was on for two years and loved. I used it in between having my two kids and had absolutely no problems with it whatsoever (remember: I didn't have my *"Holy sh**! I have spent a decade of my life half-asleep!"* epiphany until *after* I was off all hormonal contraception altogether). Well, my friend had a *very* different experience with this pill than I had. But before I get to the punch line, it's worth mentioning that this friend of mine is someone who is otherwise emotionally stable and does not have a history of psychological problems.

Then came the new pill.

Within forty-eight hours of going on the new pill, she experienced a very scary psychotic episode, during which she became super-anxious and paranoid. She started to believe that everyone she knew was actually an imposter, and not the real people they said they were. This five-day-long ordeal came to a head when one of her friends took her to the emergency room for a psychiatric evaluation after she texted him, asking if she could cut him open to make sure he was real!

I promise you that I am not making this up.

After arriving at the ER and going through the "Have you had any changes in your health recently?" checklist, the only thing that the doctors could put a finger on that was different between the time of her ER visit and before her breakdown was her new birth control regimen. Even though no one thought that her birth control could possibly be responsible for her psychotic episode, they advised her to at least try going off it, since they couldn't think of any reason why she was having this psychotic break from reality.

Twelve hours later, she was back to her old self.

Now, my point here isn't that the pill is a horrible drug that will make you go crazy and you shouldn't use it. Most women do *not* have this experience with this pill, and many women love it. *I* loved it. The point is that hormones influence *billions* of cells at once, and exactly what they do to each of those billions of cells differs somewhat from woman to woman. Whether it's weeping uncontrollably while on pill X, being hugely anxious on pill Y, or feeling like you don't have a conscience when on pill Z, I have heard pretty much every type of story that you might imagine about every type of pill out there. And for every horror story I've heard, there is also a line of women eagerly waiting to tell me that the exact same pill is the best thing that's ever happened to them.

And you know what?

They're *all* right.

The specific way that your body will respond to the pill's hormones depends on a whole bunch of things that are you-specific. Things like your pre-pill hormonal profile, your age, your health, your brain's neurotransmitter profile, your genes, and probably a bunch of other stuff that we don't yet know. This means that as we move forward and I tell you women's stories and discuss what research finds about how the pill changes women, you'll likely find that you recognize yourself in some things but not others. Each of us is unique, so what works for you might not work for your best friend. So if you're going to take the pill, I urge you to troubleshoot, troubleshoot, and troubleshoot some more until you find the one that works best for you.

THIS IS YOUR BRAIN (UTERUS, OVARIES, AND EVERYTHING ELSE) ON DRUGS

A big takeaway from this book is that the person you think of as you (capital Y-O-U you) is a product of the biological processes going on in your body. And huge among the mediators of these processes are your hormones. Although the pill was created to have a very specific, targeted effect on women (preventing ovulation, which means no pregnancy—brilliant!), hormones simply cannot work this way. There is no "magic bullet." You cannot (I repeat: *cannot)* send a "targeted" hormonal message to one part of the body and not to others. Although this is true of any medication you might take (side effects* and all that), this is *especially* true for medications that influence your hormones. No matter where you administer the hormones (whether you are wearing the vaginal ring, having a birth control implant in your arm, or getting a shot of Depo-Provera in your a**), they all end up in the same place.

And that place is everywhere.

Any hormone in your body—whether the real deal (we call these endogenous hormones) or one of the artificial (exogenous) hormones in the pill—will get picked up by all the cells in your body that have receptors for that hormone. They're able to turn billions of switches on and off throughout your body at one time, influencing which version of yourself your body creates. This includes whether or not you mature and release an egg (which is how the pill prevents you from getting pregnant), but also a whole bunch of other stuff, too. It's sort of like dropping an atomic bomb on your house to blow out a candle. Dropping a bomb on a house *will* blow out a candle. It's just that its effects are sufficiently . . . nonspecific . . . to make this a fairly unpopular way to deal with one's candle-extinguishing needs.

Over the years, the primary focus of doctors and medical researchers looking at the potential side effects of the pill has been on things that pose an acute threat to survival. We're talking about blood clots, stroke, changes in blood lipid profiles, dangerous changes in bodily electrolyte balance. And I think that we can agree that this sort of research is a very good thing for women. You can feel confident about the safety of the hormonal contraceptives that are out there (with all the fine print and

....

* Although, there's really no such thing. Medications only have *effects*. Calling the I-didn't-ask-for-this-to-happen effects *side* effects is a clever smoke-and-mirrors trick aimed at making medications appear more targeted than they are and minimizing our attention to the stuff we don't like.

caveats about not being an over-thirty-five-year-old smoker and that sort of thing). The reason for this confidence is the result of decades of thoughtfully conducted medical research. Doctors have been trained to protect the health and safety of their patients, and the research that has been conducted on the pill has reflected this focus.

However, until very recently, very little attention has been paid to what the birth control pill does to the *brain*—and therefore what it does to women: what it does to the *person*. There has been such a focus on safety (which, again, is huge, and the first thing that *should* be considered with a medication!) that very few people thought to consider the big picture.

Who does a woman become on the pill?

The brain and the rest of the body are too flush with hormone receptors for the pill *not* to change women. And it's not just the areas of the brain and body that are directly responsible for orchestrating your cycles and coordinating pregnancy. We're talking about areas of the brain that are responsible for things like emotional processing, social interactions, attention, learning, memory, facial recognition, self-control, eating behavior, and language processing. And we're also talking about non-brain body parts like the immune system, the stress response, and your gut hormones. This means the pill will have a ton of different effects on your whole body, from top to bottom. And the way that the pill influences these outcomes is often sufficiently downstream and indirect that we can't always say that the pill *directly caused* the outcome, because not much in biology actually works that way.

Take weight gain, for example.

Whether we like it or not, the idea of unintended weight gain is kind of a big deal for most women. Because of this, when considering their contraception options, many women wonder whether the pill will cause weight gain, because weight gain is something that they hope to avoid.

So, does it?

Maybe. But probably not for the reasons you think.

When most people think about medications causing weight gain, they usually imagine a scenario in which some chemical enters the body and then screws around with their metabolism or fat cells or whatever to cause fat accumulation. But this isn't actually the way this sort of thing works much of the time. Fat accumulation that occurs in response to things like medications, hormonal changes (including things like menopause and pregnancy), or having certain genes are oftentimes mediated by changes in *behavior*,* rather than being solely the result of some sort of unavoidable biochemical change. So if there's a medication out there that's known to be associated with weight gain, there's a good chance that the chemicals in the medication aren't *causing* it directly. Instead, they may be making you feel hungrier or sleepier, which causes you to eat more or work out less, which are actually the things that cause fat to accumulate.

So what about the pill and weight gain?

Well, a number of studies show that the pill, per se, does not *cause* weight gain. But a lot of research out there suggests that if you are on the pill and *do* gain weight, the hormones in the pill might have something to do with it.

The reason I say this is that a great deal of research in humans and other animals shows the estrogen surge that prompts ovulation predicts decreased food intake. This decrease is believed to reflect an unconscious motivational trade-off in which women's increased sexual motivation (all that fun stuff we talked about in chapter 3) comes at the expense of decreased motivation to do other things, like eat and digest.

Consistent with this interpretation, research finds that when estrogen and sexual motivation are at their highest across the cycle, hunger and food intake are at their lowest (see my picture on the next page). Conversely, food intake is highest when progesterone peaks during the

....
* There are exceptions to this, of course. Some genes and medications promote weight gain independent of changes in behavior. These are the exception, though.

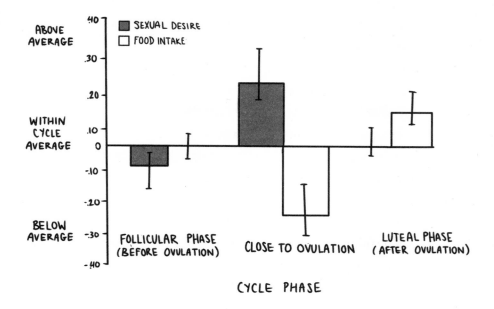

When conception is possible, women eat less and want sex more.

second half of the cycle (when women's bodies are preparing for the possibility of needing to provide an uninterrupted supply of energy to a developing fetus for nine months).

Now, this is all well and good across a typical ovulatory cycle. If women eat less during the first half of the cycle and more during the second, over time their weight will remain relatively stable. But pill-taking women don't have regular cycles. They are stuck in an artificial approximation of the luteal phase, with progestins being the predominant hormone. And the strongest evidence of hormonal contraceptives being linked to weight gain are in those types that have the highest ratio of progestin to estrogen. So using hormonal contraceptives like the pill might not *cause* weight gain in the strictest sense of the word (and enough research shows no link between pill taking and weight gain to suggest that this is the case). However, there is good reason to believe that, for women who aren't aware of the effects of hormones on eating behavior (and therefore don't monitor themselves for changes in food intake that could occur on the pill), being on the pill might prompt behavioral changes that cause weight gain. This means for some women the pill might be associated with weight gain (for those in whom it increases eating behavior), but for other women, it might not.

The effects of the pill on women and the world (I'm talking big picture here) are necessarily going to be far greater than the individual effects of the pill on specific parts of women (little picture, sensu stricto). As you'll see, changing a woman's hormones will change what she does. And when a woman's behavior changes, it can also change what other people do. And when these individual-level changes repeat themselves in women around the globe, this means that it can change the world. Sometimes for better, and sometimes for worse.

In the following chapters, we'll go over the different ways in which the pill changes women. We'll talk about how the hormones in the pill have downstream consequences on how women think, how they feel, how they experience stress, how they choose their romantic partners, how satisfied they are in their romantic relationships, how much they desire sex, and so on. Then we'll talk about the (much) broader ramifications. Some of this will come from the pages of research journals, some from the stories that women have shared with me, and some from the research conducted in my own lab. Although the science is still new and there are a lot of questions about some of the details, we know enough for you to be able to make more informed choices, not just about your health but about who you want to be.

Progestins and Estrogens in Some Frequently Used Hormonal Contraceptives

BRAND	ESTROGEN (AMOUNT)	PROGESTIN TYPE	GENERATION	PROGESTIN (AMOUNT)
Alesse	0.02 mg	levonorgestrel	Second	0.10 mg
Apri	0.03 mg	desogestrel	Third	0.15 mg
Aranelle	0.035 mg	norethindrone	First	0.50 mg;* 1.00 mg
Aviane	0.02 mg	levonorgestrel	Second	0.10 mg
Azurette	0.02 mg; 0.01 mg	desogestrel	Third	0.15 mg
Beyaz	0.02 mg	drospirenone	Fourth	3.00 mg
Camila	N/A	norethindrone	First	0.35 mg
Caziant	0.025 mg	desogestrel	Third	0.10 mg; 0.125 mg; 0.15 mg

* Pills listing multiple dosages vary the dosage across the twenty-eight-day pill cycle.

BRAND	ESTROGEN (AMOUNT)	PROGESTIN TYPE	GENERATION	PROGESTIN (AMOUNT)
Depo-Provera	N/A	medroxy progesterone	First	150.00 mg/every 3 months
Desogen	0.03 mg	desogestrel	Third	0.15 mg
Enpresse	0.03 mg; 0.04 mg	levonorgestrel	Second	0.05 mg; 0.075 mg; 0.125 mg
Errin	N/A	norethindrone	First	0.35 mg
Estrostep Fe	0.02 mg; 0.03 mg; 0.035 mg	norethindrone acetate	First	1.00 mg
Gianvi	0.02 mg	drospirenone	Fourth	3.00 mg
Heather	N/A	norethindrone	First	0.35 mg
Jencycla	N/A	norethindrone	First	0.35 mg
Jolivette	N/A	norethindrone	First	0.35 mg

BRAND	ESTROGEN (AMOUNT)	PROGESTIN TYPE	GENERATION	PROGESTIN (AMOUNT)
Kariva	0.02 mg; 0.01 mg	desogestrel	Third	0.15 mg
Lessina	0.02 mg	levonorgestrel	Second	0.10 mg
Levlite	0.02 mg	levonorgestrel	Second	0.10 mg
Levora	0.03 mg	levonorgestrel	Second	0.15 mg
Lo/Ovral	0.03 mg	norgestrel	Second	0.30 mg
Loestrin	0.02 mg	norethindrone acetate	First	1.00 mg
Low-Ogestrel	0.03 mg	norgestrel	Second	0.30 mg
Lybrel	0.02 mg	levonorgestrel	Second	0.09 mg
Mircette	0.02 mg; 0.01 mg	desogestrel	Third	0.15 mg
Mirena	N/A	levonorgestrel	Second	Approx. 0.02 mg/day

BRAND	ESTROGEN (AMOUNT)	PROGESTIN TYPE	GENERATION	PROGESTIN (AMOUNT)
Natazia	3.00 mg; 2.00 mg; 1.00 mg	dienogest	Fourth	0.00 mg; 2.00 mg; 3.00 mg
Nor-QD	N/A	norethindrone	First	0.35 mg
Nora-BE	N/A	norethindrone	First	0.35 mg
Nordette	0.03 mg	levonorgestrel	Second	0.15 mg
NuvaRing	Approx. 0.015 mg/ day	etonogestrel	Third	Approx. 0.12 mg/day
Ocella	0.03 mg	drospirenone	Fourth	3.00 mg
Ortho Tri-Cyclen	0.035 mg	norgestimate	Third	0.18 mg; 0.215 mg; 0.25 mg
Ortho-Novum	0.035 mg	norethindrone	First	0.50 mg; 1.00 mg
Ortho Micronor	N/A	norethindrone	First	0.35 mg

BRAND	ESTROGEN (AMOUNT)	PROGESTIN TYPE	GENERATION	PROGESTIN (AMOUNT)
Previfem	0.035 mg	norgestimate	Third	0.25 mg
Reclipsen	0.03 mg	desogestrel	Third	0.15 mg
Safyral	0.03 mg	drospirenone	Fourth	3.00 mg
Seasonale	0.03 mg	levonorgestrel	Second	0.15 mg
Seasonique	0.03 mg	levonorgestrel	Second	0.15 mg
TriNessa	0.035 mg	norgestimate	Third	0.18 mg; 0.215 mg; 0.25 mg
Triphasil	0.03 mg; 0.04 mg	levonorgestrel	Second	0.05 mg; 0.075 mg; 0.125 mg
Velivet	0.025 mg	desogestrel	Third	0.10 mg; 0.125 mg; 0.15 mg
Yasmin	0.03 mg	drospirenone	Fourth	3.00 mg
Yaz	0.02 mg	drospirenone	Fourth	3.00 mg

CHAPTER 5: SEXY IS IN THE EYE OF THE PILL-TAKER

Most of us would probably agree that attraction, love, sex, and marriage are the kinds of things that qualify for "big deal" status in a person's life. And since they're a big deal, these aren't the sorts of things that we would want our birth control pills to mess with.

But of course they do.

Consider the experiences of Olivia and Anneliese,* two women who were on the pill when they chose their partners and then went off it.

Olivia is a thirty-five-year-old attorney who has been married for ten years. She met her husband in law school and married him a few years later. At the time she met him, she was on the pill, as she had been since her senior year in college. Although her relationship with her husband had never been intensely passionate, she never felt it needed to be. She actually prided herself on the fact that she was no longer distracted by men and sex the way she had been in her early college years. She was very

....

* Each of these women is actually a fictional composite character made up using elements from several women's stories (along with some made-up details to personify the characters). Characters of this sort will be used throughout the book to help personify women's experiences with the pill without compromising the confidentiality of anyone who has shared their story with me.

focused on her career and felt like she couldn't be bothered by the types of intensely sexual relationships that she'd had earlier. She had sex with her husband regularly, but she was indifferent about it. She didn't spend time thinking about sex, and she regularly told her girlfriends that she could never have sex again and it wouldn't bother her at all. She felt like she had moved beyond the whims of attraction and desire, both of which took up a lot of her mental energy when she was younger.

She went off the pill after the birth of their first and only child when her husband had a vasectomy. And although she didn't feel different at first, she began to notice that she was thinking about sex a lot more frequently than she used to. More startlingly, she found that she was thinking about sex with men who were not her husband. She was finding herself sexually attracted to men she met when traveling for work and while at the park with her son. She remembers vividly when it struck her that something was going on: "I was on a plane to L.A. to give a presentation. As I was walking through the first-class cabin, I found myself making eye contact with some of the attractive men in suits who were sitting there looking so sexy and self-assured. This is when I knew that I was in big trouble. I felt like this sexual tigress, and it was so startling to me. I wondered whether everything that I thought to be true about me in the last decade was a lie."

Soon after that, Olivia began to question her relationship with her husband. Because she was now having all these feelings for other men—feelings that she'd never had for her husband—she wondered whether maybe she had married the wrong man. She'd thought for so long that she was just totally past all the messiness of sexual desire, but she started to realize that these feelings had just been buried by the pill. Her desire for her partner remained flat, which she soon remedied by getting involved in a sexual relationship with an attractive judge she met at a party. She suspected that going off the pill may have played a role in her desire reawakening, and because of this, she continues to toy with the idea of going back on it to get her life back in order, but she always hesitates. "I don't want to feel like I'm asleep anymore," she says. Both relationships are ongoing, and she continues to struggle with knowing what to do next.

Or consider twenty-three-year-old Anneliese. Like many women her age, Anneliese began taking the pill at seventeen to normalize her periods. During her third year in college, she began a relationship with a guy she'd met during a study-abroad trip. Although he was also an American, he lived three states over. After returning home, they spent some time doing the "long-distance thing" before he finally moved in with her.

This relationship was in year three when she went off the pill. Before she'd gone on it, she used to love to exercise and go shopping, and spent a lot of time putting together funky outfits from vintage clothing stores and doing her makeup and hair. Her interest in these types of activities had subsided as she was getting ready to graduate from high school and enter college, which she assumed was the result of becoming more mature and serious about her schoolwork. After she went off the pill, she felt like she didn't know who she was anymore. First, she noticed that her disgust sensitivity was now off the charts; she found smells and sights that she hadn't noticed previously totally disgusting. This included the smell of her boyfriend's dogs and (much worse!) her boyfriend. She also found that she was interested once again in shopping and exercise. She lost five pounds. She later got a breast-augmentation procedure and broke up with her boyfriend (and his dogs). She feels like herself again.

Before I throw us both in the deep end with what the research says about all this, I want to remind you that the birth control pill is made of artificial sex hormones and that sex hormones flip billions of switches on and off in cells throughout your body, influencing the version of yourself that you are. This means that—*of course*—the pill will mess with all your love- and sex-related brain circuitry. It would be impossible for it not to. And if this all seems super-obvious to you, you're two steps ahead of where I was when I first learned about it. Despite my two decades of research looking at biological influences on women's relationship psychology, I managed to be totally blindsided by the research we're going to go over in the next couple of chapters. This research, although still in its infancy, suggests that the pill has the potential to influence who you're attracted to, the dynamics of your relationships, the quality of your sex life, how you respond to your partner's face, how sexy *you* are to others, and your likelihood of getting a divorce. In other words, the pill influences pretty much everything that matters when it comes to love and sex. This is pretty provocative stuff, as it suggests that the pill may be changing the face of modern women's relationships.

Maybe yours.

Let's start by talking about attraction. We've already talked a fair amount about the various ways that women's hormones influence who they're most attracted to. As we've discussed in the preceding chapters, decades of research suggest that as estrogen increases across the cycle, so, too, does sexual motivation and attunement to cues of good genetic quality in men. In particular, this research finds that at times in the cycle when estrogen is high—which naturally happens mid-cycle—women have a stronger preference for men whose faces, voices, and behaviors have testosterone markers (we're talking square jaws, deep voices, and swagger) than they do when estrogen is low. Remember: Estrogen loves testosterone. The research also finds that estrogen tends to heighten women's preference for the scent of men who possess testosterone markers, whose faces and bodies are symmetrical, and/or whose immune genes are different from their own. The latter is something that helps prevent inbreeding (as if we really need additional reinforcements against *that* . . . yuck!) and promotes the health of any resulting children by increasing the number of pathogens the body is able to recognize and eliminate, thus decreasing the risk of infection and illness.*

....

* I'm talking about the genes from the major histocompatibility complex, or MHC (in humans, these are also referred to as the HLA genes). The MHC is a set of genes that codes for cell surface markers that your immune system uses to discriminate its own parts and peptides (the parts in your body that make you, you) from those belonging to things like parasites, viruses, and bacteria that make you sick. MHC loci are highly polymorphic, which means that there are a ton of different versions of them floating around the gene

But what happens, then, to women's mate preferences when they're on the pill? Since (a) pill-taking women don't ovulate, and (b) the artificial hormones in the pill fake out the brain by making it think that it's in the progesterone-dominant luteal phase of the cycle (or some approximation of this, anyway), this raises the possibility that birth control pills might have the ability to influence the types of men that women choose as their partners.

Holy sh**!

Scientists have only recently started to explore this possibility. And although this research is new and the results are mixed, the picture that is beginning to emerge is fascinating. They suggest that the birth control pill might influence everything ranging from who you pick as your partner to the likelihood that you'll get divorced.

THIS IS YOUR MATE ON DRUGS

In light of what the artificial hormones in the pill do (make every day the same, hormonally), it's probably not terribly surprising to learn that pill-taking women don't experience any cyclicity in their mate preferences. Instead of experiencing an increased preference for sexy men at high fertility like naturally cycling women do, pill-taking women exhibit an unwavering preference for men with *less* masculine faces and voices, which are preferred by naturally cycling women during the second half of their cycles, when progesterone is high.

....

pool—so many, in fact, that unrelated people are very unlikely to possess identical MHC genes. The cool thing about MHC genes (and the reason we should want partners who have different genes than we do) is that they are expressed co-dominantly. This means that both sets of genes (the ones from mom and the ones from dad) get turned on. The current wisdom is that having variable (rather than similar) MHC genes allows a person to present a wider range of pathogen-derived peptides to patrolling T cells, improving immune defense and making for a healthier you.

For example, in one study, researchers brought two groups of women into a research lab during the follicular phase of their cycles and allowed them to use a special computer program to manipulate the appearance of photographs of male and female faces. They could alter the appearance of the men and women in the photographs by clicking on a computer mouse that masculinized or feminized the facial prototype by changing things like the jaw height, face width, and cheekbone prominence of the faces in 10 percent increments. Unbeknownst to the women in the study, these are the types of facial features that tend to vary as a function of a person's levels of sex hormones. The researchers asked the women to manipulate the male face to look like that of their ideal short-term and long-term romantic partners. They also asked them to manipulate the female face to create the face of a maximally attractive woman. After their first laboratory session, half the women started taking hormonal contraceptive pills (the experimental group), and the other half did not (the control group). Both groups of women came back to the lab three months later and completed this task a second time.

When the researchers compared the two sets of images created by the naturally cycling women (the control group), they found no differences between the faces they created during session one and session two. However, for the women who started the pill, they found that these women's ideal male faces became significantly less masculine during the second session. Once these women were on the pill, the faces they created became more feminized, with narrower jawbones and rounder silhouettes, than the ones they had created just three months prior. This was true both for the faces the women made to represent their ideal long-term and short-term mating partners. Importantly, the researchers didn't find a similar effect when comparing the ideal female faces that the women designed. They were the same across testing sessions, suggesting that the effect of the pill on masculinity preferences is specific to their preference for *men*.

In a second study, these same researchers wanted to test whether women on the pill actually choose less masculine men as relationship partners relative to their non-pill-taking counterparts. Like, in real life. To this end, they recruited a large sample of men who were in relationships with women. Half of the sample was made up of men who were chosen by their partners when their partners were on the birth control pill. The other half of the sample were men whose partners were *not* on the pill at the time that they met. The researchers then took the men's photographs so that they could compare the average facial masculinity of the sample of men chosen by women on the pill with the average facial masculinity of the men chosen by women who weren't. They measured the men's subjective masculinity (how masculine their faces look to outside raters) and also their objective masculinity (which is calculated by assessing cheekbone prominence, the ratio of jaw height to lower-face height, and the ratio of face height to width).

Have you anticipated the punch line?

The men chosen by pill-taking women had significantly less masculine faces than those men who were chosen by non-pill-taking women.

Now, even you if you saw that one coming, you have to admit that this is pretty intriguing stuff. The idea that women might choose different partners when they are on the pill than when they are off it suggests that the pill may have rippling effects on the quality and dynamics of women's long-term relationships. Maybe even the risk of divorce or infidelity. It also raises a number of provocative questions that researchers hadn't even considered asking until now. For example, if pill-taking women aren't really all that interested in sexiness when choosing partners, what exactly *are* they looking for? And if the pill makes women focus their mate choice on one set of qualities but not another, this raises the (potentially more serious) question of what this might mean for women's relationships when one set of hormones chooses their partner (the hormones in the pill, for example), but a different set of hormones is stuck in a relationship with him (the naturally cycling version of yourself).

To address the first question, researchers conducted a survey of relationship quality on a sample of more than two thousand women, each of whom had at least one child. Half the women in the sample were on the

ITEM	WHO IS MORE SATISFIED?
Partner's financial provisioning	On Pill > Off Pill
Partner's intelligence	On Pill > Off Pill
Sexual arousal	On Pill < Off Pill
Sexual adventurousness	On Pill < Off Pill
Sexual proceptivity	On Pill < Off Pill
Sexual attraction	On Pill < Off Pill
Partner's support	On Pill < Off Pill
Partner's body attractiveness	On Pill < Off Pill
Orgasm with partner	On Pill = Off Pill
Partner's loyalty	On Pill = Off Pill
Partner's ambition	On Pill = Off Pill
Partner rejection	On Pill = Off Pill
Compliant sex	On Pill = Off Pill
Partner's facial attractiveness	On Pill = Off Pill

How satisfied women were with different aspects of their relationships depending on whether they picked their partners while on or off the pill.

pill when they met their partners, and half were not. The survey asked women questions about the quality of their relationship with the man who fathered their first child, regardless of whether they were still involved in a relationship with the guy.

You can see the results of this survey in the table above. The white items are those areas of relationship satisfaction that were greater for the women who chose their partners when they were on the pill. The light-gray items are the aspects of relationship satisfaction that were higher for the women who were not on the pill when they chose their partners. The dark-gray items are the aspects of relationship satisfaction that didn't differ between pill-takers and non-pill-takers.

Naturally cycling women—in addition to choosing sexier partners—seem to be enjoying better sex-related . . . well, pretty much everything when compared with women who chose their partners while on the pill. This makes a lot of sense when we consider all the research showing that naturally cycling women—at least for the phase of their cycle when estrogen is dominant—are particularly attuned to sexiness. And it also makes a lot of sense that women who are paired with sexy partners would be more inclined to want to have sex with their partners than would women paired with less sexy men. They're sexy, for crying out loud. It's what you do. Choosing your partner when you are on the pill appears to predict less long-term attraction and sexual satisfaction than what you might get from a relationship initiated by the non-pill-taking version of yourself.

[INSERT DISAPPOINTED TRUMPET SOUNDS HERE.]

Now, the good news is that everything in life is a trade-off. And this means that there will be an upside to having a partner who was chosen by your birth control pill. And the upside, it turns out, is one that is pretty meaningful to a lot of women.

As you can see in the table on the previous page, women who chose their partners when they were on the pill were more satisfied with their partners' financial-provisioning ability and intelligence than were the women who chose their partners when they were off it.* This result is

....
* Although you may tire of my dichotomizing investment with sexiness (dads or cads; Madonnas or whores; Berts or Ernies, etc.), these trade-offs are par for the course in the world of biology. Life history theory (which is a big-deal theory in evolutionary biology) is all about predicting how organisms (or individuals) will invest their limited time and

believed to emerge from the (artificial) progesterone-a-rific hormonal profile of pill-taking women, which is reasoned to cause their brains to emphasize qualities that would have helped to keep them safe and secure when preparing for pregnancy. Such an interpretation is echoed in the results of brain-imaging research. When compared with naturally cycling women, pill-taking women exhibit less activity in the reward centers of the brain when looking at masculine faces, but more activity in these centers when looking at money. This is nothing to sneeze at, because money and financial security matter. So being on the pill probably doesn't make women choose partners who are any better or worse than they would have chosen if they were off it. It just makes them prioritize different things. And this small shift in priorities may come with benefits of its own when it comes to the divorce rate.

Despite the whole my-sex-life-is-meh-and-I-am-not-that-attracted-to-my-partner thing, another pattern observed in this study was that women who chose their partners when they were on the pill were significantly *less* likely to divorce than women who chose their partners when they were off it(!!!). So maybe the key to long-term marital bliss (or at least long-term marital married-ness) is choosing a partner for his brains and provisioning ability rather than sexiness. Or maybe the pill makes women zero in on some other unmeasured quality that is the key to long-term matrimony. Regardless of the reason, the pattern is intriguing. Even more intriguing yet was the fact that when these pill-taking women *did* get divorced, they were overwhelmingly the ones who

....

energy budgets in doing all the things that are required for survival and reproduction. Things like growing, maturing, mating, and parenting. One of the key resource-investment trade-offs that organisms are confronted with is whether to invest in mating or whether to invest that effort in resource acquisition, caregiving, or parenting. If you make a trade-off that prioritizes mating (which life history theory predicts that sexy men should because they're likely to be more successful and produce more robust offspring than less sexy men), this means that you're necessarily going to have less time and effort available for other things, like caregiving. This is why mating or parenting and caregiving are almost always dichotomized in art and literature. Art imitates life. And life is filled with trade-offs. You'll find the Madonna-whore dichotomy in species ranging from honeybees to human beings, because mating and caregiving cannot simultaneously be maximized.

initiated it: They were the initiators 84.5 percent of the time, compared to being the initiators 73.6 percent of the time among those who chose their partners when not on the pill. So although prioritizing financial security (at the expense of sexiness) may lead to more stable marriages, one of the biggest threats to these marriages is that a woman herself will become dissatisfied. And this research suggests that the most reasonable culprit in this dissatisfaction is lack of attraction and sexual satisfaction.

!!!!! . . . !

The idea that the quality and longevity of women's long-term relationships might be impacted, for better and for worse, by their method of pregnancy prevention is just so . . . *big*. It's almost unbelievable. But before we get too carried away, it is worth noting that the results of this study are open to interpretation. The scientist in me is obliged to point this sort of thing out, even in the face of exciting research results.

For example, because this research compared the relationship outcomes of women who were on the pill when they chose their partners with women who were not, it's possible that the results reflect preexisting differences in the types of men preferred by these different groups of women. For example, women who stay on the pill even when they're not in a relationship (remember that our pill-takers were already on the pill when they met their partners) may be more inclined to choose romantic partners for reasons of the head (*Is he a good provider and likely to be faithful?*) rather than reasons of the heart (*Is he so delicious that I want to bite him and sit in his lap all day?*). So we can't know for certain whether the pill is responsible for the differences observed between these two groups of women. It's also hard to know whether any differences that we see between these two groups of women are the result of *being* on the pill, *going on* the pill, or *going off* the pill, because the researchers didn't measure women's usage of birth control pills over the course of their relationships.

To answer these questions, a separate group of researchers looked at data collected from two samples of married couples who were followed over a period of one to four years. The researchers had information about whether the women in the samples were on or off the pill when they chose their partners, whether they subsequently went off it or on it, and whether they experienced any changes in their sexual and marital satisfaction as a result of this change.

The first thing these researchers found was that women who were not on the pill when they chose their partners, but *then* went on it, reported a decrease in sexual satisfaction as a result. We will revisit this issue in greater detail in the next chapter, but this is pretty much what a person would expect to see, given what the artificial hormones in the pill do to women's libidos. These women reported no changes in marital satisfaction in response to starting the pill, which suggests that going on the pill might diminish the quality of women's sex lives, but it does so without harming how they feel about their partners or the relationship itself. The sex thing is a bummer for sure, but in the grand scheme of things, these results suggest that initiating pill use after a relationship begins isn't likely to cause enough of an earthquake to put a permanent crack in the relationship's foundation.

Takeaway (Part I): No pill to pill—sexual satisfaction may decrease, but there are ways around that if you like everything else the pill affords you.

So, what about the women who were *on* the pill and then went *off* it?

If we look at this question from a strictly biochemical perspective, we should expect that when women go off the pill, the amount of satisfaction they feel with the sexual aspects of their relationship should *increase*. As I've already alluded to once before, the hormones in the pill can throw a big wrench in the works when it comes to the hormones that regulate sexual desire and bonding. So women who meet their partners while on the pill and subsequently go off it—all else being equal—should experience an increase in sexual satisfaction.

But this research found that they didn't. In fact, these women experienced a *decrease* in sexual satisfaction, which doesn't seem to make any sense at all. Why on earth would stopping the pill cause women's sexual satisfaction to decrease?

Although we can't know for sure, the data strongly suggests that this effect might have something to do with the fact that the pill-version of a woman and the non-pill-version of a woman may want to have sex with different types of people. Remember: Pill-taking women don't exhibit the preference for masculinity that is observed in naturally cycling women, and they prefer rounder, more feminine faces. If that's the sort of man a woman chooses as her partner when she is on the pill, there's a chance that the non-pill-taking version of that same woman might not be all that attracted to him. As unsettling as this interpretation may be, it is echoed in the pattern of marital-satisfaction changes observed among these women when they went off the pill. Here, the researchers found that going off the pill led to changes in women's marital satisfaction, but whether these changes were positive or negative depended on . . . drum-roll, please . . . how attractive their husbands were!

Given that pill-taking women seem less tuned in to sexiness cues than naturally cycling women, the researchers suspected that the attractive-ness of the husbands would influence what happens to relationship satis-faction among women who go off the pill after getting married. So they had photos of all the men's faces in both studies rated on attractiveness to test whether this had any impact on how women felt about their relation-ships after going off the pill. They found that women with more attractive husbands reported *increased* marital satisfaction after going off the pill than they reported while on it. Women with less attractive husbands, on the other hand, experienced a *decrease* in relationship satisfaction after going off the pill.

This tells us that if pill-taking women somehow manage to stumble into a relationship with an attractive man (despite not prioritizing attrac-tiveness), once they're off the pill, they feel happier about their marriage. And I guess we would all probably feel that way if we suddenly realized that our romantic partners possessed this positive quality that we never knew we wanted but are now glad we have. Women who weren't as fortunate, on the other hand—who didn't serendipitously somersault into a relationship with a hot guy without even trying—became *less* satisfied with their partners once they were off the pill and sexiness started to matter.

Interestingly, since the time I began drafting this book, some new research has failed to find differences between women's facial preferences or relationship satisfaction based on their pill-taking status. And this is the way that science works. Learning about the ways of the world through science is something that unfolds in a series of shuffle steps forward, followed by shuffle steps backward, followed by more steps forward . . . But this doesn't mean that you need to forget everything I just told you. Instead, it just means that we're still in the early phases of the science, and you might want to take these results as being preliminary. It will probably be years before we have definitive answers about the reliability with which the pill influences women's facial preferences and relationship satisfaction. And it will be longer yet before we know whether these effects vary depending on the hormonal composition of the pills that the women are on (which I suspect play a huge role in driving the contradictory results). Until that time, you can use this information to help you know what to look for in your own relationships. Each woman's pill experience will be a little different from everyone else's, and the only one who can tell you whether these results are meaningful to you is you.

SCENTS OR SENSIBILITY?

Taking the pill might change the traits that women prioritize in their partners. Because pill-taking women don't ovulate, they don't experience the pre-ovulatory estrogen surge that increases attention to markers of genetic quality in men. So being on the pill is—at a minimum—probably going to decrease the priority that women place on a partner's sex appeal when choosing mates. And it's easy to assume that this sort of shift is something that occurs because women on the pill are deliberately choosing not to prioritize sexiness in a sort of cerebral, not-judging-a-book-by-its-cover approach to mating. In this scenario, pill-taking women downplay the importance of sexiness in their partners because they have instead chosen to prioritize caregiving qualities in response to the progesterone-dominant hormonal profile mimicked by the pill.

However, research in neuroscience and psychophysics suggests that the lack of preference for sexy, genetic-quality markers on the part of pill-taking women may actually run far deeper than a this-for-that, book-over-cover trade-off. Rather than being something that women *notice* but choose to ignore, this research suggests that pill-taking women might not actually notice these differences at all. The pill might actually blunt women's sensory acuity in a way that renders them *unable* to tell the difference between men who have markers of high genetic quality and those who do not.

For example, in one study, researchers measured women's sensitivity to six different scents. Three of the scents—peppermint, rose, and lemon—didn't have a whole lot to do with sex or mate choice (unless you've got a thing for candy canes). The other three were scents that are believed to play a key role in women's ability to discriminate between high- and low-quality partners. These were a musk odorant (similar to the scent of men's naturally occurring body odors) and two testosterone metabolites, androstenone and androsterone. Researchers measured sensory acuity to each of these types of scents in three groups of women: pill-taking women, naturally cycling women during the periovulatory (estrogen-dominant) phase of the cycle, and naturally cycling women during the luteal (progesterone-dominant) phase of the cycle.

When it came to the non-sex-related scents, there were no differences among the groups of women. Pill-taking women were just as sensitive to the scents of peppermint, rose, and lemon as both groups of naturally cycling women were. When it came to the sexy scents, though, clear differences emerged between the pill-taking and naturally cycling women. The naturally cycling women were significantly more sensitive to the scent of musk and the two testosterone metabolites than women who were on the pill were. The pill-taking women didn't start to detect these scents until they were more or less being hit over the head with them. Follow-up analyses found that the differences between the pill-takers and non-pill-takers were most pronounced when the pill-takers were being compared with the naturally cycling women during the periovulatory phase of the cycle (when conception risk was high). Women were less sensitive to each of these scents during the luteal phase of their cycles, with their sensitivity thresholds becoming more similar to pill-taking women's (although never reaching the same nadir).

Although it may seem a little surprising that your sense of smell is influenced by sex hormones (whether your own or those in the pill), it actually makes a lot of sense when we think about what your different sensory systems do. A major charge of these systems (which includes your sense not only of smell but also sound, sight, and taste) is to notice and discriminate between things in the environment so that you can parse the world into meaningful categories, like good/bad, hot/not, and approach/avoid. The sharper your senses are, the better you are at discriminating between things that co-reside in the same stimulus category.* For example, if you have a sensitive palate, you are better able to discriminate between the taste of a cabernet sauvignon and a cabernet franc. If you have a good sense of hearing, you can tell the difference between the music notes C and D (and the difference between an A-sharp and an A-flat).

....

* There's a learning component to this, too, of course. You can actually increase your ability to discriminate between stimuli with experience and discrimination training. For example, if you take a class on wines, you can train your brain to tell the difference between a cabernet and a Malbec (and between a $9 Malbec and one that costs $150). This training will lead to an increased number of synaptic connections in the areas of your brain that are responsible for enjoying wine. Cheers to your brain!

Now, given what sensory systems do, it makes good sense for these systems to be sensitive to the presence of sex hormones. Because relatively high levels of estrogen tell the body that it's running the "conception is possible" software program, it makes good sense for the brain to throw all its efforts behind increasing our sensory system's ability to discriminate between high- and low-quality men at this time. Remember: The process of evolution by selection—the process that designed you and all your amazing traits—works its magic on the basis of a process of inheriting traits that helped promote *reproduction*. Because of this, the ability to discriminate between partners (and the quality of their genes) is one of the most valuable functions that your brain will ever perform. *Especially* when conception is possible. We're talking about decisions that influence which genes will become intertwined with your own and impact your ultimate evolutionary fate here. This isn't the sort of thing that natural selection is going to f*** around with.*

It makes good evolutionary sense for our brain to throw all available resources into maximizing our brain's ability to discriminate between high- and low-quality partners when estrogen is high and conception is possible. Experiencing increased sensitivity to sensory cues at high fertility is the sort of thing that would have offered women a distinct mating advantage, helping them separate the men from the boys. And given the research demonstrating cycle-based changes in women's preference for both vocal and facial masculinity, it's likely that we'll soon find women's sex hormones increase their sensitivity to sights and sounds, too. Your

....

* If you don't believe this, consider the male redback spider. These males often allow themselves to be eaten alive by their lovers while they're still inside them! They do this because the likelihood of insemination actually increases when the males allow the female to do this (apparently, the spastic convulsions that accompany being cannibalized allow for deeper penetration of sperm—fertility doctors, take note). The males that do this have inherited their deadly kink from their successful fathers, which passed it down in greater numbers than copies of genes coding for safer, more-vanilla sexual practices. When traits are shaped by evolution by selection, sex almost always wins. Even if it kills you.

brain should be its smartest, most sensitive self at times when conception is possible.

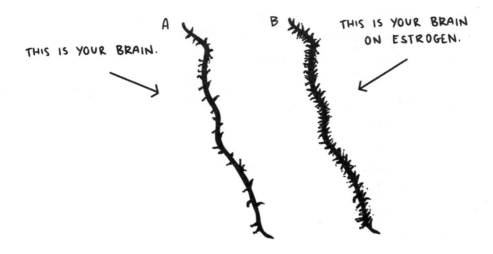

A THIS IS YOUR BRAIN.

B THIS IS YOUR BRAIN ON ESTROGEN.

A visualization of the differences in the number of dendritic spines on women's brain cells when estrogen is present versus absent.

This idea that women's brains should go full tilt at high fertility is supported by research in neuroscience, which shows that estrogen acts like fertilizer on multiple regions of women's brains. Although we tend to think of the brain as being a stable entity that doesn't change a whole lot over the course of weeks or months, it's actually a very dynamic system that changes continuously. And one of the things known to be a significant player in this dynamic is the presence of estrogen. For many key populations of brain cells—including those involved in olfaction, learning, and memory—estrogen works like Miracle-Gro, causing brain cells to sprout new connections (see the picture above) and making them more excitable and responsive to their environment. So for the brain, estrogen ushers in springtime, when everything blossoms into its most beautiful form, increasing sensitivity to the environment during times when conception is possible. And then when estrogen levels fall, these connections retract to their dormant state, ushering in your period of hormonal winter.*

So, although it is possible that pill-taking women simply care less about the cues to high genetic quality than naturally cycling women do (valuing, instead, cues to earning potential, caregiving, or witty conversation), it's also possible that pill-taking women simply don't notice the difference between men who have these good genes markers and those who do not (or both!). And because they don't notice them, they don't exhibit a preference for them. Because pill-taking women's brains are in a perpetual state of hormonal winter, their sensory acuity may not be attuned to genetic quality and compatibility cues in the same way that naturally cycling women's brains are.

Regardless of the reasons, these differences can potentially mean trouble for women if they choose their partners while on the pill and then go off it. Aside from the problems encountered by the Olivias and Annelieses of the world, if we are to take the research on women's cyclically changing mate preferences seriously, ovulation increases our preferences for qualities in men that will help promote the continued replication of our genes. The idea that there is innate wisdom in our mate preferences— and that they help guide us toward those men with healthy, compatible genes—raises the possibility that choosing our partners when we are on the pill may cause problems when it comes to reproduction.

....

* The link between fertility and sensory acuity is also well illustrated by the changes that occur in sensory acuity over the life-span. For example, humans lose more than thirty decibels of sensitivity to sound by age sixty-five. This same pattern is observed with the other senses, like our visual and olfactory acuity. This is why people tend to wear glasses, talk louder, and wear increasingly intense perfume as they age. And before you accuse me of ageism and the perpetuation of stereotypes, let me add that we see the same patterns in birds and other animals (I could go on and on about the research into this sort of thing in songbirds). One of the most important jobs that our sensory systems do is help us discriminate between genes we want and genes we don't—making our sensory systems highly sensitive to our sex hormones and reproductive status.

WARNING: THE FOLLOWING SECTION IS SUPER-SPECULATIVE.

If we naturally prefer men whose genes are well suited to commingling with our own, then it may be more difficult for women who met their partners on the pill to get pregnant. Women's bodies screen embryos for health before allowing them to implant themselves (all that grisly stuff we talked about in chapter 1). So if women on the pill are at a greater risk for choosing genetically incompatible partners than non-pill-taking women, it's not wholly unreasonable to think that women who chose their partners when on the pill may have more difficulty becoming pregnant than women who chose their partners when not on the pill. We'll talk a lot more about this possibility in chapter 9, but for now, it's just a little food for thought as you consider what all this research might mean for women who pick their partners while on the pill.

A second possibility that gets raised if we are to accept the "wisdom of our ancestors" approach to mate preferences is that the children born to women who chose their partners on the pill will be less healthy than those chosen by women who were not on the pill. Although there is very little research on this topic, one recent study suggests that choosing your partner on the pill could be predictive of more health problems for your children. In this study, the researchers conducted a survey of 192 mothers who each had a child age one to eight. They were given a twenty-three-item questionnaire about the health of their child and whether they'd met the father while they were on or off hormonal contraceptives. Although most of the women in the study reported that they began their relationship with the father of their child when they were not on the pill, a third of them reported that they were. When comparing the health of the children born to couples who met on the pill with those of couples who met without it, the researchers found that the children born to couples who met on the pill had the poorer overall health. Their children were more prone to infection, had worse perceived health than their peers, had taken more trips to see the doctor in the past three months and in the past year, and were sick more often than the children born to couples who met without the influence of the pill.

Given that this study was just putting a toe in the water in terms of understanding whether there are differences in reproductive outcomes that stem from pill taking, we need to be cautious. The differences between these two groups of children could have resulted from a million different things, including the preexisting differences between the types of women who are long-term pill-takers and those who are not. For example, maybe the pill-takers were on the pill to help with irregular cycles, something that is itself linked with poorer health. Or maybe they were older, since pill-taking women often go on the pill to build their careers before having babies. It's also possible that women who are chronic pill-takers are just more inclined to think about things related to health and, as a result, perceive more illness in their children. There is no way to know for certain at this point, as the necessary research hasn't been done yet.

Do you need to be alarmed about the health of your (future) children if you met your partner while on the pill?

The short answer is no. We don't yet understand whether choosing a partner when on the pill increases a woman's risk of infertility with her partner or increases her children's risk of health problems. And even if the research eventually finds conclusive evidence that it does, it's not a doomsday scenario. The research that has been done on pill-based partner choice suggests that being on the pill may increase women's *risk* of choosing a partner with less-compatible genes. Sort of like how eating processed foods increases your *risk* of getting type 2 diabetes. These things are good to know and take seriously, but they don't imply that you are totally screwed if you chose your partner when you're on the pill (just like you aren't totally screwed if you eat more cookies than carrots). This is just good information to have—and information that you deserve to know—when you are making decisions about the pill and your approach to choosing long-term partners.

Which brings me to takeaway point part two.

Takeaway (Part II): Pill to no pill—there's no need for alarm, but you might want to proceed with caution. Although the jury is still out about how the pill impacts mate choice, if you meet your partner when you are on the pill, it probably can't hurt* to see how you feel about your partner when you are off the pill before making anything permanent. Having both sets of hormones test-drive prospective long-term partners will reduce the likelihood of any unpleasant surprises after you've said, "I do."

IF YOU'RE FREAKING OUT OR FEELING DEPRESSED ABOUT THIS

Look, I get it. The idea that your birth control pill might influence your choice of relationship partners in a way that could mean trouble down the road is scary. But relationships are always scary. This just adds a new wrinkle to the mix. Whether you choose your partner while on or off the pill, you're always trading one set of pluses and minuses for another. If you chose your current partner while you were on the pill, this doesn't mean that your relationship will fall apart if you go off the pill or that you and your partner are genetically incompatible. It also doesn't necessarily

....
* But, for the love of God, do this only if you are protecting yourself against an unwanted pregnancy in some other way. Getting pregnant at the wrong time by the wrong guy is far, FAR worse for you than any problem you could possibly encounter from choosing your partner when you are on the pill. This is why, if you are looking for a long-term romantic partner, it might be a better choice to be off the pill until after you have initiated the relationship. This would help minimize your risk of having picked a partner your naturally cycling hormones will disapprove of *and* allow you to protect yourself from pregnancy once the relationship becomes sexual. If you are *not* looking for a long-term partner but want to keep yourself open to the possibility of having sex when you want to without getting pregnant, you can forget about the desires of your naturally cycling hormones and just keep yourself safe.

mean that you will have trouble getting pregnant or, if you do, that your children will be unhealthy. Most women who choose their partners while on the pill don't have problems down the road. It's just worth noting that some of them do. And although the research suggests that the pill may have an impact on what trade-offs women make when choosing their partners, these are trade-offs that women have been making since the beginning of time—it's just that, in the past, they were less unwitting.

It's also noteworthy that for every Olivia and Anneliese, there are plenty of women who chose their partners on the pill who didn't have these outcomes. Many women's pill story is "I chose my partner on the pill and then went off it, and now my life is pretty much exactly the same as it was before." And for some women who meet their partners when they're on the pill, going off it actually *increases* relationship satisfaction.

In fact, although being on the pill when you choose your partner may increase your risk of some types of relationship problems, it dramatically decreases your risk of others. For example, being on the pill decreases women's risk of *needing* to get married out of financial necessity or because of an unexpected pregnancy. While there has been no research comparing the relationship satisfaction of women who chose their partners on the pill with women who chose their partners out of financial necessity or because they became pregnant unexpectedly, I would be willing to bet that the former would be happier than the latter. Being on the pill grants women the opportunity to take their time in finding the right partner and allows them to meet their career goals and be less financially dependent on men. Both these things increase women's ability to find satisfying relationships. And they put women in a position of being better able to walk away from relationships that don't meet their needs. In the grand scheme of things, the pill has undoubtedly done more good than harm for the quality of women's relationships and marital satisfaction.

Knowing what the pill does when it comes to choosing men means that you get to choose who you want to be and what you prioritize in your partner. And that's empowering. Whether you are on or off the pill, *you* get to pick what happens next.

CHAPTER 6: SEX ON DRUGS

If you go on the pill, there's a pretty good chance that you're sexually active (or at least aspiring to be). They're called birth control pills, after all, and the thing they're best at doing is preventing you from getting pregnant from all the sex that you're having . . . or hoping to have. Given that the birth control pill is a great facilitator of sexual behavior, it might just go down as one of the great ironies of our time that it can have the effect of making women lose interest in sex altogether. And it might even influence how sexy your partner finds you.

Consider what happened to Katie, who was twenty-two when she went on the pill after getting into a serious relationship with her boyfriend of six months. She hated having sex with condoms (her boyfriend wasn't a huge fan, either), and she and her boyfriend would often find themselves unprepared for sex when they wanted to have it. This would usually result in sex, regret, and a trip to the drugstore for the morning-after pill. Katie hated the morning-after pill. It was expensive, it made her feel sick, and she hated having to go into the pharmacy to pick it up. Even though she wasn't ashamed of having sex with her boyfriend, she always felt like she was being judged by the pharmacist (who had to be at least 107 years old and probably thought Katie was going to hell). After one too many unpleasant experiences with all this, she decided to go on the pill (which she chose to get filled at a different pharmacy, thank you very much).

It wasn't long after Katie went on the pill that she noticed she wasn't all that interested in sex anymore. It happened gradually, but she reached a point where she just Did. Not. Want. It. And when she was feeling this way, she had a really hard time talking herself into having sex, even though she wanted to want it. She couldn't understand why she managed to do *other* things that she didn't want to do (like her stupid accounting homework), but couldn't get herself to have sex with her boyfriend, whom she loved, without getting upset about it. She hated herself for not being able to just go with it anyway, and resigned herself to the idea that her boyfriend would probably cheat on her or break up with her. She just had no interest in sex and felt like the world would be a much happier place if sex weren't a thing that people were expected to do.

Katie talked to her doctor about her wilting desire for sex because she wanted to see if there was something she could take to make things better. Katie's doctor told her that the pill might be part of the problem, but that it was normal for couples in long-term relationships to have their sexual activity drop off after a while. He told her that her lack of sexual interest was something that she should learn to expect if she was going to be in a long-term relationship. Katie thought her doctor was probably right. This was the longest relationship that she'd ever been in, and maybe that was her real problem. Nothing else felt any different to her since going on the pill. Katie left her doctor's office thinking that her problem was probably just a long-term relationship thing.

Soon after her visit with her doctor, Katie and her boyfriend did break up. At that time, she'd just started a new job and didn't want to deal with dating, so she went off the pill and focused on work. The only difference she noticed after going off the pill was that her periods became harder to predict.

This all changed, though, when she ran into her ex-boyfriend at Starbucks on her way to work a few months after going off the pill.

> When I saw him, I felt like I'd been struck by lightning. He
> was just so hot! Being near him made my whole body feel like

I'd been electrocuted. I couldn't believe that I would ever NOT want to have sex with this beautiful man. We started talking and texting; it wasn't long before we got back together. This was two years ago, and things have been amazing ever since. Our relationship isn't perfect, but it's crazy how much of a difference wanting to have sex makes in a relationship. Things are so much easier now that I have my [copper] IUD. I can't believe that I thought that my lack of sex drive was normal. My doctor was talking to me like I was a postmenopausal woman who'd been married for fifty years. I was twenty-two. And in an eight-month-old relationship. How could I have been so stupid?

Although not every woman who goes on the pill becomes a Katie, a number of women do.* And this can become a big deal in women's relationships because for women, having low sexual desire can quickly turn into a full-scale sexual lockdown. Women's "I don't want to do this" response to sex is much more assertive than their "I don't want to do this" response to needing to load the dishwasher or put away laundry. Women's sexual decision-making has been programmed by natural selection to have an element of consequentiality that is missing from other types of things that we might not want to do.

Loading the dishwasher when we don't feel like it will, at worst, get our hands a little dirty. A non-life-changing prognosis rectified by a little hand soap and water. Having sex when you don't want to, however, could

....

* And some cool work in chimpanzees suggests that whether you are a Katie or not might be influenced in important ways by the quality of the relationship you had with your partner before going on the pill. In particular, these researchers found that female chimps' sexual swellings and sexual behavior decreased on the pill, but the magnitude of this decrease was directly related to the quality of the social and sexual relationship of the pair *prior* to treatment. The more compatible and frequently copulating couples continued to copulate once the females went on the pill (although at lower rates). The less compatible and less frequently copulating pairs? Once the females were on the pill, they ceased having sex altogether.

mean having to invest a minimum of nine months in a child you aren't ready for and the potential of death from childbirth. This is a much bigger deal than dirty hands. Because of this, evolution by selection has programmed our sexual psychology to have a very firm brake pedal that makes it difficult for women to talk themselves into having sex they don't want to have, even when they wish they wanted to have it. For women's brains, *I don't feel like doing the dishes* feels like *I don't feel like doing the dishes*, but *I don't feel like having sex* can feel like **I. ~~DO. NOT. WANT. TO.~~ WILL. NOT. HAVE. SEX.**

Modern women—even when we're on the pill and pregnancy isn't possible—still have this brake pedal as part of our sexual psychology. It's all part of that inherited wisdom from our ancestors. Having a powerful "no" response to sex helped our ancestors prevent pregnancies they weren't ready for and helped protect them from sexual aggression (which is, unfortunately, something that women have had to deal with since the dawn of time). However, it can make things really difficult for women in relationships when they are experiencing low desire. Women get frustrated with themselves because they don't understand why their brains and bodies rebel at the thought of having sex that they don't want (but wish that they wanted). And men get their feelings hurt because they don't understand why their partners would be more willing to do the dishes or put away laundry than to have sex with them.

This is also undoubtedly why some women, like Katie, feel that their doctors don't take their sexual-desire concerns on the pill very seriously. Historically, most doctors have been men. And a lot of men out there—even those who are non-Neanderthals and actually listen to women—don't fully understand what it means for a woman not to want sex. This is because men have a totally different sexual brake pedal than we do.* Evo-

....

* I recognize that men can experience low sexual desire, too. This can be a huge deal for men because—in addition to not wanting sex—men have to deal with all the cultural expectations for men as being wellsprings of sexual motivation. And this is so not a good

lutionarily, men have had almost nothing to lose and everything to gain from having sex. Since their minimum level of investment in reproduction is so small, even bad sex with someone they don't really like all that much has the potential to be an evolutionary win. Because of this, when men put on the sex brakes, it's less likely to turn into the sexual lockdown that it is for women.

Considerable research finds that women on the pill have lower sexual desire than what is observed in naturally cycling women. It also shows that they tend to have sex less frequently and are more likely to have problems with pain or discomfort from sex than non-pill-taking women do. This pattern is observed when making comparisons between groups of women who are either on or off the pill (called a between-subjects research design) and also when observing changes in individual women's sexual functioning after starting the pill (a within-subjects design). Together, this body of research suggests that going on the pill—which is so often done in the name of sex—can have potent anti-sex side effects in some women.

And it's not just that it can make women feel like they don't want to have sex. It also influences the degree to which our brain even wants to entertain sexualized thoughts that are thrust upon us.* Take, for example, the results of a study in which researchers had pill-taking and naturally cycling women look at almost one hundred sexually explicit photographs while wearing an eye-tracking device. They wanted to see whether the pill had an impact on women's interest in sex, even at the level of attention. So they showed the women pictures of couples engaged in various sexual acts and recorded where everyone's eyes went.

What did they find?

Well, the first thing they found was that *all* the women in their study

....

time. However, men are much less likely than women to go into full sexual-lockdown mode, even if they don't feel much like having sex.
* There was simply no way to avoid that pun.

spent most of their time looking directly at the genitals.* This was a result that surprised everyone because not even men are so crass when it comes to looking at explicit pictures. Men—despite their reputation for sexual depravity—spend most of their time looking at the depicted women's *faces* when they look at erotica. Nobody was expecting women to out-perv men when it came to getting down to business with the pictures.

But they totally did.

Which is kind of a big moment for us as a gender.

In addition to discovering that little conversation starter, the researchers also found notable differences in the looking behaviors of the pill-taking and naturally cycling women. Although both sets of women's eyes went first to the genitals (now, now, ladies), pill-taking women were quicker to lose interest and start looking elsewhere. And rather than looking at the faces or bodies of those engaged in the act, their eyes were more likely to wander to aspects of the photographs that had absolutely nothing to do with sex. They were more likely to have their attention captured by things like the clothing worn by the models or the objects in the background. This suggests that pill-taking women's brains—even at a preconscious level—may be less captivated by things related to sex and quicker to return to more pedestrian concerns (. . . *is she being bent over a Victorian-era chaise longue? God, that would look great in my living room* . . .) than their naturally cycling counterparts.†

So, the pill can make your brain less interested in sex. And that's not a lot of fun. In fact, it can be incredibly stressful. And if you find yourself in this situation, remember to be gentle with yourself. It's hard enough being a woman, and it's even harder being a woman without any sexual motivation. You're not crazy and you're not broken. Be patient with yourself (and your partner) as you both work together to troubleshoot your

....
* Interestingly, cycle phase did not affect naturally cycling women's looking patterns. They tested these women at three separate occasions for cycle-phase effects and didn't find any.
† It's like Grandma always said: You can lead a pill-taking woman's eyes to genitals, but you can't make them stick.

birth control options. Although this is a scary thing to go through, remember that you're not alone with this. The solution may be as simple as finding a new doctor, a new pill, or a new form of birth control.

But there's more.

You see, sex is more than just sex. Sex is also shopping and makeup, exercising and creativity, and a whole bunch of other things that you probably haven't considered until now. Because sex is ultimately at the heart of so many things that we do (you can thank evolution for this one, too), the pill may change more than just your activities in the bedroom. We'll turn to this idea now.

SEX IS MORE THAN SEX

Even though this might feel like a reductionist way to see the world, sexual motivation is, ultimately, at the heart of many things we do.* It's one of those pesky by-products of being designed by a process that rewards gene transmission. A lot of our traits—especially those traits that come into full bloom right around the time in our life when fertility is high—are maintained as part of the human nature playbook because they helped one of our ancestors reproduce. This means that sexual motivation—which is a psychological program coordinated by our sex hormones—is related to a lot of things that don't feel like they have anything to do with sex.

Now, some things that we do to attract partners are pretty obvious. Like, making ourselves look attractive. This is something that women do for lots of reasons, but one of those reasons is that it increases attractiveness to men. And this isn't me being sexist; this is just what the research tells

....
* I recommend Geoffrey Miller's *The Mating Mind* if you have any interest in this sort of thing. He does a really great job of unpacking the evolutionary link between sex and our giant brains, our almost limitless vocabularies, and the ability to create and enjoy art.

us. When women are looking to attract a man's attention or entice a partner they already have, one of the first (and most effective) things that most women do is spend a little extra effort on their appearance. For example, research finds that women's mating motivations are at the heart of things like clothing choice and cosmetics use, as well as dieting, exercising, and visiting tanning beds. Mating effort begets beautification effort,* so it's possible that women's appearance-enhancement efforts may also diminish somewhat on the pill.

But it probably goes even deeper than this. Because sex is at the heart of less obvious behaviors, too.

Take music, for instance.

Music is interesting because it's one of those things that all cultures create, but without an obvious survival purpose (you can't French-horn your way out of a wildebeest stampede). This is usually the hallmark of a behavior that is maintained to serve a courtship function.

Consistent with interpretation, almost all organisms that create complex acoustic signals do so for the purposes of mate attraction. This is why birds sing, howler monkeys howl, and red deer roar. Acoustic signals make a nice medium for discriminating between potential partners because they provide all sorts of information that is useful for females (they're usually the choosers) to use to determine whether a male is of high quality or not. This is because rhythm is a product of the nervous system. And nervous systems that are well put together can produce more coordinated, complex rhythms than nervous systems that aren't as well put together. This is why so many species use rhythmic displays such

---

* Now, please note what I am *not* saying here. I am not saying that any of these behaviors are motivated by you lying on your fainting couch, hand to forehead, thinking, "Oh, heavens to Betsy! Whatever can I do to attract a man? I'm just a feeble little woman whose life is incomplete without a man to take care of me." I don't think that most of us work this way anymore. Instead, this is to say that natural selection has programmed us in such a way that the behaviors that increase our desirability to partners are fueled by sexual motivation.

as song and dance as a means of mate attraction. They tell us something about the individual's motor control, as well as their self-confidence and creativity, which are other traits that bespeak high genetic quality.

There is no reason to think that humans are any exception to this rule.* Rhythmic displays created by whales, wrens, frogs, flies, honeybees, *and* humans all show off the functioning of the nervous systems to prospective mates. And females pay attention to them. The Keith Richards effect—where a kind of road-worn guy with good musical skills could, if he chose, have access to an almost alarming number of sexual partners—is no joke. This is why almost all adolescent males eventually try their hand at the guitar. A well-executed rhythmic display attracts mates. If you don't believe me, ask Keith.

Now, given that any courtship display worth doing will have an audience that is attuned to all its brilliant rhythmic nuances, we should also find that women's attunement to rhythmic displays is similarly tied to mating effort. Although this is a relatively new idea (we're actually actively researching this question in my lab right now), there is good reason to anticipate that fertility will increase females' attunement to the quality of rhythmic displays. Women's ability to discriminate between high- and low-quality displays should be more pronounced at high fertility and lower at other times in the cycle because conception is possible.

So what does all this mean for women on the pill? Well, a lot more research needs to be done on this topic before we can know for sure. But I think there's a good chance that the pill might influence women's direct mate-attraction efforts (beautification and the like), as well as their attunement to courtship cues, like music.

I say this for a couple of reasons.

First, this is what theory would suggest. Sex hormones fuel mating

....
* Others find that mating effort is also at the heart of creativity, humor, and trying new things. These are some other areas that may feel the long reach of the pill.

effort. Mating effort drives mate-attraction behaviors and attunement to courtship cues. It doesn't take a huge leap of the imagination to predict that preventing the hormonal surge that prompts mating effort (both in terms of releasing an egg and wanting sex) will also suppress behavioral offshoots of this same motivational pathway.

Second, although we need more hard data on this, this idea is something that has come up more times than I can count when talking to women about their experiences of being on and off the pill. Many women I have interviewed have told me that they noticed an uptick in their interest in their appearance after going off the pill that coincided with the return of their sexual desire. For some, this meant that they started clothes shopping again and growing their hair long after it being short for years when they were on the pill. For others, this has meant a renewed interest in healthy eating and working out. For others yet, this has meant cosmetic surgery and teeth whitening. Now, I don't know for certain whether the pill, per se, was responsible for any of this. Right now, this evidence is anecdotal. And I'm also not saying that it's bad to care less about your desirability. Most of us would probably benefit from a healthy dose of "I don't give a sh** about my appearance." This is just something that might be worth noting as you consider your options and your experiences.

For me, the most noticeable change was the music thing. And I have since heard this repeated back to me by several other women.

To provide you with some context, I loved listening to music all through high school and my early college years and then, I just . . . stopped. I never questioned why this happened. I didn't even notice. I just stopped listening to it, favoring podcasts and NPR when on an airplane or in my car. Although I don't have perfect documentation of any of this, this change in listening habits corresponded to the time that I began taking the pill.

Now, flash forward ten-ish years (a couple of months after going off the pill), when I started downloading new playlists to listen to in my car for the first time in forever. I got a subscription to Spotify. I finally downloaded Pandora. It was only after a friend had commented on my rekindled interest in music that my attention was even drawn to this fact. Even then, I figured that my renewed love of music was probably just a byproduct of needing more things to listen to since I was working out a lot more than I used to (that happened to me, too). And although I can't be 100 percent certain about the pill's involvement in any of this (you can bet we're collecting data on this, too), I would be very surprised if it wasn't. Mating effort and attunement to courtship cues are driven by sex hormones. There is good reason to think that—at least for some women—these things might change on the pill.

So, sex is more than just sex. And having a diminished desire for actual sex (like, sex-sex) may be a canary in the coal mine of much more pervasive changes in women's motivational states. While a lot of this thinking is still in its infancy, it's worth considering if these outcomes might be meaningful to you.

A RECIPE FOR SEXUAL ANTIVENOM

So why does the pill mess around with women's sexual motivation?

When women are on the pill, at least three things can put a wrench in their sexual motivation. And the first of these is the very thing that makes the pill so effective at preventing pregnancy.

As you might recall, the pill works its magic by suppressing the hormonal cascade that sets in motion the release of a mature egg. The whole "no egg, no pregnancy" thing. Unfortunately, as you also might recall from chapter 3, the pre-ovulatory estrogen surge, which is a key part of this hormonal cascade, is also known to fuel women's desire for sex. Conception risk and sexual motivation go hand in hand because (let's face it) evolution by natural selection would have it no other way. We have inherited traits that promoted our ancestors' successful reproduction, and there are few things that encourage reproduction more than sex at times when conception is possible. So, although lacking an estrogen surge is a pretty surefire plan to avoid releasing an egg, it can also sound the death knell of your sex drive. Both things are powered by estrogen. Pill-taking women's estrogen levels stay relatively low and stable across the cycle, which means that they don't get to enjoy the natural boost in libido that occurs when your body is in egg-fertilization mode.

One reason the pill can kill your sex drive, then, is its suppression of ovulation and the estrogen surge that precedes it. This is great for preventing pregnancy, but can be bad for sex.

Biology can be a cruel and uncaring force.

The pill can also mean bad news for your sex drive because of its influence on testosterone (T). Although we tend to think about T as being a guy thing, women have it, too. And just as it does for men, T plays an important role in women's sexual function. It plays a role in sexual arousal and sexual responsiveness, and it's necessary for the body to synthesize estrogen, which is another big driver of women's sexual motivation. And there's a pretty substantial body of research showing that the pill can cause women's levels of free T (which is the stuff that the body can actually use—think of it as usable T) to steeply decline. How steep is steep, you ask? Well, most research finds that pill-takers' levels of free T are somewhere on the order of 61 percent lower than the levels of naturally cycling women.

I'd say that's pfs.*

This happens to pill-taking women for a couple of different reasons. First, the pill causes your ovaries and adrenal glands to produce less T. Because all sex hormone synthesis is orchestrated by the same pituitary hormones, inhibiting these hormones to prevent ovulation (which the pill does) is pretty much guaranteed to mess with T production, too. This

....
* pfs = pretty f***ing steep.

is strike number one for pill-taking women. Less T is produced, meaning there's less T to go around.

The other thing that causes women's levels of free T to tank on the pill is that the hormones in the pill increase levels of sex-hormone-binding globulin (SHBG).* This charming molecule binds to T and makes it inactive. So even though the T is there, it can't actually do anything. It's like the queen of England. Or nonalcoholic beer. By increasing the levels of SHBG, the pill makes more of pill-taking women's T biologically unusable.

And it's not just baseline levels of T that seem to be affected by the pill. Women's T *response* to sex-related things also seems to be negatively affected by the pill. For example, in one study, researchers had women watch a love scene from *The Notebook* or one of three control videos that had nothing to do with love or sex. They measured the magnitude of women's T response to each of the different movie clips. For most women, watching the love scene caused an increase in T. As brains do, they responded to the fact that there seemed to be a little sex in the air by ordering the release of T to help their bodies prepare for the possibility that they might be the next up to bat. For the pill-taking women, though, their T response to the video clip was blunted. And this was true despite the fact that their T was significantly lower to begin with. Others doing similar studies have found that pill-taking women's T *decreased* in response to sexual scenarios.

Although this isn't life threatening or anything, your T is important stuff. Lack of usable T in the body can cause your sex drive to tank and your arousal response to diminish. In addition to decreasing your desire to have sex, lower T has been linked to diminished vaginal lubrication

....

* Research suggests that women taking pills containing 20 to 25 milligrams of EE have less of an increase in SHBG than those taking formulations with 30 to 35 milligrams of EE. Progestin generation also seems to matter, with second-generation progestins showing the least increase in SHBG and third- and fourth-generation progestins showing the biggest increase.

and an increased risk of pain during sex. These types of things aren't exactly helpful in terms of getting you to want to have sex.* And what's scary about this (although not in a "let's freak out and get alarmed about this" kind of way, but just in a "let's take this seriously" kind of way) is that some research suggests that women's levels of SHBG (that stuff that binds to T and makes it inactive) may continue to remain elevated in women even *after* they go off the pill.

So the pill can cause your levels of T to drop rather dramatically, which isn't good for sex. This is reason number two that the pill can hurt your sex life—maybe even after you go off it.

The next thing that the pill might do to mess with your libido is something that has only recently been considered because of some provocative new research on oxytocin signaling in pill-taking and naturally cycling women.

Oxytocin is a hormone that plays a super-indispensable role in regulating sex, bonding, and social interactions. When oxytocin is released, it tells your brain that the person you are with—whether it is your newborn baby, your best friend, or your romantic partner—is someone special you love and cherish, and whose welfare you are concerned about. Because of this, it plays a key role in your ability to bond with others, including your romantic partner. Oxytocin makes your brain's reward centers light up like a Christmas tree in response to your romantic partner's face, helping to reinforce your brain's belief that he's the number one guy for you (as in, XOXO; true love always). It separates your partner from every other man

---

* I'm sure that it hasn't been lost on you that women on the pill get the worst of both worlds when it comes to T. On the one hand, the progestins in the pill can bind to T receptors, which can put hair in embarrassing places and make you break out (a side effect of too much T). But on the other hand, it can kill your sexual motivation and lead to painful sex (a side effect of too little T). Although the reasons for this cruel paradox aren't all that well understood, it probably means that the T-derived progestins are binding to women's T receptors in a different way than they get bound by actual T. This is why they cause your body to do some T things (hair and acne), but not others (sex).

in the world and earmarks him as someone who is different, special, and worthy of your undying devotion.

Since oxytocin promotes romantic coupledom, researchers find that if you give someone a dose of internasal oxytocin, it will cause them to see their romantic partner as being more attractive than other people they're looking at. This is part of the whole "earmarking your partner as someone special" thing. It also causes the reward centers of the brain—including the nucleus accumbens, which is the big cheese of the brain's reward pathway—to get activated in response to their partner.

Unless you're on the pill.

When pill-taking women are given a dose of internasal oxytocin, they don't see their partners any differently from the way they do in the absence of oxytocin. Pill-taking women also don't experience increased activity in the reward centers of their brain when looking at pictures of their partners. Instead, when pill-taking women view photographs of their partners, they may as well be looking at the face of a stranger. The normal biological processes that go on in response to oxytocin to help label your partner as someone special and flag him as a reinforcer (like food, sex, or morphine) don't happen in women on the pill.* In addition to throwing a wrench in the works of women's relationships by messing with the signaling pathways that promote bonding,† there is good reason

....

* Although researchers aren't positive why this happens, it may be because sex steroids in the pill antagonize normal oxytocin effects in the brain, or bind to oxytocin receptors, which makes the receptors less sensitive to oxytocin.

† This research is also really provocative in terms of what it might mean for women's ability to bond with their babies if they go on the pill soon after giving birth. For example, we all know that oxytocin signaling plays an important role in women's responsiveness to babies. Just as with the studies of romantic partners' faces, research finds that internasally administered oxytocin increases women's responsiveness to the faces and sounds of babies. If oxytocin signaling is disrupted in pill-taking women's responses to babies, too, this could mean an increased risk of postpartum depression among pill-taking women. Although there hasn't been any experimental research yet examining this possibility, I would be really careful with the pill postpartum if you have a family history of postpartum depression or depression. Oxytocin signaling is oxytocin signaling. I can't think of any

to believe that this also has the effect of messing with sex. Feelings of emotional closeness and attachment can grease the wheels of a sexual response, especially for women, making dysregulated oxytocin signaling in pill-taking women another potential culprit in low libido.

Finally, research in nonhuman animals suggests that the pill might also lead to decreased concentrations of allopregnanolone in the brain. Allopregnanolone is a neurochemical involved in mood and memory that also has a hand in motivating sexual behavior. We'll talk about this one in a little more detail when we talk about mood. For now, it's worth noting that decreases in the neurochemical allopregnanolone in response to the pill might also have a negative effect on your desire for sex.

And you know what? There are probably dozens of additional ways the pill can mess with your sex drive.

Given that the hormones in the pill flip billions of switches on and off throughout the body, what we know about the ways that the pill influences women's sexual functioning is vastly less than what we don't know. But even though we still have a lot to learn, you can use what we know to help you make a decision about whether the pill is going to work for you. If you are suffering from sexual side effects on the pill, but you like everything else about it, troubleshoot. The solution may be as simple as modifying your pre-sex routine in a way that helps kick-start sexual arousal.* Or it might mean talking to your doctor about trying a new pill. For example, some research finds that fourth-generation pills (with either 20 or 30 milligrams of ethinyl estradiol) might be a good choice for women experiencing sexual side effects on the pill. These studies find that fourth-generation pills may cause women to have increased sexual functioning and satisfaction and may improve symptoms among women with a history of pain during sex. They probably aren't a magic bullet, but

---

reason the pill would do weird things to this signaling system when it comes to romantic partners but not to babies.

* You can use your imagination here, but this could include anything from getting a massage to indulging in any of the many forms of commercially available erotica.

it's at least good to know that there are options out there. And by the time you read this, I'm hoping that there will be more options yet. Talk to your doctor about the latest research developments in this area (research moves faster than book publishing) to see if there are other options that might be worth trying. Being protected from pregnancy and having a fulfilling sex life should not be mutually exclusive.

UNF***ABLE ME

So we've been talking about how the pill can make *you* less interested in sex, but research suggests that the impact of the pill on things related to sex might cut both ways, potentially making *men* less interested in sex with *you*.

Which is so not okay for most women.*

We know from the research that we discussed in chapter 3 that the periovulatory phase of your cycle (the window of time prior to ovulation when estrogen is dominant) is generally when women look and feel their sexiest. Men find women's faces, voices, and body scents most attractive at high fertility. And for their part, women dress sexier and act more flirtatious at this time, too. This is because the periovulatory estrogen surge tells women's bodies to pull out all the stops to make them the sexiest, most alluring version of themselves that they can possibly be.

Those eggs aren't going to fertilize themselves, you know.

And since pill-taking women don't ovulate, they miss out on this all-natural, free-of-cost (certified-fair-trade and organic) mid-cycle sexiness boost. Although this might not be a big deal for everyone, it might be for

....
* Not that a woman's worth should be tied to her attractiveness, of course. But I think that most of us want to be the best version of ourselves that we can be, and for many of us, this includes feeling like we look our best.

you. Most of us want all the sexiness boosts we can get. And pill-taking women don't get this monthly sexiness spike from their sex hormones.

So, the pill might make you lose a little bit of your sexiness edge across the cycle because you miss out on your estrogen surge. How all this plays out in men's and women's sexual dynamics can be difficult to study, though, because it's hard to observe human sexual behavior in the wild, so to speak. Thankfully, someone was clever enough to realize that this is the sort of research question you can study in nonhuman primates (other species of non-us apes and monkeys) who use the same birth control pills that we give humans.

That's right: Monkeys go on the pill.

In addition to preventing unintended pregnancies in populations of primates living in captivity (which is why they're given the pill in the first place), giving primates the pill also sets the stage for some interesting research into how male primates respond sexually to female primates on the pill. Obviously, this isn't a perfect analog to what goes on in humans, but we can learn a few things about how men might respond to women based on their pill-taking status from observing the sexual immodesties of our closest living relatives.

The results of this research show pretty unanimously that being on the pill* decreases females' likelihood of being chosen as a mate. For example, in female chimpanzees and rhesus macaques, being on the pill is found to decrease the likelihood of being approached by males for sex, and also decreases the number of spontaneous mounting attempts they receive. Although you and I might find the latter to be a terrible breach in dating etiquette (particularly when done without warning or introduction), this is a huge compliment to females in these species, for whom a mounting attempt is high romance. An even more egregious reduction in sexual interest is observed in the male cynomolgus monkey (*Macaca*

----

* Although in some cases, it wasn't the pill, per se, but instead a dose of synthetic hormones similar to the pill.

fascicularis). Although these males are equally likely to have sex with naturally cycling and pill-taking females, when they have sex with the pill-takers, they don't ejaculate. They can't be bothered. It's almost as if they have some level of awareness that the pill-taking female is a reproductive dead end and would rather save the energy that would be required to punctuate their sexual behavior with gamete release to do something else. Like going to look for a snack, or trying to attract a partner who might eventually ovulate.

Interestingly, research in humans suggests that human males (those slightly less hairy apes that we call men) might also change their partner-related behaviors depending on the reproductive dead-end status of their mates.

Consider one study that was done on a sample of newlywed couples to look at the connection between women's level of commitment to their partners and the mate-guarding behaviors of men. *Mate guarding* is a term used to describe the whole smorgasbord of activities that people in relationships might do to keep their partner from straying. For example, when your partner texts you to ask who you're out with, that's mate guarding. Mate guarding is also the thing that's happening when you find yourself grabbing your boyfriend's hand whenever there are attractive women around. We mate guard to help keep our romantic relationships intact in a world full of sexual opportunities and mate poachers.

Now, normally, there is a relationship between low commitment in one partner and increased mate guarding in the other. This makes good sense. Uncommitted partners are more likely to stray than committed partners, making it a good idea to up your mate-guarding game when your partner seems less committed to the relationship. So we shouldn't be terribly surprised that this was the exact pattern observed among many of the newlywed couples in this study. Low commitment on the part of the wives predicted increased mate guarding by their husbands.

That is, unless the men were married to women on the pill.

For men married to women on the pill, although there was an uptick in jealousy that occurred in response to their partner's low commitment (which was also observed in the other couples, too, as you might expect), there was no increase in mate-guarding behaviors. Even though these men felt more jealous than men with more committed partners, they took fewer actions to do anything to keep their partner away from other men. It's like they just can't be bothered if the integrity of their partner's empty womb isn't at stake. Just like the non-ejaculating cynomolgus monkeys, men seem to change their behavior toward their partners when conception isn't possible. They might decrease mate-guarding behaviors in response to the diminished risk of their partner becoming pregnant with some other man's child.* Although this might be good in some ways (it frees you up from having to worry about an overbearing partner, which is a context that can be linked to violence and abuse), it may be bad in others. Mate guarding can prompt great acts of romance targeted at keeping women happy and satisfied.

So the takeaway here is that being on the pill may put you at a sexiness disadvantage by suppressing a naturally occurring boost in attractiveness that accompanies the periovulatory estrogen surge. This little boost in sexiness may be the thing that helps you catch the eye of an attractive stranger who will whisk you away to Paris for the most amazing weekend of your life. Alternately, this might be something that you wish to avoid because you have more pressing things to worry about and don't want to be bothered by unwanted advances, mate-guarding behavior, or (if we are to take the chimpanzee research seriously) spontaneous mounting attempts. It's also possible that having or eliminating a cycle-based

....

* This idea is also supported by research showing that men's mate-guarding behaviors are sensitive to their partners' changing fertility status across the cycle. Of course, it's also possible that these men mate-guard less because their partners aren't giving off fertility cues, so the men don't worry about them being desired by other men. Or that they are less worried their partners will stray because their partners desire sex less, which is something that we know can also happen on the pill. It could also be something else altogether. Regardless, it's an interesting pattern of results and suggests that the pill might influence relationship dynamics in ways that we haven't even started to consider.

beauty boost might not impact you in any meaningful way at all. Still, this information is worth knowing when it comes to the pill. You can use it to help make you into the version of yourself that you most want to be.

ONE MORE THING BEFORE
WE MOVE PAST SEX

As a scientist, I come across some research every once in a while that I just have to tell people about. And this is one of those studies. It's about what happened to a group of female ring-tailed lemurs when they went on a hormonal contraceptive shot containing a first-generation progestin (medroxyprogesterone acetate, or MPA).

I won't bore you with a bunch of details about ring-tailed lemurs that you didn't ask for, but it's worth noting that (a) we're primates, (b) they're primates, and (c) because of *a* and *b*, we have a lot in common. We're both highly social, we both like hanging out and basking in the sun with our friends, and we're both highly attuned to scent cues. In both humans and lemurs, scent cues provide others with information about identity, genetic quality, and fertility status. This makes the lemur a nice animal model for understanding the impact of hormonal contraceptives on females' olfactory signals.

The researchers in the lemur study were interested in whether hormonal contraceptives might be disruptive to naturally occurring scent cues that lemurs use to identify one another and help inform their mate choice. And, as in humans, one of the areas of the body richest in the release of these unique and informative scent cues is the genital area. Given that humans' scent cues can influence mate attraction in significant ways, too, if the composition of chemicals in a female lemur's vaginal secretions changes in response to the artificial hormones in the pill, this is something that you probably want to know about.

To test whether hormonal contraceptives influence females' scent cues, researchers looked at the chemical makeup of the labial secretions released by females when they were on hormonal contraceptives and when they were off them. Looking at the same group of females both on and off hormonal contraception allowed researchers to see the changes that take place within each female. They measured the chemical "richness" or diversity present in the females' labial secretions, as well as the relative abundance of each type of chemical in the secretions.

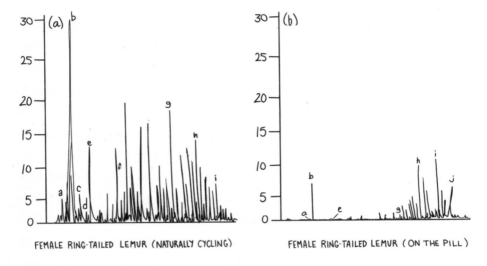

FEMALE RING-TAILED LEMUR (NATURALLY CYCLING)   FEMALE RING-TAILED LEMUR (ON THE PILL)

The number of different chemical components (and their amounts) in a female lemur's labial secretions based on pill-taking status. Each letter corresponds to a unique chemical component. Note that some chemical components are only present in females on hormonal contraceptives, while others are only present in naturally cycling females.

In the figure above, you can see the differences in the chemical profile of one of the females in the study. Each letter in the histogram corresponds to a chemical compound found in the secretions. On the left (histogram a) is the diversity and abundance of different chemical compounds in her labial secretions when she was off birth control. On the right (histogram b) is what it looked like after she went on birth control.

As you can see, being on hormonal contraceptives decimated the number of chemical components in the olfactory profiles of the female lemurs. It also depleted the richness of the different chemical components that made up their scents. And there was one chemical (represented by the letter j) that was *only* found in the contracepted females. Being on hormonal contraceptives also eliminated each female's unique chemical scent signature, replacing it with a generic "random contracepted female X" scent. Interestingly, the generic chemical signature of the contracepted females wasn't found to resemble that of a naturally cycling female at any point in her cycle. Instead, it's specific to females on hormonal contraceptives, eliminating the otherwise reliably occurring relationship between the complexity of the females' scents and their genetic quality.

These changes didn't go unnoticed by the males. The male lemurs demonstrated a clear preference for the females' scents when they were not on hormonal contraceptives. This was found to be true regardless of whether the naturally cycling females were at high or low fertility.

Now, we need to consider some caveats with all this. To start with, I am assuming that you are not a lemur. And if my assumption is correct (and I'm not making an ass of U and ME), this means that we don't know for certain whether the same pattern would hold for you. Second, there's also the whole "does this happen on all forms of hormonal contraception?" thing to consider. These lemurs were all on medroxyprogesterone acetate, and it's possible that this pattern is observed only with this specific progestin. We can't totally dismiss the possibility that this research is relevant only to those lemurs (specifically) on MPA.

However, although this is a possibility, I would say that it's doubtful. We know that women's sex hormones influence the composition and scent of their vaginal secretions. We know that the pill changes women's hormonal profile. And now we know that lemurs on hormonal contraceptives experience changes in the chemical composition of their labial secretions. It's not too far of a stretch to predict that the pill will do something to the uniqueness and complexity of women's chemical signatures . . . both in all the areas down below and in other places on the body, like on our skin and in our saliva. It's just one of those things that we don't yet know for sure. You get to decide if you want to take it seriously. And you get to decide what this means for you. If you are someone who would like to maintain your unique scent signature, this might be a minus. If you're more of a status-quo kind of girl and would prefer to be as un-unique as possible when it comes to the composition of your vaginal and labial secretions, this might be a plus. What this all means for you depends on who you are and who you want to be.

CHAPTER 7: THE CURIOUS CASE OF THE MISSING CORTISOL

The stress response is something that most people don't spend a whole lot of time thinking about. We don't have to. It's one of those rare, beautiful features of our bodies that does what it's supposed to without us having to think about it. And just as with breathing, digesting, and falling in love, knowing how it works doesn't make us any better at it. With all the things that most of us have going on in our lives, this is a pretty sweet arrangement and not one that most of us would have any intention of messing with.

As you can probably guess, this is where I tell you about how my own benign neglect of the stress response came to a halt because of an unexpected, precipitating event. For me, that event was a methodological footnote in a research presentation about something else altogether.

Now, to appreciate this story, you first need to know that a key marker that scientists use to define the experience of stress is the release of the stress hormone cortisol. More on what this hormone does in a minute, but for now, you just need to know that a cortisol surge is so characteristic of the stress response that it's one of the ways that scientists are able to gauge whether something stressed someone out. If cortisol was released, we know that a person was experiencing stress. If it was not released, we assume that they weren't. Stress begets cortisol, and its release is part of how we define and measure stress.

The research presentation in question was on the effects of childhood adversity on cortisol release in response to the Trier Social Stress Test (TSST), an experimental procedure for activating a stress response in a research lab. And it's hugely effective. The TSST requires people to prepare and deliver an impromptu speech about their suitability for employment to a panel of unsmiling experts and a video camera. They then have to count backward from 1,022 in steps of thirteen without making any mistakes. It's the gold standard for activating a stress response in the lab because it's pretty much torn directly from the pages of everyone's nightmares. For most people, it produces a two- or threefold increase in salivary cortisol levels, which is the typical response for someone who is stressed the f*** out.

But not for everyone.

As the researcher went through his method of data collection, he casually mentioned that he'd used only men in the final data analytic sample because most of the women in their study were on oral contraceptive pills. Women on oral contraceptive pills, he went on to explain, although they reported *feeling* stressed out in response to the TSST, didn't experience any changes in cortisol. Since a change in cortisol was their key measure of interest, they tested their predictions only in men since there weren't enough naturally cycling women—who did release cortisol in response to stress—to include in their analyses in a thoughtful way.

. . . ?!

Although the idea that the pill might kill women's cortisol response to stress wasn't the point of the talk (it was a throwaway line from the methods section), this was all I could think about for the rest of the day. This might not sound like that big of a deal on the surface (it might even sound like the best effect of hormonal contraceptives since clear skin, predictable periods, and pregnancy prevention), but it probably is. Our ability to respond to stress allows us to adapt to whatever type of situation we get ourselves thrown into. Lacking this capacity isn't a "get out of jail free" card for stress. Instead, it means that when we're stressed out, we're less able to cope. It predicts problems with emotional regulation, learning, memory, and social functioning. Even though stress seems bad, I promise you that lacking a stress response is decidedly worse.

With all this in mind, once I got home from the conference, I became a little obsessed with trying to track down what happens to the stress response in women on the pill. I couldn't get over the fact that (a) this might happen, and (b) this was the first time I'd heard about it.* So, I did the thing that nerds do when they become obsessed with something: I started reading. A lot. We'll talk about what I found shortly, but first I'll give you a little background on how your stress response works. It's more interesting than you might think, and it will help you draw your own conclusions about what the pill might mean for you.

STRESS FOR BEGINNERS

We all know that stress has a bad reputation. And this bad reputation isn't altogether unwarranted. Modern stress—the type of unrelenting pressure that is so common among contemporary people with contemporary problems—is bad for us. In addition to being associated with weight gain, anxiety, heart and reproductive problems, impaired immune function, insomnia, and migraines, stress can make you tired, irritable, and miserable for other people to be around. Few among us wouldn't benefit from taking a long-overdue vacation from stress and all its crappy, health- and relationship-harming sequelae.

But stress is actually a little more nuanced than that. Although too much stress is bad for us, too little stress is bad for us, too. Even though too much stress can make us feel cranky, irritable, and overwhelmed, too little stress can make us feel sad, bored, and like we're living in blahsville. So rather than being something that we want to avoid altogether (like

....
* I'm a psychologist, for Chrissakes.

square dancing, the plague, or having to look at pictures of your colleague's cats), stress is something best experienced in moderate doses. Too much stress is ghost-pepper hot wings. Too little stress is Pablum.

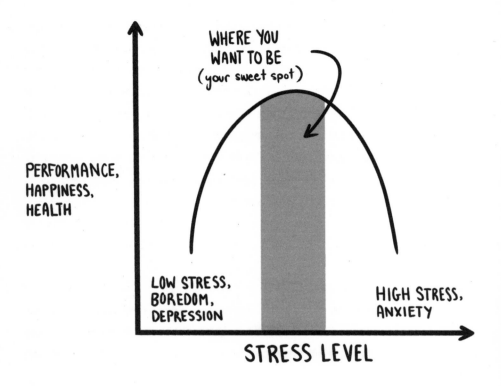

Although too much stress is bad for you, too little stress is bad for you, too.

A second nuance is that stress isn't necessarily synonymous with the sh** hitting the fan. Sex, physical attraction, getting exciting news, and Christmas morning are also powerful elicitors of stress. And this is true despite the fact that these are the kinds of activities that people generally enjoy. So, stress doesn't always mean bad. Stress just means biologically meaningful. It means that something consequential is happening and that your body needs to change what it is doing to deal with it. Sometimes the consequential event is that you are having sex or are on the cusp of an exciting new business opportunity (which is good). Sometimes the consequential event is that you've found yourself on the business end of a wildebeest stampede (which is bad). Regardless of whether these consequential events are good or bad, the way that our bodies deal with them is through the activities of the stress response.

The specifics of the stress response differ a bit depending on what's going on (e.g., sex versus wildebeest stampede), but any stress response has a few common ingredients. The first is that stress kicks your sympathetic nervous system (SNS) into gear. The SNS response carries out its objectives through the release of norepinephrine and epinephrine, and is responsible for the fight-or-flight response. It's characterized by the "my heart is racing, I can't breathe, and I'm freaking the f**k out right now" feelings that we have when stressed. Most of our stress feelings are courtesy of the SNS.

If you've been on the pill, it will probably not surprise you to learn that the SNS part of the stress response seems to remain completely intact in pill-taking women. Women on the pill *feel* just as stressed out as everyone else does in response to stressors, and their ability to fight or flee seems to be totally uncompromised. And this is good news for women on the pill. Although the fight-or-flight response is aggravating—and can feel downright cruel when we're sitting in unmoving traffic—it's something that most of us want to keep in our back pocket to pull out in case of an emergency.

The second key ingredient common to most stress responses is activation of the hypothalamic-pituitary-adrenal (HPA) axis. This magnificent mouthful is made up of three systems working together: your hypothalamus (part of your brain), your pituitary gland (just south of the brain), and your adrenal glands (atop your kidneys).

The activities of the HPA axis (just like those of the HPG axis, its sex-hormone-releasing cousin) are initiated in the brain by the hypothalamus, and are executed via another three-person telephone game (see picture on the next page). First, the brain releases corticotropin-releasing hormone (CRH), which stimulates the pituitary gland. Next, the pituitary gland passes this information to the adrenal glands through the release of

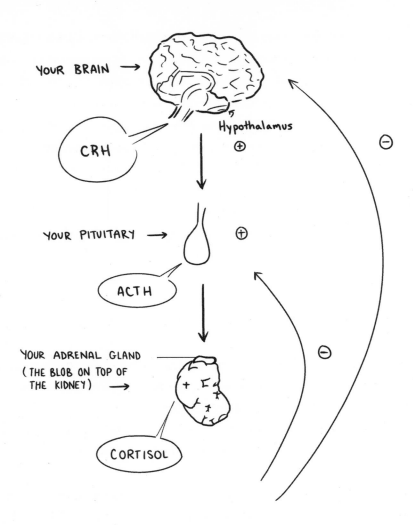

YOUR BRAIN →

Hypothalamus
⊕

CRH

⊖

YOUR PITUITARY →
⊕

ACTH

YOUR ADRENAL GLAND
(THE BLOB ON TOP OF
THE KIDNEY) →

⊖

CORTISOL

The signaling of your HPA axis.

adrenocorticotropic hormone (ACTH). Finally, ACTH stimulates the adrenal glands, which prompts the release of the stress hormone cortisol into the bloodstream.

Because the probability is very low that any human being would ever be able to remember all these ungainly acronyms* without a few reminders—I

....

* Which are surpassed in their ungainliness only by the words they stand for. More people would study neuroscience if everything was given a normal name. Like, say, Steve. If the

offer you a table that you can refer back to as often as necessary as we talk about all this stuff.

The Primary Hormones of Your HPA Axis— and from Whence They Came

HORMONE NAME	WHERE IT'S FROM	WHAT IT DOES
CRH (corticotrophin-releasing hormone)	Hypothalamus (brain)	Triggers the release of ACTH by the pituitary gland.
ACTH (adrenocorticotrophic hormone)	Pituitary	Triggers the release of cortisol from the adrenal glands.
Cortisol	Adrenal glands	Runs the body's stress program. Dumps fat and sugar into the blood to allow for quick escape, alters the activities of the immune system, stimulates the birth of new brain cells, and helps embed experiences into your brain.

Steve released Kevin, we would all remember it a lot better than the hypothalamus releasing corticotrophin-releasing hormone. I don't know who named this stuff, but they obviously had no interest in generating mass appeal.

The primary biological signature of the HPA stress response is a surge in cortisol, which is usually detectable in blood and saliva within three to five minutes of encountering a stressor. And although cortisol release isn't directly associated with any specific, noticeable stresslike feelings, the way the SNS response is, it plays a key role in managing the big picture in the stress response. It does things like redistributing energy that was being used for fueling growth and bodily repair to the parts of the body needing an energy boost to deal with the stressor. It also has a lot of important effects on the activities of the brain. For example, cortisol promotes perceptual vigilance and revs up the neural processes involved in learning and memory so that we can better embed, or consolidate, the stress-eliciting events into our brains for later use. Earmarking biologically relevant events in this way helps us adapt to our environments by allowing us to more effectively deal with similar situations in the future.

But poison is all about the dose. Although dynamic bursts of HPA-axis activity are part of what it means to be a well-stimulated person with a meaningful life, *chronic* activation of the HPA axis wreaks havoc in the body.* It keeps all the body's resources tied up with the messy business of stress management, which prevents investment in life-sustaining activities like digestive, immune, and cardiovascular function. It also increases the risk of infection, disease, weight gain, and a bunch of other stuff you probably don't want happening,† including diminished neurogenesis

....

* To understand just how powerful the destructive potential of HPA-axis dysregulation can be, consider for a moment the Pacific salmon. We all know about their heroic journey upstream, navigating dangerous waters to return to their natal streams to spawn and then *DIE*. But I'll bet you didn't know that the reason they die is because their trip upstream puts their HPA axis into complete hyperdrive, which causes their bodies to totally fall apart. As Robert Sapolsky notes in his smart-funny-awesome book *Why Zebras Don't Get Ulcers*, if you take out a salmon's adrenal glands (those blobs on the kidneys that release cortisol), they'll continue to live after spawning. The journey isn't what kills them. It's having their body running the stress program for a prolonged period of time that does.
† This is because cortisol increases levels of triglycerides and glucose in the blood. Although these things provide fuel to the brain and muscles when dealing with a stressor (which is good), they also can put you at risk for a heart attack, type 2 diabetes, infection,

(making new brain cells), brain cell damage and cell death, and reductions in brain volume.

Chronic cortisol signaling is so deleterious to the functioning of the body that when the HPA axis is chronically active, the body will do everything it can to try to shut it down. The hippocampus (which has more receptors for cortisol than any other part of the brain) will start screaming at the hypothalamus to stop releasing CRH (the primary initiator of HPA-axis activity). The pituitary and adrenal glands will start ignoring the signals telling them to release more hormone. And if this isn't enough to lower cortisol levels, the liver will start releasing a bunch of corticosteroid-binding globulins (CBGs) to inactivate a portion of the cortisol, dampening the strength of the signal to the rest of the cells in the body. It does this because the body can't function in a chronic state of OMG(!!!). This is why it is common for people's HPA axes to go into shutdown mode when they've experienced chronic stress or trauma. And this is also why I found it so alarming that pill-taking women's HPA axes appear to be doing the very same thing.

HYPOTHALAMIC HIGH JINKS

After going back to my research lab, I discovered that the methodological footnote about pill-taking women lacking an HPA-axis response to stress is, in fact, a *thing*. Several studies have now documented this effect. The figure that you see on the next page is taken from a research paper looking at women's cortisol release in response to the TSST (recall my

....

and even cancer (which is bad). One of the ways that your body helps protect itself from potentially nasty bacteria and neoplastic growth (a.k.a. cancer) is by keeping blood sugars relatively low most of the time. Since cortisol causes blood sugars to rise—and both bacteria and cancer cells thrive in sugar-rich environments—chronic activation of the HPA axis can make your body a more hospitable place for the nasties that you don't want taking up residence.

earlier description of the lab paradigm that requires public speaking and backward math). The bar on the left represents the cortisol response of the non–pill-taking women to the TSST. The bar on the right represents the cortisol response of the pill-taking women in the study.

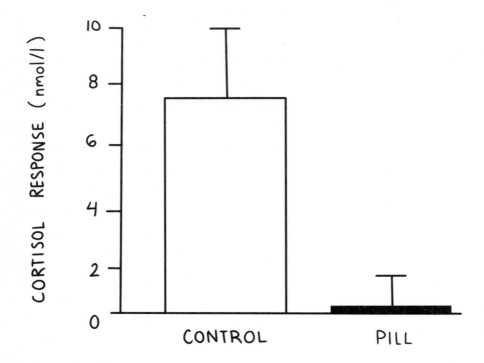

Cortisol response (measured as nanomoles per liter [nmol/l]) to the Trier Social Stress Test (TSST) in pill-taking women and a control group of naturally cycling women.

You don't need a Ph.D. in neuroendocrinology to see that these two groups of women look very different from each other. And this general pattern has now been observed in several studies. Sometimes the researchers find that pill-taking women have a blunted cortisol response to stress (relative to naturally cycling women), sometimes the pill-takers have *no* cortisol response to stress, and sometimes—as was found in one recent study—levels of cortisol actually *decreased* in response to stress, which doesn't make any sense at all. And the research shows that this isn't just a matter of pill-takers being more poised under pressure in the context of the TSST. Pill-takers also don't exhibit much of an HPA-axis response to the stress-inducing drug naltrexone or to strenuous exercise, both of which regularly elicit a strong HPA-axis response in most healthy adults.

In one such study, researchers had a sample of pill-takers and non-pill-takers ride an exercise bike until the point of physical exhaustion. They then measured the women's cortisol levels, mood, and heart rate. They found that both groups of women felt less anxious, sad, and angry after exercising than they did beforehand. This is typical because exercise is an amazing mood-booster. Both groups of women also experienced similar SNS stress responses—their heart rates and respiration rates increased the way they're supposed to when exercising. But the pill-taking women's cortisol response to this stress was a mere shadow of that of their naturally cycling peers. No matter which way you slice it (or what testing protocol you use to measure it), pill-taking women seem to lack an HPA-axis response to stress.

Their HPA axes are dysfunctional in other ways, too. For example, research finds that pill-taking women also have an entirely different daily cortisol rhythm than other people. Cortisol follows a circadian rhythm, reaching its daily peak thirty minutes or so after we wake up and gradually declining throughout the day. When women are on the pill, though, their morning cortisol peak is lower and their daily cortisol curve is flatter than what is observed in most healthy adults. Pill-takers are also less able to regulate cortisol that is administered to them in the lab than natural cyclers are, and continue to exhibit differences in HPA-axis function even during a week when they were given a hormone-free sugar pill. This latter result suggests that whatever is going on with the pill and the HPA axis may continue after a woman stops taking it. Rather than simply blunting the stress response (as I first learned about at that fateful conference talk), the pill might totally redefine the functioning of women's HPA axes.

WHEREFORE ART THOU, CORTISOL?

As of this writing, we don't know a whole lot about why pill-taking women's HPA axes seem to go into complete disarray. Despite the fact that researchers have known about this general pattern for more than two decades, very few non-academics know about it, and fewer yet have tried to develop a comprehensive, big-picture answer for why it happens. Currently, the research is in a state where we know bits and pieces about *what* happens—like how peptide X or protein Y changes in women on the pill, thus contributing to HPA-axis dysfunction—but we know very little about *why*.

For example, there's been quite a bit of research into the role that corticosteroid-binding globulins (CBG) play in blunting pill-taking women's cortisol response to stress; CBG is the protein that binds to cortisol and makes it biologically inactive. If pill-taking women have more CBG, this could explain why women's cortisol response to stress appears to be blunted. More CBG = less biologically active cortisol = blunted cortisol response to stress.

You with me so far?

And it's true. Pill-taking women *do* have higher levels of CBG than naturally cycling women. Like, 170ish percent more. And that's a sh**load of CBG. Certainly enough to make it reasonable to expect that CBG plays a role in blunting pill-taking women's stress response. How can it not when its levels are more than twice that of non-pill-takers?

But there's a lot more to it than that. Pill-takers don't just exhibit higher levels of CBG than non-pill-takers. Their HPA axes show dysregulation at every turn. This suggests that something much bigger is going on with the pill and the HPA axis, and as of right now, we don't have a clear idea what that is. For example, here are some of the big differences that we see in pill-taking women's HPA axes when we compare them with those of naturally cycling women.

- Pill-taking women have a blunted free-cortisol response to stress, when compared with that of men or naturally cycling women. Their daily cortisol rhythms are also blunted, with their daily curves looking more like a plateau than a mountain.

- Although pill-taking women's free-cortisol response to stress is lower, their levels of total cortisol (which includes both free, biologically active cortisol as well as that which has been bound up with CBG and made inactive) are *higher*.

- Pill-taking women's levels of CBG (the binding globulin that makes cortisol inactive) are significantly higher than those in naturally cycling women.

- If you give pill-taking women a dose of CRH (a peptide released by the brain that triggers the pituitary gland to initiate release of ACTH), they release less ACTH than men or naturally cycling women do in response to the same dose of CRH. In other words, their ACTH response is blunted.

- If you give pill-taking women a dose of ACTH (a hormone produced by the pituitary to stimulate cortisol release by the adrenal glands), their subsequently measured levels of free cortisol are lower than those of naturally cycling women who are given the same dose.

- If you give pill-taking women a dose of cortisol (which you can do with a hydrocortisone pill) and then measure their unbound levels of the hormone, the levels are higher than those of naturally cycling women who are given the same dose, suggesting their ability to manage excess cortisol is already maxed out.

When you lay out all these pieces, two things seem pretty clear. The first is that pill-taking women's HPA axes march to the beat of their own drum. Whether looking at the brain-to-pituitary signal (CRH), the pituitary-to-adrenal-glands signal (ACTH), or the release of cortisol itself, there is no part of the signaling pathway that looks like it does in naturally cycling women. Top to bottom, side to side, it's different.

The second thing that's clear is that each link in the HPA-axis communication pathway seems to be trying to quiet the stress signal. The adrenal glands are releasing less cortisol than they should in response to a fixed dose of ACTH. The pituitary gland is releasing less ACTH than it should in response to a fixed dose of CRH. And the liver is releasing tons of CBG to render inactive the cortisol that's already been released.

Putting all this together suggests that the blunted stress response that's generally observed in pill-taking women might not be the result of the pill itself dialing down the activities of the HPA axis. Instead, the pill-taking women's pattern of HPA-axis function looks suspiciously similar to that of someone who has experienced chronic stress, suggesting that the pill might actually cause the HPA axis to go into overdrive, requiring it to take coordinated action to blunt *itself*.

To test this idea, researchers recently looked at whether pill-taking women exhibit four well-established biological markers of chronic stress exposure. These include (1) increased expression of genes associated with cortisol signaling (trauma predicts having a greater number of cortisol-triggered genes turned on); (2) higher levels of blood lipids (cortisol dumps fat and sugar into the bloodstream, making levels higher in those experiencing chronic stress); (3) reduced hippocampal volume (chronic stress predicts having a smaller hippocampus, since this area of the brain is highly vulnerable to cell death and diminished neurogenesis in response to chronic stress); and (4) attempted silencing of genes that get turned on by cortisol among those with a genetic risk factor for major depression* (a pattern that is observed when the HPA axis has difficulty shutting itself off). These markers are generally found only in populations of people who have suffered some serious, chronic stress.

The results of these studies found that pill-taking women didn't just exhibit one or two of these biological markers of chronic stress. They exhibited *all four* of them. Although the research is still new and there's a long way to go before we understand this fully, the picture that is beginning to emerge is that the pill might overwhelm the body with cortisol signaling to such an extent that the HPA axis needs to turn itself off.

Despite the fact that too much cortisol signaling can increase women's risk of brain-volume loss, serious depression, and certain health problems (more on all this in a bit), no one really knows why this happens, how it unfolds, or whether it is reversible. Researchers have just now barely begun to consider the possibility that any of this might go on at all. The next frontier in birth control pill research needs to identify why the pill causes the HPA axis to go into overdrive and what we can do to stop it. We're also hugely in need of research telling us whether these effects vary depending on the types of progestins used and whether they persist once the pill is stopped.

Although the science is new and there are a lot of unanswered questions about what this all means for women, it is never too soon to put what is known to good use. HPA-axis dysfunction can wreak havoc on your brain, your moods, and your immune system, and may even sap you of your joie de vivre. And since the sympathetic nervous system part of your stress response remains fully intact on the pill, all these problems occur without so much as a minor reduction in how stressed out you *feel*. Knowing that the pill may cause changes in this major modulator of

....

* Having the TT allele for the *rs1360780* gene is linked to a greater risk of developing major depression.

bodily activities can help you keep an eye out for trouble if it starts to brew. We'll talk about what to look for now.

WHAT THIS MIGHT MEAN FOR YOU

As with many hormones, cortisol has mostly modulatory effects on the body and brain. This means that, rather than being responsible for doing one or two big, noticeable things (like growing breasts or walking), cortisol does a whole bunch of subtler things to several different body systems at once. Because of this, the impact of having too much or too little cortisol signaling isn't something that most people would notice the way they would if their boobs suddenly disappeared or they grew a tail. Instead, it's more like death by a thousand cuts.

First, let's talk about what happens to the brain when too much cortisol signaling is going on in the body. This is likely the initial state of affairs for pill-taking women, before their HPA axes go into shutdown mode.

Too much cortisol exposure is bad news for the brain. It can cause structural and functional changes in areas of the brain like the hippocampus, which can mean bad news for women's cognitive and emotional health. The hippocampus plays a super-important role in our ability to learn and remember, and a ton of research in both humans and animals links hippocampal damage to learning and memory problems. Since pill-taking women have lower hippocampal volume than those who are naturally cycling, this could mean trouble for women on the pill.

For example, a hallmark of Alzheimer's disease—a devastating neurological disorder that is characterized by its negative effects on the memory—is hippocampal shrinkage. A pretty substantial body of evidence also links hippocampal shrinkage to more everyday cognitive and emotional problems, like social anxiety and memory problems. Although we don't know whether the pill has an impact on the likelihood that a woman will experience any of these outcomes, it doesn't take a huge leap of imagination to predict that it might. It might also influence women's ability to learn and remember things in more subtle ways.

One of my graduate students, Hannah Bradshaw, has preliminary results suggesting that this very thing might go on. Across two studies, she found that pill-taking women performed worse than naturally cycling women on a difficult exam and were quicker to give up on unsolvable word puzzles. Although it is as of yet unclear whether these effects are driven by changes in the pill-taking women's stress responses, hippocampi, or something else altogether, these results are consistent with the idea that the pill may harm the capacity to regulate learning, which could make it more difficult for these women to meet their educational and career goals. Structural changes in the hippocampus (and other parts of the brain that are impacted by the pill) might also have a hand in the feelings of fuzzy-headedness and brain fog that some women report having while on the pill, or the onset of depressive symptoms (something we'll talk about in more detail in the next chapter). Although these possibilities are more hypothesis than truth at this point, they are worth considering in your own experiences with the pill.

Hyperactivation of the HPA axis may also have meaningful implications for women's blood sugars and fats, as well as their tendency for weight gain, especially around the stomach area. Cortisol—because it prepares the body for needing to be quick on its feet—elevates levels of fat and sugar in the bloodstream. And this makes good sense in the context of acute stress. Outrunning a wildebeest stampede requires a pretty substantial increase in energy availability, after all. In the long term, though (as in the context of chronic cortisol signaling), this isn't great for the body. Higher-than-normal levels of fat and sugar in the bloodstream can increase the risk of glucose intolerance (pre-diabetes), weight gain (especially abdominal fat), and coronary heart disease. Even though the research isn't yet in a place where we can know for certain whether these are things to be concerned about on the pill (although some evidence suggests that women on the pill do show stress-related changes in lipid profiles), they're worth noting if you have a personal history of glucose intolerance or higher-than-normal levels of triglycerides. You may want to have your doctor keep a close eye on you when starting or changing your birth control regimen.

But this is only half the story. Because after the HPA axis goes into overdrive, it will eventually shut itself down. And, as you might recall from our previous discussion, this seems to be exactly what pill-taking women's HPA axes do. Although this will prevent women from succumbing to death by HPA-axis overdrive (as happens at the crescendo of the salmon's fateful trip upstream), it comes with its own set of problems. Our HPA axis plays a vital role in the body's ability to respond to threats and opportunities in the environment. Lacking the ability to experience dynamic changes in cortisol release in response to stressors might therefore decrease women's ability to cope, learn, and adapt to their environments.

For example, in one study, researchers had pill-taking and naturally cycling women listen to a short narrated story. Half the women heard a story that was full of emotional elements; half heard a boring, blahsville story about nothing. Immediately after hearing the story, half the women in each group were exposed to a stressor, but the other half were not. Cortisol was then measured, and everyone went home and then returned to the laboratory a week later.

When they arrived for this second session, they were surprised with a pop quiz that asked them to recall the details in the story they'd heard the week before. The researchers expected to find that the women who had been exposed to the stressor would have a better memory of the emotional (but not the boring) story. This is what stress should do, because one of cortisol's jobs is to transfer emotionally charged events from our short-term into our long-term memories.

And this was exactly what they found. Just not for everyone. Although the naturally cycling women were better able to recall details of the emotional story after the stressor, the pill-taking women were not. The pill-taking women remembered as little about the emotional story as both groups did about the boring one. And the secret sauce that made these two groups of women so different in their ability to remember the emotionally charged information? Cortisol. Naturally cycling women experienced changes in cortisol in response to the stressor, but pill-taking women did not. So even though the pill-takers paid just as much attention to the story and felt just as stressed out as the natural cyclers did to the stress manipulation, lacking a cortisol surge made it so that pill-taking women's brains didn't soak up the details of the emotional story in the way they were supposed to.

Lacking a stress response in contexts in which a stress response is called for could also potentially impair a woman's ability to recognize compatible mates. One thing that's known to elicit a strong cortisol surge in healthy adults is sexual attraction. This is part of the way that our brain earmarks a potential mate as being someone worth paying attention to. But if pill-taking women's bodies aren't flagging some men as being more salient than others, this could make it more difficult for women to choose partners. Rather than relying on the biological processes that have been shaped by millions of years of evolution to help guide partner choice, pill-taking women may find themselves having to rely more exclusively on reason-based decision-making when it comes to picking partners. This could lead them into relationships that "look good on paper" but lack sexual attraction. Although this possibility has not been tested, it could play a role in some of the pill-based relationship-satisfaction differences that we talked about in chapter 5. Lacking sexual chemistry (but being more satisfied with a partner's earning potential) could be a symptom of partners being chosen without the help of the HPA axis (in addition to the HPG axis).

In a bigger-picture kind of way, not having the brain flagging events and people as meaningful may cause women to feel the low-level blahs all the time. Because when nothing is being biologically flagged by your brain as a threat or an opportunity, it might lead women's brains to believe that they are living in an unstimulating world that lacks the promise of exciting new possibilities and challenges.

This idea—although it hasn't been researched scientifically—is very much consistent with my own experiences on the pill. It just wasn't something that I'd been able to pinpoint until after I went off it.

Going off the pill, to me, felt like slowly waking up. I found that I was feeling things more deeply—both good and bad—once I was off it. The result was that I felt three-dimensional in a way that I have a hard time articulating without the help of a metaphor about . . . of all things . . . records.

At some point in your life, someone has probably told you that music sounds better on LPs (records) than it does on digital recordings like MP3s. Although there's a good chance that your LP-loving friend is just saying this to sound cool or impress women (maybe you), there is actually some truth to this argument. Sound travels in long, beautiful, curved waveforms. And analog recordings mirror the waveform of sound. So when you listen to a song on a record, you hear the true sound of the song. It's rich, saturated, and textured. If you haven't listened to anything on vinyl in a while, it's something worth doing. It really does have nice depth, which makes for a satisfying listening experience.

A song recorded digitally, on the other hand, is a little bit less satisfying. This is because it's recorded in bits, not waves. It tries to mirror the shape of sound by taking thousands of digital snapshots of the analog signal and piecing them together to try to approximate the actual sound wave. But it's never quite the same. Although the end result *feels* like complete sound, it actually isn't. There are pieces that—unbeknownst to almost all of us—are actually missing from our listening experience.

Now, most people who listen to digital music don't have any idea that this has gone on and don't feel like they are missing anything when listening to their favorite songs. It's the type of thing that a person would probably never notice until they listened to the same song on both types of recordings, one right after the other. Even then, the difference is

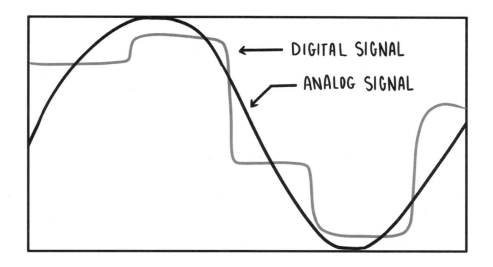

The difference between analog and digital signals.

almost imperceptible. The music on the record just sounds a little more three-dimensional and satisfying than the MP3 version.

Get where I'm going with this?

For me, going off the pill felt like moving from MP3s to records. I didn't *feel* like anything was missing when I was on it. I was only able to recognize the differences in how I was experiencing the world once I was off it. Even then, the differences were hard to describe. They still are. The best I can offer you is that, to me, transitioning off the pill felt like gradually climbing off the page of a book and coming to life. It gave me a feeling of dimensionality that I didn't have when I was on it. I felt things more fully, and life felt more interesting and filled with opportunities and meaning than it did when I was on it.

Having dynamic bursts of HPA-axis activity is one way that our brain knows that we are living meaningful lives. It helps us process emotionally complex information and embed it into our long-term memories. When it's not functioning properly, meaningful, emotional events in our lives— both good and bad—are less able to become a part of who we are. And when this happens, we're no better or wiser for having gone through them.

Our experiences—all the good and bad things that we go through—become shallow. Harming our brains' ability to grab on to all the emotionally complex moments in our lives and move them into our long-term memories may make our lives feel more one-dimensional and flat.

So another possibility is that the pill may change the way that women experience the world. And although these changes are subtle, they may have far-reaching implications for women's mood, well-being, and quality of life. The pill, by taking away the ability to biologically absorb meaning from their environments, may make women feel emptier than they would without it. We still have so much to learn about what this means for women, but it's something that you can be on the lookout for now.

Finally, I want to venture outside the brain here for a moment and raise one last possibility about the effect that a blunted stress response might have on women: It may dysregulate the immune system, increasing a woman's risk of developing autoimmunity. The body deals with infection and injury through inflammation. Although inflammation is hugely necessary to prevent the body from getting sick, it's something that the body has to regulate carefully. Prolonged exposure to inflammation is bad for the body. It contributes to a host of nasty outcomes, like DNA damage, cell death, tissue degeneration, and premature aging. It can also cause problems like fatigue, depression, chronic pain, and memory impairment, and increase the risk of developing cancer, Alzheimer's, and autoimmune diseases. So inflammation is something that needs to be kept in careful check, or the body will increase its risk of suffering any of these inflammation-driven pathologies.

And guess which signaling molecule plays a starring role in our body's ability to regulate inflammation?

Although inflammation is regulated by a whole bunch of different things in the body, a key player in this process is cortisol. When cortisol signaling is out of control or totally shut down, it can promote dysregulation in the body's inflammatory response. This could potentially increase pill-taking women's risk for inflammation and the development of autoimmunity (which is often driven by inflammation). Though we are far from knowing for certain whether the pill and its effects on the HPA axis contribute to misbehavior on the part of the immune system, at least some evidence suggests that it might. And pill use has now been linked to the development of multiple forms of autoimmunity, suggesting that the pill may have implications for women's health. This is critical information to know, since 78 percent of people suffering from autoimmune diseases are women.

Does the birth control pill contribute to these high numbers?

We don't yet know.

Although we don't know for certain what it means for women to have HPA axes that get put through the wringer on the birth control pill, this should give you some ideas of things to look out for. It is never too soon to be proactive with your health.

If you feel like you have been suffering from any of the issues that we've talked about in this chapter, listen to what your body is telling you. It may be time to try a new pill or even a new form of birth control. It may be time for you to take a break from the pill for a while and let your body reset.

The general attitude with women's health has long been that if what a woman is feeling isn't written somewhere in a medical textbook or on a package insert, it's not real. But our bodies sometimes do things that aren't yet fully understood by medicine. Just because the way you feel hasn't been well characterized by research doesn't mean that it's not real or not important. Science hasn't totally figured out women, and research is just beginning to uncover the different ways that the pill changes us. This makes it doubly necessary for you to keep on top of how you feel. Listen to your body and become an advocate for how you're feeling and how you want to feel.

We've covered some pretty scary-sounding ground here, but the overall message is hopeful. I graduated summa cum laude and earned a Ph.D., *both* while on the pill. And there are many women (maybe even you) who've been able to do a whole lot better than that. If my hippocampus is or was smaller than it would have been in the absence of the pill, it hasn't harmed me in any noticeable way.* Women are performing better than ever before in history, so whatever the pill might be doing to our brains, it's not hurting us too badly. But you do deserve to know what you're getting into. Having a modified HPA axis might change how you experience the world. And although the research in this area is still in the super-early phases (meaning we know almost nothing), it's worth considering as you determine whether the pill is working for you.

....
* Although I lock myself out of my office with suspicious frequency . . .

CHAPTER 8: WHAT THE FUNK?

If you're somebody who watches or reads the news, you've probably seen the stories that pop up every year or so about the pill and mood. Sometimes the stories report that the pill is linked to depression. Sometimes they report that the pill is decidedly *not* linked to depression. Other times they report that the pill may be linked to depression in some people but not others. In addition to being confusing, this type of information is hard to take seriously. Studies on health seem to be in a state of perpetual contradiction. For example, in the past ten years alone, wine has been bad for us, good for us, bad for us, and then good for us again. Now it's believed that wine is good for some of us, but only when the wine is red, served in a cup made from a dried sow's ear, and consumed in 1.7922-ounce portions on Sunday and Tuesday afternoons (as long as it's not a leap year, in which case, all bets are off).

It's hard to know what to worry about and not worry about when it comes to health research. And research about the pill is no exception. It can feel like we simultaneously know way too much and way too little about what the pill can do to our moods. Here, we'll go through what the research actually says (and doesn't say) about what the pill can mean for your mental weather forecast . . . and what you can do if you find yourself with more clouds than sun on the horizon.

THE TRUTH ABOUT THE PILL
AND YOUR MOOD

Most women know at least one or two other women who have had a bad reaction to the pill. And most of the time, these bad reactions have been related to unpleasant changes in mood.* Consider Leah's story.

Leah spent most of her early twenties trying to find a method of birth control she liked. The first type of hormonal contraception she tried made her cry all the time (like, *ALL* the time). It was so bad that she became utterly convinced that the way it prevented pregnancy was by making women such emotional basket cases that no one in their right mind would sleep with them.

The second one she tried wasn't a whole lot better. Even though her best friend swore by this one (and her doctor told her that it had a low dose of hormones), it made her super-anxious. For the first time in her life, she missed deadlines at school and work because she was paralyzed with fear about everything not being perfect.

> I have this extremely vivid memory of crying hysterically on the floor of the kitchen in my apartment the night before I had a class project due. It was a group project, and I was so afraid that my portion wasn't going to be good enough and that the other girls in my group were going to hate me. I was freaking out. My mom had to spend an hour on the phone with me trying to talk me out of dropping out of school because I felt like I just wasn't good enough to be there. I felt like I wasn't cut out for school because the stress was too much for me. The crazy thing was that I didn't even know how much of a mess I'd become. I thought that I just had too much on my plate. It was my roommate who told me that she thought something might be going on with me and that I

* Of course, we both know that "unpleasant changes in mood" is just a more delicate way of summarizing what women say to themselves about their experiences on the pill. The latter sounds more like *"Oh, the pill? Yeah, I can't take it because it makes me batsh** crazy."*

wasn't myself [since starting my new pill]. At first, I thought that she was crazy, because I didn't feel any different. I just felt like I was under a lot more stress than I ever had been before in my life. It had never occurred to me that I might be the problem, not my workload.

After more than two months of this sort of thing, Leah switched birth control pills again. This most recent pill (which uses a different type of progestin from that in the first two pills she tried) has been a lot better for her. She feels more like herself again and doesn't feel so stressed out anymore. Although she prefers the way she feels off the pill to the way that she feels on it, she feels pretty normal. And the benefits of not getting pregnant make it an easy choice for her to stay on it.

Interestingly, I've also heard the opposite story from women. Although women's stories about all the different ways that the pill made them crazy are usually the ones we talk about, for some women, the pill is a mood-related godsend. When you talk to these women, they'll tell you that they feel better and more stable on the pill, and feel crazy when they're off it. Take Sophie's story. Sophie was on the same pill (the very first brand she tried) for seven years and loved it. She decided to go off it after her aunt had a stroke. Although her aunt wasn't on the pill, this new piece of family history motivated her to take a break. She wasn't in a relationship, anyway, and because the pill can increase the risk of blood clots, she figured it probably wasn't worth the risk.

This turned out to be hugely disruptive.

Going off the pill made Sophie feel like she was coming unhinged. Although she had always prided herself on her ability to think calmly and rationally, she felt like this wasn't true anymore. She felt emotional. She found herself crying at the drop of a hat, and she no longer felt the ambition and drive that she used to feel at work.

> I used to think that I was so above the fray when it came to getting emotional about things or PMS or whatever. I

remember listening to my coworkers talk about their hormones and how sad or moody they would be at this time or that time of the month and thinking, "Does. Not. Compute." I couldn't remember having ever experienced anything like that before. I'm ashamed to admit it, but I thought they were making it up. Was I ever wrong. When I went off the pill, it was like my body was trying to make up for all the PMS I missed when I was on it. I found myself getting weepy about everything and thinking about how much I wanted to have a baby. I was appalled by my own thoughts. Here I was, climbing the corporate ladder with my business degree, and thinking about babies. I felt like I was turning into a cliché about women in their late twenties and was singlehandedly setting women's lib back sixty years.

After spending a lot of time deliberating about it, she decided to go back on the pill.

Even though I thought the idea that my birth control pills were responsible for my success at work was crazy, I was willing to try anything. And I don't know if it's just a psychological thing, but I have to say, I have my focus and drive back now that I'm on it again. And my moods aren't all over the place. Even though I wouldn't have believed it if someone else would have told me that the pill made them perform better at work, for me it's true.

Before we get into what the research says about all this, let me just go ahead and address the elephant in the room. And that is the whole thing about women's sex hormones influencing mood. Which they do. And this might be the world's oldest cliché about women—and you might hate it—but that doesn't make it any less true. Women's sex hormones influence women's moods. Men's sex hormones affect men's moods. It would be impossible for them not to. The job of hormones is to influence the activities of *everything* that goes on in the body. So of course they are going to influence the brain and the moods the brain creates. Let's all just take a moment to get over this so that we can move forward.*

. . .

Our moods are influenced in significant ways by our hormones. And because of this, the pill can change the way that we feel. Sometimes the changes are for the better (the pill has been successfully used by women for decades to alleviate symptoms of PMS). But sometimes the changes are for the worse. And this is where we'll start our conversation right now, since this is the question that many women have about the pill: *Why does the pill make me crazy?*

To start with, you're not crazy.† All of us feel a little crazy sometimes. Life is hard, and trying to keep as many balls in the air as most of us do can make anyone feel anxious and overwhelmed. And for some women, being on the pill can magnify these feelings, leading to anxiety disorders and depression. But if these things happen to you, it doesn't mean that you're crazy. It just means that you're on the wrong pill. Because some pills make some women's brains do things that happy brains don't usually do. And these things most frequently manifest themselves as anxiety and depression.

Although anxiety and depression lack the kind of family resemblance you get when comparing things like binge-eating disorder and bulimia, these two mood disorders are actually sisters from the same (neurobiological) misters. They involve the same brain regions and signaling pathways, they respond to the same treatments (selective serotonin reuptake inhibitors, used to treat depression, are also effective for treating anxiety), and they tend to cluster together within families (families having members with depression also tend to have members with anxiety). So, rather than being two distinct issues that emerge from two different sets of

----

* If this idea still makes you queasy, you might want to reread chapter 2. It's so necessary for us to embrace our biology and really get that we *are* our hormones.
† Unless you are.

mechanisms, depression and anxiety are better thought of as two sides of the same coin. They just manifest themselves differently in different people and situations. Some people with mood-related vulnerabilities react to life stressors by experiencing anxiety. For others, anxiety turns into the feelings of despair and helplessness that we call depression.

And, as you're probably aware, mood-related issues like anxiety and depression are super-common among women who go on the pill. Almost half of all women who go on the pill stop using it within the first year because of intolerable side effects. And the intolerable side effect that is most frequently cited among those that caused them to quit is unpleasant changes in mood. Sometimes they quit because of intolerable anxiety. Sometimes they quit because of intolerable depression. Sometimes they quit because they were one of those unfortunate souls who is able to experience both simultaneously. And even though some women's doctors continue to tell them that those changes in their moods aren't real or that they aren't important, a growing body of research suggests otherwise. For some women, being on the pill can increase the risk of anxiety and depression. And the results can be devastating.

LESSONS FROM DENMARK

Denmark is a beautiful Scandinavian nation located on a peninsula in the North Atlantic Ocean. In addition to being the birthplace of writer Hans Christian Andersen, the Lego company, and roughly one-quarter of my ancestors,* Denmark is also home to a number of nationwide registers, which are collections of data from all the nation's citizens on a number of health and social issues. For example, the Danish Psychiatric Central Research Register keeps track of the incidence of all psychiatric disease diagnosed in Denmark; the National Prescription Register keeps track of all the prescriptions that are filled in Denmark; and the Cause of Death

....
* That's right, Grandma.

Register keeps track of who dies when, and from what. And because all Danish citizens have a unique personal identification number, researchers are able to link individual people's data across these different registers. This gives researchers access to tons of information about patterns of health and social behavior in a *whole population of people*. All of them. The benefits of this register to science are nothing short of huge.

Perhaps not surprisingly, it is from these health registries that we've learned some of the most critical and valuable lessons about the powerful effects that the birth control pill can have on mood. In the first of these studies, the researchers tracked changes in the risk of being diagnosed with depression on the basis of whether women went on the pill or not. They looked at the health and prescription records of *all* the healthy, non-depressed women living in Denmark between the ages of fifteen and thirty-four. They then followed the prescription and mental health records of these women (more than a million of them) for fourteen years to see whether going on hormonal contraceptives influenced the likelihood of later being diagnosed with depression or being prescribed antidepressants.

What they found is some of the most powerful evidence demonstrating a link between hormonal contraceptives and depression risk to date. The researchers found that women who were on hormonal contraceptives were 50 percent more likely to be diagnosed with depression six months later, compared with women who were not prescribed hormonal contraceptives during this time. They also found that the women who were on hormonal contraceptives were 40 percent more likely to be prescribed an antidepressant than were women who were not prescribed hormonal contraceptives during this time.

You can see a breakdown of the results by product type and age group in the table on the next page. The numbers in each row tell you the degree to which the depression risk increased for women on each type of hormonal contraceptive relative to naturally cycling women. The column on the left shows the results pooled across all women in the sample. The column on the right shows the results for the women ages fifteen to nineteen (who were hardest hit by an increased depression risk).

Type of Hormonal Contraceptive

COMBINATION PILLS	% INCREASED RISK OF DEPRESSION*	
ETHINYL ESTRADIOL (50 MG)	**ALL WOMEN**	**WOMEN 15–19**
Norethisterone	30%	20%
Levonorgestrel	†50%	†120%
ETHINYL ESTRADIOL (30–40 MG)		
Norethisterone	-10%	50%
Levonorgestrel	0%	†70%
Norgestimate	0%	†80%
Desogestrel	†10%	†100%
Gestodene	0%	†80%
Drospirenone	†20%	†100%
Cyproterone acetate	†20%	†50%

* Note that these numbers are telling you how much higher the risk of depression was for each group of women on each type of contraceptive compared to that observed in women who were not prescribed hormonal contraceptives. You can use these numbers to mentally fill in the blanks in the following sentence: Women in this age range on this type of hormonal contraceptive exhibited a risk of depression that was _____ percent higher than was observed in comparably aged, naturally cycling women.

† Indicates the result is statistically significant (i.e., not likely to have been found by accident).

ETHINYL ESTRADIOL (20 MG)		
Desogestrel	0%	†60%
Gestodene	0%	†60%
Drospirenone	†20%	†70%
ESTRADIOL VALERATE (30, 20, 10 MG)		
Dienogest	†80%	†160%
NON-ORAL PRODUCTS		
Patch (norgestrolmin)	†90%	†180%
Vaginal ring (etonogestrel)	†50%	†170%
IUD (levonorgestral)	†40%	†220%
PROGESTIN-ONLY PILLS		
Norethisterone	0%	30%
Levonorgestrel	30%	N/A
Desogestrel	†20%	†130%

The results of this study, as well as others, suggest that the pill can increase some women's risk of depression. And this seems to be particularly true for non-oral products (a patch, vaginal ring, or hormonal IUD) and for young women (ages fifteen to nineteen), whose brains are not yet done developing and may be more prone to the influence of hormonal signaling. These results represent a huge step in our understanding of the potential link between hormonal contraceptives and problems with mood.

Now, because I'm a scientist, I'm contractually obliged to point out that—although these researchers found a relationship between being prescribed hormonal contraceptives and depression risk—we don't know for sure that the pills themselves *caused* this increase. Correlation doesn't equal causation. It's possible, for example, that the researchers found pill taking and depression to be related to each other because they were each related to some other third variable, making it look like they're related even though they're not. For instance, women who seek medical interventions to prevent pregnancy may be more likely to seek medical interventions for depression, or getting into a new sexual relationship (which often prompts a pill prescription) could be what's increasing women's depression risk. Although relationships typically make our lives happier and fuller, not all of them do. It's possible that the women of Denmark might have had a run of bad luck and just happened to find themselves in some crappy relationships at the time of the study.

Although it would be impossible for third variables not to have influenced the results of this study at all (surely, they did), I urge you to take these results seriously. The researchers statistically tested for the influence of a number of third variables, and each of these tests found that hormonal contraceptives predicted depression risk even after statistically controlling for the impact of these third variables. Further, it's hard to imagine a reasonable third-variable-based explanation that would account for the fact that the risk of depression differed—sometimes in pretty dramatic ways—depending on the specific product that was used. There's no reason, for example, that women prescribed non-oral products (which pose a greater depression risk) would be more eager to visit a doctor about depressive symptoms (one third variable) or have crappier relationships (another third variable) than women using oral products (which predict a lesser depression risk). This suggests that something in the products themselves is changing a person's depression risk.

So, even though this wasn't a double-blind, placebo-controlled experiment (which is the gold standard in research and is the only way to make bold claims about cause and effect*), the researchers took great care with their study design and data analysis, and the results were published in the top medical journal in the United States. And although these researchers weren't able to deliver a smoking gun, this was a thoughtfully done, well-executed science. And the results suggest that the pill might have undesirable consequences on some women's moods.

More recently, the same research team decided to take this finding one step further: to look at whether hormonal contraceptives might also increase women's risk of suicide. Suicide is a tragic, irreversible outcome that often stems from problems with mental health that have gone unaddressed. In this study, researchers tracked hormonal contraceptive usage and suicide attempts and deaths in all Danish women who'd turned fifteen between 1996 and 2013.[†] They followed all the women for an average of eight years and then compared the likelihood of having attempted or successfully committed suicide among the women who were prescribed hormonal contraceptives and those who were not.

....

* Which most studies on the pill don't do, by the way. It's a weakness in much of the work that has been done. Double-blind, placebo-controlled research is the exception in the world of birth control pill research.

† As in their prior study, they did not include any women who had previously diagnosed psychological problems or who had used antidepressants. They also didn't include women who were already on hormonal contraceptives when they entered the study at age fifteen.

When comparing these groups of women, the researchers found startling differences in their risk for suicidal behavior. The women who were on hormonal contraceptives were twice as likely to have attempted suicide in this period of time than the women who were not on hormonal contraceptives. And this is eye opening on its own. But the risk of successful suicide attempts was actually even higher than that. It was *triple* that of women not on hormonal contraceptives. And, as they found with depression risk, the biggest negative impact of hormonal contraceptives on suicide risk was found for young women (ages fifteen to nineteen) on non-oral products.

This is an absolute tragedy. Although suicide is something that happens for a variety of reasons, our failure to take mental health concerns seriously is one of them. And there is no group of people on this planet whose mental health concerns have been taken less seriously than women. This is especially true when these concerns are related to hormones or the birth control pill.

Although things have gotten better for women, for a very long time doctors didn't take women's mood-related concerns on birth control seriously. Women were often told that they were imagining how they were feeling or that their symptoms were "all in their heads" (as if they'd emerge from anywhere other than the location of the brain). Even today, when women's mood changes on the pill are more likely to be acknowledged by their doctors, the seriousness of these changes is too often minimized, treated as being a nuisance side effect like bloating or bleeding between periods. And, to some degree, we've all been complicit in being treated this way. Somewhere, somehow, we've all agreed that it's okay for ourselves and for other women to live with mental health problems, as long as no one is getting pregnant unexpectedly. This is—quite literally—complete insanity.

Your mental health is a very serious and significant matter, and your desire to feel balanced and happy is not a character flaw. Anyone who makes you feel like it is doesn't have your best interests in mind. If you have mental health concerns on the pill, you should absolutely talk to your doctor. And if your doctor doesn't take your concerns seriously, it's time to find a new one. Getting depressed or anxious on the pill doesn't mean that there's anything wrong with you or that you're mentally unstable. It just means that your body might not be very tolerant of having its hormones monkeyed with. You need to take how you feel seriously and make sure that your doctor does, too. As the women of Denmark have shown us, failure to take it seriously can have the most tragic consequences of all. Women shouldn't be losing their lives because of their birth control.

SO, WHY MOOD?

When it comes to the reasons that the pill can mess with your mood, the two systems that shoulder most of the blame are the HPA axis (which, at this point, you probably know more about than you'd ever wished to be true) and some of our neurotransmitter systems. In particular, the research finds that the neurotransmitters that influence our brain's ability to slow itself down, as well as those involved in our ability to feel rewarded, may be altered in the face of the pill.

First, the HPA axis. We've already talked about this, so I won't spend too much time going over what you already know. It is worth mentioning again, though, that the type of blunting of the HPA axis that we tend to see in pill-taking women is a known contributor to mental health problems, including the types of mood disturbances characteristic of post-traumatic stress disorder (PTSD). Stress hormones like cortisol help our bodies deal with stress. And because lacking the biological tools necessary to deal with stress *literally* harms your ability to cope, having a broken stress response might be a key player in the development of anxiety and depression.

In addition to harming mood in direct ways, by making us less able to cope, having a blunted stress response could also harm emotional well-being in more indirect ways through its negative impact on our ability to absorb emotionally meaningful events from our environments. As you might recall from the previous chapter, lacking a cortisol surge in response to stress impairs the brain's ability to encode emotionally valenced events into our memories. It's possible, then, that the pill may decrease women's ability to shepherd meaningful life events from their short-term memories into their long-term memories. Over time, it's possible that this could cause their brains to believe that their lives lack meaning and excitement. And there are few things more depressing than this.

Changes in the HPA axis are just the first piece in the puzzle, though, when it comes to the pill and mood. The second piece—and the one that's been given the most attention in the research world—is the role that neurotransmitter systems, like those involved in GABA* signaling, play in making women feel lousy on the pill. To get into this, though, I need you to know three quick things about neurotransmitters.

- Quick Thing 1: Neurotransmitters are chemicals that the brain uses to communicate with itself and the rest of the body.

- Quick Thing 2: Excitatory neurotransmitters tell your brain cells to get ready for action, making them more likely to fire off messages to other cells in the brain. These are your alert, ready-for-action neurotransmitters.

- Quick Thing 3: Inhibitory neurotransmitters, on the other hand, tell your brain cells to slow their roll, making them less likely to fire off messages to other cells in the brain. These are your relaxed, kumbaya neurotransmitters.

The most prevalent and frequently used inhibitory neurotransmitter in the brain is GABA. And as the star inhibitory neurotransmitter in the

....
* A.k.a. *gamma–aminobutyric acid*. Like any of us would ever call it that.

brain, it's often on the scene in a big way when your brain is trying to slow itself down. For example, GABA gets released when you're relaxing in your PJ pants in front of the fire, and it also gets released when doing things like meditation and yoga. When GABA receptors are stimulated, it causes powerful anti-anxiety effects in the brain, helping you feel like the calmer, more relaxed, kumbayaed version of yourself.

Interestingly, you can get a nice, relaxed, GABA-rific experience not only from GABA but also from other things that stimulate GABA receptors. This is how alcohol and benzodiazepines like Xanax work. They do their seductive black magic by prompting the action of your GABA receptors, slowing down synaptic firing in your brain and making you feel . . . Ahhhhhhhhh. This is why having a drink at the end of a stressful day can help take the edge off. It slows down your brain, making all that dumb little sh** that you were worrying about on your way home seem like much less of a big deal than it was before the cork was popped and the wine was poured.

Now, the cool part about this is that our bodies actually produce a variety of compounds that work like alcohol and Xanax, but without all the calories or potential for addiction. One of the most powerful of these comes in the form of a neurosteroid called allopregnanolone. Allopregnanolone gets synthesized when progesterone is broken down in the body and has the effect of kick-starting action by your GABA receptors. Just like alcohol and Xanax! But from progesterone! This is part of the whole mom-jeans part of the cycle, with women's bodies doing things to prepare for the possibility of egg implantation. It's believed that allopregnanolone is synthesized to slow women's brains down such that they're more inclined to relax at home than do the kinds of activities that could knock a newly implanting embryo out of place. So, an upside of the luteal phase and its relatively high levels of progesterone is that it allows for the synthesis of more of this calming neurosteroid.

Unfortunately for women on the pill, it doesn't seem that the artificial progestins in the pill offer this same type of benefit. In fact, the research suggests that women on the pill may have lower levels of these naturally occurring sedatives relative to what's observed in its absence, regardless of the point in the cycle. This could mean less naturally occurring kumbaya for pill-taking women.

In one particularly well-executed study, researchers looked at the effect of the pill on levels of progesterone's calming derivative, allopregnanolone, in both rats and women. Both sets of females were put on a pill containing ethinyl estradiol (EE) and the progestin levonorgestrel (LNG) for a series of three cycles. The researchers then measured levels of allopregnanolone in the blood (humans and rats) and brain (rats only).

Going on the pill was found to decrease levels of allopregnanolone in the rats' brains by a staggering 79 percent relative to the levels observed in the non-pill-taking rats. They also found that the pill-takers had a lot more GABA receptors in their brain than the untreated females did. This happens when there is a shortage of GABAergic* activity, as it's a sign that the brain is trying desperately to slow itself down by grabbing on to as many GABA-receptor-stimulating molecules as possible in the face of a major shortage.

The results from the human females in the study told a similar story. Although the researchers couldn't directly assess the levels of allopregnanolone in the women's brains, their blood levels of allopregnanolone were significantly lower after three months on the pill than they were prior to treatment. Other research has also found this result. And because the brain is usually harder hit than the peripheral blood when it comes to levels of allopregnanolone in response to the pill, the situation in pill-taking women's brains is probably far worse.

All this can mean really bad news for women's mental health. When GABA receptors aren't being properly stimulated, it's known to make

....

* Quite possibly the ONLY way to make the ungainly acronym GABA less aesthetically pleasing is to add the suffix -ergic to it (especially when all it means is that it uses the neurotransmitter GABA).

people feel anxious, overwhelmed, and depressed. Not surprisingly, a number of mental-health-related issues, including panic disorder, depression, bipolar disorder, and the mood-related symptomology of PMS are characterized by lower-than-average levels of GABAergic activity. Lack of GABAergic activity can also increase a person's risk of alcohol dependence, as alcohol is a tempting surrogate to an anxious brain that's desperate for calming. Although no published studies link birth control use to the risk of alcohol dependence, this is something that might be worth paying attention to if you have a family history of alcoholism. Women have one of the fastest-growing rates of alcohol-use disorders in the United States, and it's not too much of a stretch to imagine that a lack of GABAergic activity in pill-taking women's brains might increase their tendency to self-medicate for depression and anxiety.

In addition to the observed changes in women's GABAergic system, research suggests that changes in dopamine and serotonin signaling may also play a role in mood-related changes that we see on the pill. Dopamine and serotonin, like GABA, are neurotransmitters. And these two play a vital role in creating some of our absolute favorite psychological experiences ever. These are the chemicals that come on the scene in a big way when we're spending time with people we love, eating hot fudge sundaes, falling in love, having sex, and having orgasms. It's through the release of these neurotransmitters (which create the experience of feeling happy and blissed out) that our brain rewards itself for doing the types of things that have historically promoted successful survival and reproduction. Having sex, eating a beautiful meal, feeling loved and adored, loving and adoring others . . . All these things feel so amazing to us because our brain has been designed to release these happy-reward-pleasure chemicals when we're doing things that, ultimately, help promote gene transmission.

Not surprisingly, given their role in promoting gene transmission, these neurotransmitter systems change what they do in response to women's cyclically changing sex hormones. In particular, the research finds that estrogen makes rewarding things feel even more rewarding than they do in its absence, and that progesterone attenuates these effects. So, estrogen makes sex feel sexier, chocolate taste yummier, and getting status boosts feel boost-ier. And this makes a lot of sense. Of course, natural selection would turn up the volume on pleasure at times in the cycle when conception is possible. The better it feels, the more likely we are to do it. And when it comes to the kinds of things that influence gene transmission, the time to do them is when estrogen is high. So, estrogen makes pleasure more pleasurable, and progesterone has the opposite effect.*

Given that the pill keeps estrogen levels low across the cycle (and stimulates progesterone receptors), it's possible that the pill might have the effect of dampening reward processing in the brain. And if the world seems unrewarding, this makes us feel depressed. One hallmark symptom of depression is that people no longer find pleasure in things that they used to find pleasure in (anhedonia). So it's also possible that the pill might increase a person's risk of depression by making pleasure less pleasurable. Consistent with this idea, research finds that pill-taking women—when compared with their naturally cycling counterparts—have a blunted positive emotional response to happy things and don't experience activity in the reward centers of their brains when looking at pictures of their romantic partners (which is something that naturally cycling women do). This

....

* This is something that is often studied in the context of drug addiction. The reason for this is that drugs of abuse (cocaine, opioids, etc.) work their black magic by hijacking your brain's reward system. They're so addictive because they stimulate the sh*t out of your brain's pleasure receptors, which simulates an experience that's like winning the lottery, having the best sex of your life, and eating a hot fudge sundae all rolled into one. This makes all the everyday things that make you happy and reinforce your behavior (things like actual sex and hot fudge sundaes) seem like penny-ante bullsh*t, because there is no way they can measure up to the crazy super-stimulus stuff that drugs can do. It's hard to go back to the farm once you've seen Paris. Consistent with what you would expect, given what estrogen does to the brain's reward centers, this research finds that estrogen increases the rewardfulness of drugs like cocaine while progesterone decreases them. One interesting possibility that comes from all this is that maybe the birth control pill could help women struggling with addiction by keeping sex hormones low.

suggests that the things that normally cause brains to feel pleasure don't elicit the same response in women on the pill. Although the exact reasons for these differences aren't yet well understood, they all point to the possibility that the pill may change neurotransmitter patterns in ways that mean trouble for mental health.

AM I AT RISK?

It seems pretty clear from the research that the pill can cause some women some pretty serious problems when it comes to their mental health. What's also clear, though, is that not all women are equally at risk. For example, research finds that women who have genes that code for a specific type of mineralocorticoid receptor* seem to be protected from most of the negative mood problems on the pill. And there are probably hundreds of other genes that influence how women react to the pill that we just don't know about yet. We may never know. The only thing that is clear is that whether the pill harms or improves your mood is very person-dependent, and the science isn't yet at a point where we can make strong predictions about exactly what's going to happen to whom, and on what.

All is not lost, though. At least a few things are clear from the research, and it's never too early for you to use this information to help you make more informed decisions about your health. According to the research, you might have a greater risk of experiencing negative mood effects on the pill if:

- You have a history of depression or mental illness (although there is also evidence that the pill can stabilize mood in certain women with mental illness).

....

* In particular, this research finds that a certain set of mineralocorticoid receptor genes (haplotype II) seems to protect women from experiencing negative psychological effects on the pill. People with this haplotype also tend to be happier and more optimistic.

- You have a personal or family history of mood-related side effects on the birth control pill.

- You are taking progestin-only pills.

- You are using a non-oral product.

- You are taking multi-phasic pills (these are the pills that have an increasing dose of hormones across the cycle rather than a constant dose).

- You are nineteen or younger.

These bullet points are here to give you a starting point that you can use to initiate a conversation with your doctor about any mental health concerns you might have on the pill. They aren't your fate, though. Even if you're an eighteen-year-old with a family history of depression and are on the birth control patch, if you aren't experiencing any signs of troubled mental health, the chances are incredibly low that you're going to suddenly develop mood problems from your birth control. This is especially true if you've been on it for a while and seem to be tolerating it well. If you feel great on the pill, this is really all you need to know. You are the only data point that matters when it comes to choosing what works best for you.

It's also worth pointing out that, while some women can experience negative mood changes on the pill, some women experience the opposite reaction. Rather than feeling worse, they feel a whole lot better and mentally healthier on the pill than off it. For example, in one study, researchers took quality-of-life measures on more than three thousand women before and after starting a pill containing ethinyl estradiol and the third-generation progestin desogestrel. They found* that the women's quality-

....

* However, this study didn't use a control group (a comparison group of non-pill-starting women) to compare the pill-takers' results to. This is worth keeping in mind, since

of-life scores—especially as they related to mood—were significantly higher after going on the pill than they were before they started. Similar results have been found with pills containing the fourth-generation progestin drospirenone and the third-generation progestin gestondene. So for some women, some pills may improve mood and decrease irritability.

Research also finds that the pill can offer huge mood-stabilizing benefits to women who have severe PMS. Premenstrual syndrome (PMS) is the cornucopia of symptoms that women can experience during the late luteal phase of the cycle (the last week or so of the cycle before your period starts), including mood swings, bloating, fatigue, and a bunch of other unpleasant changes that can make women (and those around them*) totally miserable. Although some research finds that women who experience PMS may be more at risk for negative mood changes on the pill, there's also a pretty substantial body of research showing that the pill can be a godsend for women who have PMS and can even alleviate symptoms of premenstrual dysphoric disorder (PMDD), a much more serious and debilitating form of PMS.

The reason the pill can help these women is that PMS and PMDD symptoms are believed to be caused by abnormal physiological responses to changing levels of hormones across the cycle. The pill irons out all the hormonal fluctuations, keeping them stable and unchanging. This can take the edge off PMS for women whose brains and bodies don't respond well to hormonal ups and downs. This is particularly true of brands that use the same dose of hormones throughout the cycle (monophasic treatments) or those that keep you on a steady dose of hormones for three months before you have your week of placebo pills, prompting your pseudo-period. This is a good thing to keep in mind as you weigh your

....

researchers have found pretty substantial placebo effects in studies of birth control pills and mood.

* You didn't hear that from me.

different options, too. Some women swear by the pill when it comes to their mood and feel terrible when they're off it.

The most critical thing about how the pill might make you feel, though, will come from you. How do *you* feel? Each of us will have a somewhat different response to anything we take, so however you feel is your biological reality. You are the only data point that matters when it comes to your pill.

A LITTLE UNSOLICITED ADVICE

Although this book is meant to be more science than self-help, let me offer you some unsolicited advice. Any time you start a new pill, please let someone close to you know about it. Ask them to make note and tell you if they notice any changes in your behavior that might suggest the onset of depression. The thing that can make hormones' impact on our moods a little scary is that, a lot of times, we can't separate how they're making us feel from the way we see the world. Because the hormones in the pill influence what the brain does, it's almost impossible to separate out what the hormones are doing from who we are. We feel like the version of reality that is created by our brain on the pill is real. Like, objectively REAL. This can make it difficult for us to notice depression creeping in. Rather than feeling like the pill is messing with our mood, it just feels like our life is getting crappier. Or that our job has gotten more stressful. If you tell your person that you are trying a new pill, he or she may be able to help you recognize any problems that start to develop so that you can look for a new pill or an alternative means of protecting yourself from pregnancy.

On top of this, I think that you should consider keeping a journal. If possible, start before going on the pill so that you have a written log of how you were feeling before and after. The brain likes to play tricks on us when we are sad or anxious and tells us we have always felt that way. It's part of how it creates the illusion of being stable and consistent over time. Having hard evidence of your mood prior to the pill can be a good way for you to think about your past a little more objectively, making it easier to recognize any changes based on the pill. In each entry, make note of your mood, energy level, and well-being using some sort scale, like the one I have below. This will help you keep tabs on how things change for you (or not!) when you're trying out a new pill.

1   2   3   4   5   6   7

I FEEL SAD/ANXIOUS   I FEEL GREAT

Using a scale like this one to keep track of your moods when on and off the pill can help you keep tabs on whether the pill changes your outlook on life.

If you're already on the pill, it's not too late to keep track of how you're feeling. You can just make a note of your patterns. If you have more happy days than sad ones, that probably means that everything is on the right track. None of us feel happy all the time, but we should feel happier more often than we do sad when things in our lives are going well. And if you have fewer happy days than you think you should, talk to your doctor. It could be time to try a new birth control pill or address an issue with your mental health that you've let go too long. If you don't take care of yourself, you can't take care of anyone else, either. You need to make yourself and your mental health a priority, and using a journal can be a really powerful step in doing this. It can help you learn more about what makes you tick and how you feel on the pill and off it, so that you can become the version of yourself that you most want to be.

PART III—
THE BIG
PICTURE

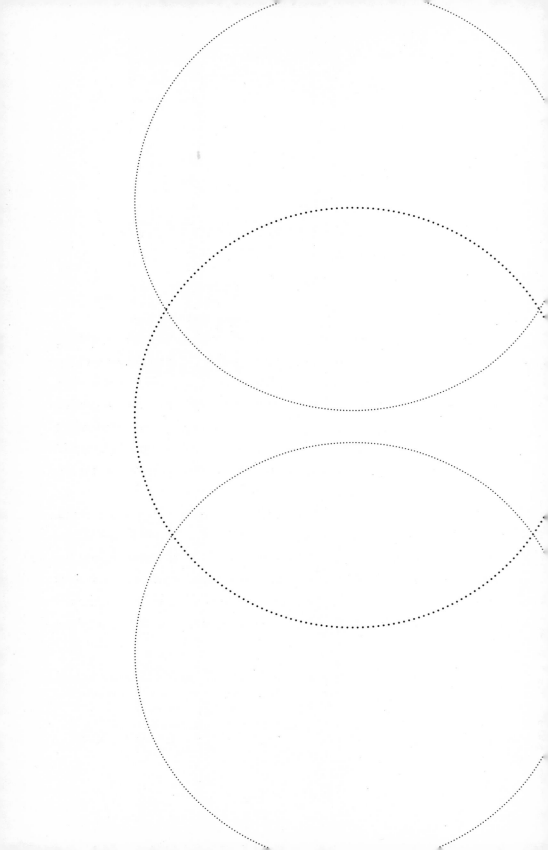

CHAPTER 9: THE LAW OF UNINTENDED CONSEQUENCES

Nature is a finicky thing. And one reason it's so finicky is that everything in it is interdependent. This means that you can't go changing one thing without it changing everything else. This is why time travel is such a bad idea and why butterflies flapping their wings in Brazil are always getting blamed for tornadoes in Texas. Whenever you have an interdependent system—which, in nature, we always do*—making one small change in point A can set off a chain of events that culminates in much bigger, widespread changes in points B through Z.

This idea is something that we've been talking about all along in this book, without actually talking about it. Everything the pill does—all the changes that it causes throughout women's bodies—happens because the body's systems are hugely interdependent and therefore prone to these sorts of "I wasn't expecting *THAT* to happen!" effects. Women's sex hormones influence a whole bunch of other things going on in the body (and those

....
* If you need evidence of this, check out the food chain sometime. The degree to which we are interdependent with other living (and nonliving) organisms borders on unsettling. This is why conservation biologists look so freaked out all the time. They have a deep appreciation for just how fragile this balance is and know better than anyone that the fate of our entire species could depend on the mating behaviors of a blue-winged cuckoo bird or the rate of photosynthesis in a slime mold.

things influence other things, which influence other things . . .), which is why the pill changes a whole lot more than our proclivity toward monthly egg release. It changes *everything*.* And this includes things that seem to have nothing to do with sex. It changes how our digestive system works, what our microbiomes look like, how our immune system functions, what our other endocrine organs do, how our metabolism operates, and—of course—what goes on in our heads. The effects of the pill echo throughout women's bodies from head to toe in ways that can mean big changes for the version of themselves that their brains create.

But the way that the pill changes women turns out to be just the tip of the iceberg. Because a woman's own body isn't really an end point at all. Each woman is a starting point in an interdependent web of people that includes her friends, family, romantic partners, coworkers, and everyone else she will ever interact with or influence. This means that when women go on the pill—which changes who they are and what they do—it can influence other people by changing who they are and what they do, too. The pill, by changing women, has the ability to have cascading effects on everyone and everything a woman encounters. And when you multiply this type of an effect by several million (the number of women around the world on the pill), the pill changes the world.

GIRL POWER AND THE ACHIEVEMENT GAP

If you've had the opportunity to spend any time on a college campus in the past twenty-five years, you've probably noticed that there aren't a whole lot of men around. This wasn't a figment of your imagination. Most college campuses in the United States have female enrollment numbers that would have shocked even the most optimistic of feminists

....
* If not *everything*, at least everything in the figurative "I'm exaggerating for effect but not that much" kind of way.

fifty years ago. In 2017, more than 56 percent of college students on U.S. campuses were women, accounting for some 2.2 million more women being enrolled than men. And it's not just that more women are attending college than men; they're also graduating at a higher rate. In 2015, 37.5 percent of women between the ages of twenty-five and thirty-four had a college degree, whereas for men, that number was 29.5 percent.

This shift in educational and job performance is usually called the male-female achievement gap. And when you look at the development of this achievement gap over time (check out my figure below), it becomes apparent that there are two sides to the story.

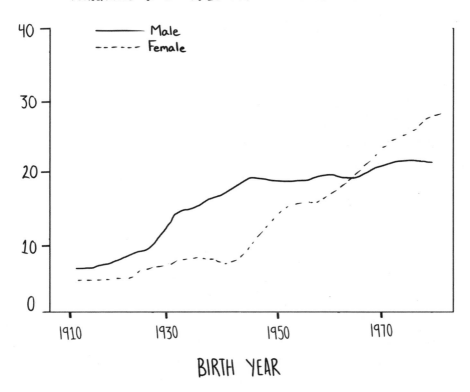

Although men used to earn more college degrees than women, women are now outperforming men by most educational metrics.

The first side to this story is that women are achieving a lot more than they used to. Back in 1940, only about 10 percent of women age twenty-six to twenty-eight had completed a college degree, whereas in 2017, that number was up by 35 percent. Women are going to college, graduating, and entering the workforce in greater numbers than they ever have in the past. And there's good reason to believe that the birth control pill has a lot to do with this. The birth control pill has made it possible for women to get degrees and climb the corporate ladder without having to worry about getting benched because of pregnancy, allowing us to kick ass and take names in ways that weren't available to our grandmothers.

The second side to the story is that men are achieving *less* than they used to. And, as you'll see in just a bit, the birth control pill might have a lot to do with this, too. Changing the consequences associated with sex, in addition to changing what women do, may also change what men do . . . or don't do.

But first, women.

Like most women I know, I've spent a good portion of my adult life taking for granted the fact that I didn't need to worry about getting pregnant from sex. But in the history of women, this has been a total game changer. Life is so much different for us now than it was for our great-grandmothers, and a lot of this is due to changes that ultimately stem from the advent of the pill.

Granting women the ability to have sex without having to worry about rushing into marriage or parenthood has allowed them to focus on educating themselves and building careers before starting families. And this has been paramount in terms of allowing women the opportunity to achieve. But perhaps even more important, the pill has allowed women—for the very first time in history—to *plan*. Knowing that the odds of an unplanned pregnancy are effectively zero has removed from women's dreams about their future a powerful storm cloud that was perpetually present for our college-bound grandmothers and great-grandmothers. For them, there was always the very real possibility that any plans they made would be laid to dust by an unplanned pregnancy.

Removing this storm cloud has been particularly beneficial in terms of getting women's faces and voices represented in fields requiring an advanced degree. Most people won't take on a huge, costly project without feeling fairly confident that they're going to cross the finish line. And there are few projects that are as costly—both in terms of having to take out loans and defer almost all forms of gratification—as getting an advanced degree.* Many advanced degrees require people to stay in school until they're close to thirty. I went to graduate school immediately after completing my undergraduate degree, and I still didn't complete my Ph.D. until I was just shy of twenty-nine. And I was one of the lucky ones who finished "quickly." For women going into fields like medicine and the physical sciences, this timeline can be stretched out well into a woman's thirties. Without reliable birth control, women choosing to go into these fields would have to be okay with the very real possibility that their investment of time and financial resources would go to waste because an unexpected pregnancy would interrupt their training. The pill changed the game for women by allowing them to feel confident that their training wouldn't be cut short by an unexpected pregnancy. And their response to this change was overwhelming.

Before 1970, almost no women went into careers requiring a postgraduate education. All that changed, however, precisely at the time in our nation's history when the pill became legally available to single women (the late 1960s and early '70s†). As you can see from the figure on the next page, as soon as women felt in control of their fertility—and knew that they wouldn't get benched mid-education because of

....
* And if you don't believe me, ask a graduate student. They'll tell you terrible tales of costly student loans, sleeplessness, stress, and how much it sucks to be broke and living in a crappy apartment when most of their friends have real jobs, money, and lives.
† Before then, it was legally available only to married women, which, I think we can both agree, is total ridiculous bullsh**.

pregnancy—their applications to postgraduate degree programs skyrocketed. Although the surge of women in these fields was also helped by decreasing sexism in the admissions process, the biggest driver of these effects was actually the huge surge in the number of female applicants.

When it is possible for women, they do.

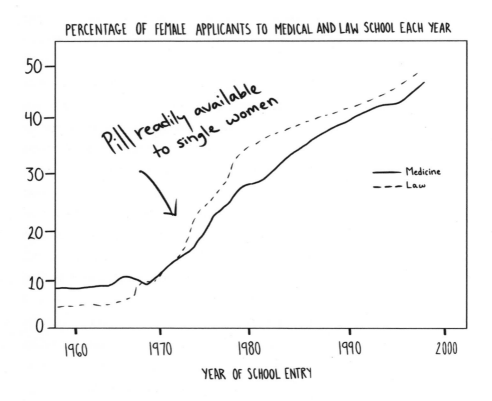

The numbers of women applying to law school and medical school skyrocketed once the pill became legally available to single women.

Women responded to the freedom granted to them by the pill not by becoming more irresponsible and reckless in their lives (which is what a lot of the abstinence-only types might want you to believe), but by becoming more educated and being more inclined to contribute to fields like law, medicine, science, government, and business. And even though you and I take this sort of thing for granted, it hasn't always been easy for women to dream this big.

Some of the most brilliant scientists I know—scientists who are doing things like discovering new ways to treat cancer and to help prevent diseases of aging—are women. And just fifty years ago, many of these brilliant women probably would have been sidelined because the demands of childbearing would have made their extensive education and training nearly impossible. The pill has opened up a huge new pool of talent to help solve some of the world's most vexing problems.

And if vexing problems aren't your thing, think for a moment about all the amazing women who have touched your own life. Maybe it was a teacher or a professor who was meaningful in shaping your career goals. Or maybe it was a doctor or nurse who made you feel comforted when you were sick or afraid. Think about all the amazing, brilliant, funny, empathetic women whose voices would have been quieted and whose contributions we would be without if they didn't have a reliable means of pregnancy prevention. We should all be thankful to be at a place in time when we all get to benefit from these women's ambitions. The world would be a much different, less brilliant place if these women weren't able to restrict their fertility in a reliable way.

The pill has changed the world by making women more present in the educational sphere and workplace. We probably owe countless specific achievements—technologies developed, cures discovered, people helped—to the birth control pill. But not all these changes have been for the better.

IS WHAT'S GOOD FOR THE GOOSE BAD FOR THE GANDER?

Unless you live under a rock (or in a Mennonite community somewhere), you're probably aware that women are a powerful source of motivation for men. Like, hugely powerful. Many of the things that men do are ultimately (although not always consciously) motivated by the desire to impress, woo, court, and have sex with women. And even though this might sound crass or sexually myopic,* mountains of data back this up.[†] Natural selection has wired men's brains to be inspired to do things that women value. This is why, in the arts, having a muse is a thing, and why Aristotle Onassis once said, "If women didn't exist, all the money in the world would have no meaning."

He was right. It's true. It wouldn't. Ask any man.

Women are so motivating to men because they are the ones who get to dictate the conditions that need to be met for sex to occur. Women are in this privileged position because their expensive sex cells and minimum nine-month investment in pregnancy have historically made sex costlier for them than for men, which makes them choosier. And in nature, whenever you have one sex that's choosy (usually females), you'll find that the other sex (usually males) is characterized by the great lengths to which it will go to try to get chosen. This means that men's brains have been designed by evolution to most want to do whatever is required of them to get access to women.[‡] If women will have sex only with men who are able to tap dance and play the piano, men will learn to tap dance and play the piano. If women will have sex only with men who can crochet and mix a decent Bloody Mary, the world will become flush with yarn-based handicrafts and breakfast cocktails. The more women require of

....

* Everything shaped by the process of evolution by natural selection is sexually myopic. Sexual myopia is literally its mechanism of action.

[†] And I can promise you that if you ask almost any man who came of age before the internet, he'll tell you that most of his problem-solving skills came from trying to find ways to catch a glimpse of a naked woman.

[‡] Women, just by virtue of being the choosier sex, have the ability to inspire men to do amazing things. And it shouldn't spoil it for us that these things are (ultimately) motivated by sex. Many of the amazing things about people—including our capacity for empathy and goodwill toward others—have been selected for, ultimately, because they helped facilitate reproduction. This doesn't make them any less commendable; it just makes them biologically explainable.

men to be considered a worthy partner, the harder they will work to be chosen.

Now, for most of human history, women's standards for consenting to sex were pfs.* And these standards were high for good reason. Sex always used to imply some risk of pregnancy, so any partner a woman was considering for sex would first have to undergo a careful vetting process to help ensure that if she got accidentally pregnant, she wasn't going to get stuck having a child with a deadbeat. Women had to be just as selective about things like commitment, ambition, and fathering potential in their choice of sex partners as they did in their marriage partners, because there was always the very real possibility that the former could turn into the latter.

But we don't have to worry about that anymore. We have the pill. Women are now in the position of being able to have sex with whomever they want to, whenever they want to, without having to worry about whether the men in question would make crappy husbands or terrible dads. Women, if they want to, can act like *men*, choosing partners with one set of qualities for long-term partners (usually a very long list of qualities, including provisioning ability and parenting potential) and another set of qualities for sex partners (usually a much shorter list, populated primarily with synonyms for the word *sexy*). Because of this, women are now having more sex, with more partners, than ever before in history, including men they wouldn't dream of marrying.†

And, in most ways, this is a great thing. Women no longer need to feel that they have the weight of the world on their shoulders when they're consenting to sex. It's also afforded women the opportunity to try out different types of relationships with different types of men before

....
* pfs = pretty f***ing steep.
† You and I both know that our sexual histories would look very different if pregnancy weren't completely off the table.

settling down and getting married. And these things are good for women *and* men.

These changes in the sexual landscape don't come without consequences, though. The desire for sex and the need to prove themselves worthy of the act has been a powerful source of motivation for men. When sex is no longer difficult to get, men lose what has been the most powerful naturally occurring motivator of achievement out there. So although the pill and the freedom it allows may be responsible for the fact that women are now able to achieve more than ever before in history, it may have the opposite effect on men.

And this isn't just my opinion about what might be going on. Experiments in my lab support this idea. We find that men's achievement motivation and self-control march in lockstep with their beliefs about women's requirements for sex. In these studies, we randomly assigned men to read one of two (fictitious—but they didn't know that) newspaper articles. One was a story about how dating and hooking up are harder than ever for men because women have gotten considerably choosier about their partners than they used to be. The other was a story about how dating and hooking up are easier than ever for men because women have gotten considerably less choosy. Afterward, participants were given tests to measure their self-control and achievement motivation.

Guess which group of men did better and which group of men did worse?

Men who believed that women's standards were high outperformed those who believed that women's standards were low. And it was only men who responded this way. When we gave the same setup to women (randomly assigning them to read an article about dating being harder or easier because of changes in men's levels of choosiness) and measured their self-control and achievement motivation, there were no differences in their self-control or achievement motivation based on the article they'd read. Men's achievement motivation is tied to women's standards for sexual partners in a way that women's is not. This isn't to say that all men take the path of least achievement when easy access to sex is on the table. But some of them do. And the growing achievement gap between men and women may be influenced, in part, by the number of men taking that path now that it's possible.

And make no mistake about it, men are achieving less than they used to. In 1970, the majority of college students were men (58 percent), but by 2000 that number dropped to 44 percent (which is where it is currently). Some of this difference is the result of women doing more, but some of it is due to men doing less (look back at the figure presented at the beginning of the chapter to see for yourself). Women are also staying in college longer and are more likely to graduate and enroll in graduate school than men. Men also have a higher unemployment rate than women do. No matter which way you slice it, men are having their asses kicked by women when it comes to educational achievement and representation in the workplace.

As a college professor, I see this everywhere. The overwhelming majority of my students are women (our undergraduate population is about 60 percent female), and three out of four of my Ph.D. students are women. And most of my graduate students are women not because I'm a woman and female applicants to our Ph.D. program want a mentor with whom they have reproductive organs in common. The graduate students of my *male* colleagues in learning and neuroscience—two areas in psychology that have historically been predominantly male—are *all* women. Every. Single. One. And this isn't by design. There just aren't a lot of men applying, and the men who do apply get outshone by their female contemporaries.

I have seen this play out in recent faculty hires, too. In the past five years, we've hired two tenure-track research professors in my department. In both cases, the majority of applicants were women, and the female candidates were the best of the bunch. This was even true in our most recent hire in the area of neuroscience, which is the research area in psychology that has the greatest male presence. In both cases, we hired women because they were the best and the brightest in the pack.

Nothing motivates and inspires boys to work hard to develop into respectable, financially independent *men* more than an unfailing commitment to the belief that to do anything otherwise would doom them to a life of involuntary celibacy. When men are able to gain access to women without having had to accomplish or commit to anything first, oftentimes this is the path they will follow.* Because sex no longer comes with the risk of pregnancy, qualities like ambition, industriousness, and fidelity, which matter hugely in the context of potential parenthood, don't always enter into the equation when women are choosing sex partners.† As Roy Baumeister and Kathleen Vohs wrote in a paper on sexual economics, "We have found no evidence to contradict the basic principle that men will do whatever is required in order to obtain sex, and perhaps not a great deal more." Perhaps not.

Now, this isn't to imply that it is somehow women's fault that men are lagging behind. It is not (I repeat, *not*) the responsibility of women to inspire the achievements of men. This is so, *so* not our job. We have enough on our plates (especially being as busy as we are outachieving men). At the end of the day, individual men are responsible for their individual choices (including the choice to live in their moms' basements and play video games all day). This is simply to say that everything that happens in an interdependent system—even the sexual empowerment of women—has the potential to have cascading effects on everything else in the system. Sometimes this is for better (more women in the workplace

....

* This idea is the subject of a series of brilliant papers on sexual economics by Roy Baumeister and Kathleen Vohs, as well as an equally brilliant book, *Cheap Sex* by Mark Regnerus.
† Even though the pill is an evolutionarily novel item, it is a product of the human nervous system and not beyond the capability of our mind to reason about. Our psychological mechanisms have been shaped by selection to make decisions about sex based on an unconscious calculation of the costs and benefits of sexual behaviors. In the context of the pill, the "pregnancy risk" cost of sex shrinks considerably, which is evidenced by women's increased willingness to engage in short-term sex.

means fewer are living in poverty). But sometimes—as is the case with men turning into boys—it's for worse.

THE BIFURCATION OF THE MATING MARKET AND CHANGING MARRIAGE PATTERNS

For much of recent history, people dated primarily as a means of determining whether someone might make a suitable marriage partner. Although many cultures around the world continue to practice some form of arranged marriage, for cultures that have embraced the "boy meets girl; boy and girl fall in love; boy and girl get married and buy an oversized house in the suburbs" marriage script, dating used to be an activity done in the service of marriage. And because for most of human history we didn't have super-effective ways to avoid pregnancy, people didn't spend too much time hanging out in the dating market before heading to the altar. People dated until they found someone they thought was a suitable marriage partner, and then—when they did—they'd generally marry that person. This is why back in 1960, before the pill was available to single women, the average age at which women were marrying was twenty, and 72 percent of all adults eighteen and older had already taken the plunge.

Flash forward to right now (as I sit at my computer writing this to you in 2018), and dating is more of a hobby or recreational sport than it is a means of finding a marriage partner. Although people do still use dating as a means of identifying who they do and don't want to marry (and learning what types of qualities will and won't work in a long-term relationship), it's also something that we do for fun. Because why wouldn't we? The pill has made it possible for men and women both to date and try out relationships with different people without the fear of pregnancy. And because it turns out that this is a fun thing to do (especially when you're young and in the flower of your youth and attractiveness), everyone is in less of a hurry to get married than they used to be. Currently, in the United States, people aren't getting married until they're around twenty-seven, and only about half of those who are eighteen or older have made the choice to do so.

With this comes a lot of good things. The ability for women to postpone marriage to get an education has played a huge role in women's growing representation in the workforce. And I would imagine that people make wiser partner choices at thirty than they do at twenty. Most people don't really know who they are yet when they're in their early twenties, making it likely that delaying marriage has improved the quality of matches that some people are able to make for themselves.

But the whole dating-as-recreational-sport thing has also made relationships harder in some ways. In particular, it has bifurcated the mating market into two distinct marketplaces: the dating-sex market, which is made up of people looking for casual dating relationships and hookups; and the marriage market, which is made up of people hoping to find a long-term, committed romantic partner. And the bifurcation of the mating market into these distinct marketplaces has had the effect of making things more difficult for women who are looking for relationships.

Although women generally move from the dating market to the marriage market once their educational goals have been attained, most men are in less of a hurry to do this. This is because men's psychology has been wired in such a way to desire sexual novelty for its own sake to a greater degree than women's. Men also don't have waning fertility to worry about, making them more laissez-faire about the timing of marriage than women are. So for every woman who enters the marriage market, there are many fewer men. And when you combine this with the fact that men are also achieving less than ever before in history, it creates a situation in which women are finding that they have to cut some pretty crappy deals if they want to get married.

Although women used to be able to expect to pair with a partner who was their equal—someone with at least as much education, earning potential, attractiveness, and world experience as they have themselves—this is becoming an increasingly elusive prospect for many contemporary women. An increasing number of women are finding themselves in the position of needing to be okay with being more educated, earning more, and doing more for their relationships than their partners if they want to get married.

Unsurprisingly, this isn't something that most women are okay with. Having more education, a better job, and a safe and effective means of regulating our fertility means that women can now avoid relationships with men that are born out of financial necessity or accidental pregnancy (men we *need*). So, if women don't find a relationship that suits them (with men they *want*), they'll just opt out. As chronicled in Rebecca Traister's (very smartly written) *All the Single Ladies*, this decision to remain single—rather than end up in a marriage with someone they don't feel is an equal match—is a choice that a growing number of women are making. For the first time in U.S. history, single women outnumber married women, and the number of adults under thirty-four who have never been married is up to 46 percent. This is a full 12 percentage points higher than it was only a decade ago. So, the pill has simultaneously made it harder for women to find a long-term relationship with a partner who suits them and also increased the ease of walking away from marriage altogether.

INFERTILITY TWO WAYS

Women's fertility is a cruel and uncaring force. It generally peaks in our early twenties (when most of us still don't have a clue what we're doing and feel like we have no business bringing life into the world) and falls off a cliff right around the time when we finally have our sh** together at thirty-five.* And this can be a tricky thing to have to navigate in a world where the age of first marriage keeps getting pushed back. Although a growing number of women are choosing to have children without being married, the majority of women in the United States still wait until after marriage to have kids. This means pushing back the age at which women are becoming mothers, too. Which they are. For the first time in history, there are now more women in their thirties having babies than there are women in their twenties or younger having babies. This is remarkable, and worth pausing to think about.

Although the trend of delaying motherhood until educational and career goals have been met has been hugely instrumental in women's success in the workplace, this has been less than amazing for women's fertility. When women delay childbearing, it comes at the risk of not being able to conceive once they're ready for children. And there is little doubt that the pill—by changing the age at which women are marrying and having children—has played a key role in the increasing need for the use of reproductive technology in people's quest to become parents. And the need has definitely grown. The infertility-treatment business has quadrupled in the past twenty-five years, becoming a $3.5 billion industry. And as women continue to delay their childbearing to accommodate their education, their careers, and their difficulty in finding an equal partner, this industry will likely continue to grow. As it goes with the pill, so it goes with IVF.

But there might be even more to it than this. The pill may also increase the need for fertility services for other, more provocative reasons. As you

....

* Nothing in this world is more ageist and sexist than women's fertility. Most of us don't have our sh** together by the time our fertility starts to decline. I had my first child at twenty-nine (which is approaching old ladyville as far as the biological clock is concerned), and the timing was terrible: I was still in graduate school at the time and in the throes of dissertation writing, job searching, and living in two cities at once (Austin, where my school and work were, and Dallas, where my husband was). Yet if I would have waited for my sh** to be in order before getting pregnant, I could have been in the unfortunate (for me) situation of not being able to get pregnant.

might recall from chapter 5, the pill can have a not-so-terrific effect on women's ability to suss out genetically compatible men. In particular, the research finds that women tend to be less attuned to subtle scent-based cues of genetic compatibility than naturally cycling women are.*

And the research suggests that one of the subtle scent-based cues that naturally cycling women seem much better attuned to than their pill-taking counterparts is the scent of men who have compatible immune genes. Although there is some debate in the literature about the reliability of these effects, this research generally finds that naturally cycling women tend to prefer the scent of men whose immune genes are dissimilar to their own. And this is a good thing, because choosing a partner with dissimilar immune genes is believed to improve the health of offspring by increasing their immune system's ability to recognize the bad guys in the body.

But pill-taking women don't seem to pick up on these scent-based cues. And when they do, it seems to lead them to choose men with *non*-complementary immune genes. If this is the case, pill-taking women could find it more difficult to have children.

Although this is mere speculation now (so I urge you not to get alarmed), research indicates that couples with similar immune genes may have more difficulty getting and staying pregnant. For example, research on couples with a history of unexplained miscarriages finds higher-than-average levels of genetic similarity in immune genes between the mom and dad from what is observed in couples without this history. This suggests that women who aren't choosing partners with complementary immune genes may have a more difficult time conceiving and maintaining pregnancies than women who are attuned to these cues and choose

....
* More purely anecdotal stuff here, but I have heard from multiple women that going off the pill greatly increased their attunement to men's naturally occurring body odors. Sometimes this worked in their favor (they found themselves increasingly attracted to their partners because they suddenly smelled totally delicious to them). Other times, it led to breakups or divorce.

genetically compatible mates. This pattern is also observed in nonhuman primates. So the pill, in addition to the changes that it has on the timing and stability of marriages, could mean more fertility problems for modern couples. This may be happening because of the later age at which women are having children and because it may decrease women's ability to choose genetically compatible mates.

These changes are just the tip of the iceberg. There are probably countless ways that the pill has changed the world that we haven't begun to fathom yet. For example, when you have a growing number of later- and never-married men and women, this might increase the demand for housing (two single people usually take up two houses; whereas two people in a couple usually take up one), as well as the demand for all the things that go into houses (refrigerators, ovens, and the like). This could have an impact on the types of jobs that are available (are there more refrigerator manufacturers and house builders than there used to be?) and the types of services that are valued. Maybe increasing numbers of later- and never-marrieds means a greater demand for things like cool museum exhibits and meal-delivery services, but a decreased demand for divorce lawyers.

This all might sound trivial and obvious, but it's remarkable, really. When you think about the possibility that a medication can have a side effect such as "cool museum exhibits in a city near you," it really highlights one of the big points of this book (and facts of the universe): There's no such thing as a small change. Especially when the change is in women's hormones.

Everything in your body is interconnected in ways that you'd probably never dreamed possible, and so are all the people in the world. So although it may sound absurd, the pill could be that thing that's initiated a sequence of events that will eventually culminate in our ability to send a person to Mars, bring world peace, and price all but the wealthiest of the world's citizens out of zucchini. And you know what? The effects will probably be larger, vaster, and more surprising than this. Some of these effects will be positive, while some of them will be negative. The good news is that—because the pill has made it possible for a record number of women to go into the sciences—we are now in a better position than ever before to understand its reach. And although we have only barely nicked the surface in terms of understanding the ways that the pill has changed the world, one thing is clear: It will never be the same.

For better and for worse.

CHAPTER 10: WHY DIDN'T I KNOW THIS ALREADY?

The story of gender in the United States and around the rest of the world is a story filled with gaps. There's the wage gap, the math and science gap, the political- and economic-participation gap, and the time-spent-on-household-chores gap. To be a woman, no matter where you are in the world, means to be on the wrong side of social and economic gaps much of the time.*

Among the most pernicious and damaging of the gaps confronting women throughout history has been the gap in knowledge about women's health. Until very recently (like, up until the early 1990s recently), most of what we have been told about our bodies and our brains has come from research conducted almost exclusively on and by men.

Consider, for example, the recommendation that we should take a baby aspirin every day for heart health. This is something that most of us (or at least our parents) have heard from our doctors based on research

----

* Not all, of course. Like the achievement gap, other gaps have women in the advantaged position. For example, the longevity gap (women live longer than men) and the not-driving-like-a-maniac-so-I-pay-less-for-car-insurance gap (women pay less than men) both benefit women.

showing that aspirin therapy decreases the risk of coronary heart disease. Which it does . . . but not in women.

It turns out that this recommendation was made by the American Heart Association on the basis of research that was done in a sample that was 80 percent male. Later research that examined aspirin therapy in men and women concluded that aspirin does *not* decrease the risk of coronary heart disease for women. In fact, for women, it may do more harm than good because it makes it harder for women's bodies to stop bleeding in the case of injury.

And there's nothing unique about coronary heart disease. Many things that you think you know about personhood and health are probably things that you know about *men.*

Although Congress passed a law in 1994 requiring that National Institutes of Health–funded research include women in clinical trials, women are still vastly understudied, compared with men. For example, although women make up roughly half the people diagnosed with HIV in any given year, women make up only 19 percent of the participants in clinical trials of HIV anti-retroviral drugs and only 11 percent of the participants in curative research. And a recent report on the state of affairs with prescription drugs found that eight out of ten prescription drugs (80 percent) were withdrawn from the U.S. market soon after release because of women's health issues, indicating a failure to study their effects comprehensively in women.

!!!! . . . !

Despite the fact that women are more likely to seek medical advice for what ails us, and are more likely to follow the advice that is given, until recently women's health has been all but completely ignored by science. And the result of this is that, more often than not, women are completely in the dark about their health and how their own bodies work. And their doctors don't always know all that much more than their female patients do.

Lacking this information has provided the perfect backdrop for the pill to arrive on the scene and to have few question the wisdom of changing a key part of what makes a woman who she is (via her sex hormones) in the name of contraception, clear skin, or more regular menstrual cycles. Few have thought to consider the breadth of the impact such a change would have on the activities of the non-ovary parts of women's bodies, including their brains. A perfect storm of competitiveness, politics, and motivated ignorance is responsible for the fact that the pill has been embraced by women and their doctors almost without question, and also the reason that we know almost nothing about who it makes us become. Here, we're going to consider all the pieces that have contributed to the lack of information about women and the drug that almost all of us will be on at some point in our lives.

ALL ELSE ISN'T EQUAL

Although there was a time and place in history when women weren't believed to be worthy of study, this is far less true now than it was even twenty-five years ago.* Academics tend to skew more left than right, and the overwhelming majority of scientists I have met in my career—both women and men—are fully supportive of women and women's rights, and proponents of women's inclusion in science. Although others might perceive the gender-equality landscape somewhat differently than I do, all else being equal, I think that most researchers would be just as inclined to study women and things that are important to women as they are to study things that are important to men. This is particularly true given the growing number of women in science.

But all else isn't equal.

....
* But make no mistake about it: Sexism is alive and well in science. There's just less of it, and it's subtler than it used to be. I've had my share of encounters with senior male scientists who felt it necessary to pat me on the head and explain to me how my own research works, despite my greater depth of knowledge in the area.

Although I don't think that it was ever intentional, science works in ways that systematically discourage research on women. Women are harder to study than men, and because science is extremely competitive and demands a rapid pace of publication, when there aren't enough checks and balances in the system to ensure that women get studied, few people will study them. Research on women and the issues that are important to us has become a luxury that many researchers can't, or choose not to, afford.

To give you the backstory on this, you first need to appreciate how hard it is to get and keep a job as a research scientist. Finding such a job—especially the type of job that has you working at a university (which is what most of us want to do)—is extremely difficult. Only about half of Ph.D.s in the sciences end up getting university jobs. And less than a quarter of these jobs are the kinds of research positions that most Ph.D. students train for during their ten-plus years of secondary education. There are too few jobs out there for the people who want them, so finding a job at a research university requires being proficient at cranking out a constant stream of research publications, which is the currency of choice in the academic job market.

If you're one of the lucky few who manages to get an academic research job, the pressure to publish papers only intensifies once you've been hired. At many research universities, if you want to get tenure (which you generally apply for in your sixth year on the job), you need to publish an average of somewhere between two and seven papers per year.* And if you don't get tenure, you get fired.† Although the pressure

....

* This range is based on conversations with my colleagues at various types of research institutions around the world, mostly in psychology, biology, and anthropology.
† There is no middle ground in academia. If you don't get tenure (which protects you from getting fired for doing controversial research that universities don't like), you get fired. And you only get tenure if you have published enough research to show that you're a researcher worth protecting. This is why the mantra in academia is "publish or perish." If you don't publish enough papers prior to tenure, you get fired. And if you don't publish enough after that, your reputation in the field flounders, which makes it more difficult to

to publish a lot of papers, quickly, abates for some once they've been granted tenure, it's not by much. Lacking a steady stream of research publications at any point can make your lab lose funding. This is bad news for any researcher, but especially those whose salaries are partially or totally funded by research grants (which is very often the case in health research). For these researchers, no grant funding means no job (and having to let go all the other research personnel who work in their labs). The pressure to quickly publish a lot of papers is intense, because to do otherwise can land you square in the middle of unemploymentville (population: you).

Behind each of these research papers that scientists must publish are hundreds (and sometimes thousands) of hours of actual research. This includes time spent developing research protocols, running participants through studies, reading others' published studies, analyzing data, and—if everything works out as hoped—writing the results up for publication. And since research has a high failure rate, for every cool discovery that a researcher makes, there are a number of failed experiments in which these same huge investments of time, money, and effort were made on something that ended up being worth doodly-squat. These results don't get published, which means that if a scientist wants to avoid getting fired, she'll need to run sh**loads of studies and work grueling numbers of hours in the lab to have enough things that "work" to write up for publication.

So, the name of the game in research science is running as many studies as you can, and doing so as quickly and cheaply as possible. It also means doing whatever you can to ensure that your results are as straightforward and as lacking in nuance as possible, as the latter two qualities are often used as ammunition in the list of reasons that the paper shouldn't be published in a top research journal. Nuance or subtlety in research results—for example showing that something works this way in women,

....

publish and get funding, which makes your reputation flounder more, and turns you into what academics call deadwood. No one wants to be deadwood.

but that way in men; or showing that something works this way in heterosexuals and that way in homosexuals—is often seen as a sign of weakness. The gatekeepers in science perceive this as a sign that your theory or the application of your results is too limited. The biggest rewards when it comes to publishing and funding go to big, simple-to-understand sledgehammer effects that (supposedly) describe what happens to everyone under all conditions.

And guess who loses in this game fueled by un-nuanced, relatively easy-to-conduct research?

Women.

To start with, men's and women's bodies and brains are different from one another, which means that they very rarely behave exactly the same way in research studies. And in science, it has historically been seen as being more forgivable to have a theory that supposedly applies to everyone but was tested only in one sex than to have a theory that was tested in both sexes but applies only to one. In the former case, the reviewers (the ones who decide whether the paper is worth publishing) are left with a feeling of hopeful optimism that the discovery characterizes all people everywhere. As long as the researchers are appropriately apologetic about the fact that they tested their ideas only or mostly on members of one sex, there is still a good chance that their research results will get published in the top research journals in their area. In the latter case—where the ideas are tested in both sexes, but support for the ideas is only found in one—the reviewers are given evidence that the effects are limited to one sex, which makes the ideas less sexy and less *big*.

So, the decision that a lot of scientists have made throughout history has been to study their phenomenon in one sex or the other. Doing it this way minimizes the risk of failure, and it also makes the research a lot easier, because it means that fewer participants are needed (you need 50 percent fewer participants when you're only studying members of one sex).

And when researchers are choosing which of the two sexes to study (males versus females), it is almost invariably males that get chosen. This is because research using females as participants requires a much bigger investment of time and cash than research using males.

Because females' hormones change cyclically, biomedical research using females as participants has to account for cycle phase. Although this might not sound like that big of a deal, the logistics of exercising this kind of control when collecting data on a large number of participants is nightmarishly tricky and can easily triple the amount of time and money it takes to answer a research question.

To give you a sense of what this sort of thing looks like in terms of day-to-day lab operations, I'll tell you about a study that we did recently looking at the relationship between immune function and decision-making in women and men. Although the immune system seems like a good candidate for being a "gender neutral" body system (like a spleen or lungs or something), its activities are actually quite variable depending on sex and cycle phase. Maintaining a pregnancy is something that has required women's bodies to find an immunological loophole to prevent their immune systems from attacking the implanting embryo, because that embryo has more than a few things in common with what immune systems are programmed to destroy: It has different genes from the mom's (one of the hallmarks of pathogens), its cells divide rapidly (one of the hallmarks of cancer), and it siphons resources from the mom's body (one of the hallmarks of parasites). These types of cues—especially when all occur at the same time—usually send the immune system into search-and-destroy mode. To keep this from happening, women's sex hormones actually modify immunological function based on cycle phase and pregnancy status.

Now, what all this meant for us and our research was that we needed to be very specific about the cycle phase of the women we included in our study. First, we needed to make sure that all the women in the study were at the same phase in their cycle so that we could accurately compare them to one another. Second, we needed to make sure the cycle phase we chose was one that would minimize the unique impact of their sex hormones on their immune-system functioning so that we could compare their results with men's. Using these two criteria as our guides, we chose to include only naturally cycling women who were in the early follicular phase of their cycles.

Our first methodological challenge was that we needed to recruit only non-pill-taking women to participate in the study. This was not an easy feat, given that the overwhelming majority of women ages eighteen to twenty-five located in proximity to a university campus (where most of our participants hailed from) are on the pill. Next, we had to schedule all these women to come into the lab four to seven days after starting their periods. This meant that, for each woman, there were only four days each month in which she was eligible to participate, and these days were not always easy to predict. Women's cycles can have a mind of their own sometimes, and not all women are great at keeping track of where they are with everything on any given day. To make sure that women would be where we needed them to be in their cycles when they came into the lab, we found that the best way to schedule them was to have them contact us as soon as they started their periods, and then we'd schedule them to come in four to seven days later. If the woman's calendar wouldn't allow for a session to be scheduled on one of those four days (which happened frustratingly often—life is busy and usually scheduled more than a week in advance), we had to wait until the next month to try again.

Once we were able to find a day that worked for our female participant's schedule, we then had to scramble to put together an on-the-fly research team to collect her data. This was a lot more complicated than it might sound, because each of our testing sessions required the assistance of eight researchers, many of whom had to schedule around classes and other experiments that they were running. And if we were able to get that to work—if the stars aligned, the light shone down from the heavens, and angels sang—we would be able to collect data from our female participant and all was right with the world. We then repeated this exercise seventy-nine times until the data collection on women was complete.

Compare this to the process we had to follow to run men through the study.

First, we had to call the men and schedule a session based on the days in which we planned to have a research team assembled (a perk of being able to schedule far in advance). Second, our team of already assembled researchers had to run them through the study.

That was it.

If we'd used only men in our study, we would have been able to complete data collection in two to three months and it would have cost roughly $12,000. Including women and exercising control over their cycle phase meant that data collection took nine months and cost nearly $30,000. And if we had wanted to look at how women's immune or behavior relationships differ across the cycle—looking at multiple cycle phases rather than just one—or to see how these women differ from women on the pill, the cost and logistical nightmare could have been doubled, tripled, or quadrupled.* Doing research using women as participants—and doing so in a way that recognizes the pervasive role women's sex hormones play in pretty much everything their bodies do—is incredibly challenging. And because of this, many researchers simply steer clear of studying issues that require women as participants or require thoughtful control of their cycles.

This is why, as recently as 1986, papers were being published with titles like "Normal Human Aging" that included data *only* on men. Although things have gotten better since Congress made it necessary for NIH-funded clinical trials to include (some) women in their research, this issue is far from solved. Females continue to be understudied in all

....

* You can divide the cycle up into as few as two phases (estrogen-dominant half and progesterone-dominant half) and as many as four (menstrual, early follicular, ovulatory, and luteal).

phases of research, including preclinical research on nonhuman animals and cells.*

Take, for example, mice and rats, which are the workhorses of the animal-research world. Female mice and rats, just like human females, have cyclically changing sex hormones. This means that if researchers are to use female rodents in their studies, they need to control for cycle phase in some way. Because most mice haven't yet mastered the art of self-report, researchers have to infer cycle phase using a procedure that involves taking vaginal smears from the females. This method is imperfect, it stresses out the females, and it costs the researchers extra time and money. They need more than twice as many females as males in their experiments to ensure that they have as many similarly phased females in their study as they do males. And—even after jumping through all these hoops—some journal reviewers and editors still perceive this research as being "mechanistically inconclusive," arguing that the females' hormonal states may have influenced the results in a way that may render the findings less interpretable than they would have been if only male mice were used.

For a very long time, the answer to this dilemma has simply been to avoid including female animals in studies at all. It speeds up data collection, and as an added benefit, it makes it easier for their papers to get published. A colleague of mine who uses mice to study Alzheimer's (a disease that afflicts considerably more women than men) was just asked for the first time *ever* by a reviewer why female mice weren't included in one of his studies. And this is 2018. This, despite the fact that he's been

....

* That's right. Before researchers get to the point of studying animals, they will often start by studying cells. For example, imagine that you developed a new drug to treat cancer. You would first test the drug directly on the cancer cells to see whether it kills them. You would also test it on normal cells to make sure that it didn't kill them as well. These studies, too, have overwhelmingly been done on cells derived from males. In cases where the researchers report the sex of the cells that they used in their research (which they don't always do—which is also problematic), male cell lines are used four times more frequently than female-derived cell lines.

in the field for nearly thirty years and has routinely tested only males.* According to his take on the state of the field, at least 90 percent of the research he reads on the mechanisms that contribute to Alzheimer's disease is done exclusively on male mice. And the primary reasons for this are that (a) females make the results too nuanced (since males and females almost never respond the same way to treatments), and (b) the results from females are mechanistically messier (since it is possible that their sex hormones may have influenced their results). These two issues make studies that include females harder to get published, disinclining researchers from studying females at all.

This shouldn't be okay. All (as in, ALL) medical research is first tested using animal models. These models are indispensable in helping researchers study new cancer cures, the progression of Alzheimer's disease, autoimmune issues, mental illness, PTSD, and pretty much anything else that might go right or wrong in the human body (including the brain). These models are the foundational bedrock of biomedical research. And because females are harder to study (and the results taken from females can be more difficult to interpret because of cycle phase), the overwhelming majority of this research has been done using only male animals. *Only males.* I have little doubt that major medical breakthroughs in women's health have been overlooked because females have been routinely excluded from the front lines of animal research. Female rodents have typically been studied second (after finding promising results in males) or not at all. If something didn't work in males, it was just assumed not to work, without it ever being tested in females.

The inclusion of females in research—done in such a way that accounts for cyclically changing hormones—is not something that should be left up to the goodwill of the researchers running the studies. When science is done this way, women and women's issues lose. There is so

....

* Although this is now changing, based on the reviewers asking for data on females. When the system changes, research practices change.

much pressure put on scientists to publish, publish, publish that many (and I have been as guilty of this as anyone else) choose to do what's fast, cheap, and easy rather than what's right. If the top research journals will publish your research that doesn't include female participants, would you go through all the trouble when you ultimately might shoot yourself in the foot? Or would you do the easier thing and collect data on men and then simply include a caveat telling the reader that the results need to be "further explored in women"? I ask these questions not to excuse science (or myself in my own research practices), but to explain how we've gotten to this place. It should come as absolutely no surprise that research has ignored women for so long because the establishment—the journal publishers, the reviewers, and the funding agencies—has rewarded it.

Although things are changing for the better (in the United States, federal agencies will no longer fund clinical trials involving humans that do not include women, and the NIH has new policies to increase the inclusion of female animals and female-derived cells in pre-clinical work), there's still a long way to go. Animal research using only males is still funded by many agencies, is readily publishable, and continues to be the norm in many disciplines. And many biomedical research journals still don't require researchers to use females in their research or to even report the sex of the study participants. Thoughtful, carefully done research on females still takes longer and costs more, and is oftentimes harder to interpret than research conducted only on males. So, when people's careers depend on their publication rate—rather than the need for answers to the questions they're asking—women, and the issues they care about most, lose.

Many research and publishing policies are relics of a time when people didn't appreciate the breadth of the differences between men and women. It used to be thought that the results of research done on males would be easily generalizable to women, because women were thought of as smaller versions of men, differing only in our reproductive organs. But now that we *know* better, we need to *do* better. When it is de rigueur for all scientists to have to include females in their studies (and to do so in a way that takes into account women's changing hormonal status), more females will be studied. And when more females are studied, female-specific health issues—including the birth control pill—will also be studied.

UTERINE POLITICS

Several negative effects have come from science's and medicine's neglect of women. One is, of course, that women know less about their bodies, their health, and their medications than men do. And this is a big part of the equation when it comes to the reasons we know so little about the pill. But it's also harmed us in other ways. In particular, it has led women to develop a wariness toward science that—while justified—ends up further harming our ability to learn about ourselves.

For a long time, being female was treated by science and medicine as being akin to having a serious psychological disorder. Women were routinely prescribed hysterectomies or anxiolytics like Valium to treat the symptoms of hysteria (which is a "syndrome" with symptoms that are suspiciously similar to the symptoms of being a human female who has to deal with stupid sexist bullsh**). Although science and medicine have come a long way since these sorts of practices were commonplace, every woman I know has had the experience of being treated as a less-rational version of a man—sometimes even by our own doctors—simply by virtue of our gender.

The belief that women are irrational and therefore undeserving of the same rights as men is something that has lingered in the public consciousness in a huge way. And women are very aware of this. We have to listen to a lot of people say a lot of dumb sh** about our hormones and about whether we deserve the right to control our own fertility. These types of claims, particularly when combined with science's and medicine's mishandling of women for so long, have made it very difficult for anyone—even female scientists—to have thoughtful conversations about things like women's hormones and fertility regulation. These topics, when addressed by science, are often met with suspicion by anyone who's ever owned a pair of ovaries (or is an ovarian sympathist).

For example, consider what happened to Dr. Kristina Durante, who is a researcher of women's hormones and a poster child for the opportunities afforded by the women's movement. She is a champion for the cause of understanding women's psychology (something that researchers had almost completely ignored until very recently) and is a pioneer in the field of ovulation research. Durante is one of the first psychologists out there to give women's hormones the treatment they deserve in research, and her studies have provided key insights into how women work—including some of the results presented in this book.

Back in 2012, Durante did a series of studies looking at how women's changing hormones over the course of the ovulatory cycle influence political attitudes. To do this, she compared the political preferences of women at high fertility across the cycle (when levels of estrogen are highest and conception is possible) with those of women at non-fertile points in their cycle (when conception is not possible). The results of her research found that single women at high fertility skewed slightly more liberal than single women at low fertility. Partnered women at high fertility, on the other hand, skewed slightly more conservative than partnered women at low fertility. These results—which were interesting for both theoretical and practical reasons—were reported on CNN online, along with an interview with Durante about the various ways that hormones influence behavior.

Although the results of the actual research were pretty noncontroversial when taken in context, reading a news story about research demonstrating that hormones play a role in shaping political *anything* pushed a lot of women's buttons. Within minutes of the story being posted, the internet exploded with comments from angry women demanding that the story be removed and, in some cases, lobbing personal attacks against

Durante. According to the vocal readership of CNN.com, she was the worst thing to happen to feminism since Barbie dolls and internet porn.

Maybe we all should have seen this coming. To people who don't study hormones or the brain for a living (which describes pretty much every person on the planet minus a handful of science nerds), the idea that women's hormones play a role in shaping political attitudes sounds like a big deal. It sounds like the type of thing that could pretty easily turn into a discussion about whether women should be able to keep the right to vote because of their fickle opinions and even fickler hormones. And, of course, *that* pisses women off.

But this isn't a conclusion that could have possibly been drawn from this research. The research showed a really straightforward, harmless "hormones nudge our preferences this way and that way" set of results. And the idea that women's hormones nudge their political attitudes—since hormones nudge *everything*—is unavoidable and not something to get alarmed about. It's just what hormones do. They don't have the ability to recuse themselves from topics like politics because the brain finds their involvement too controversial. There's really nothing special, surprising, or alarming about the fact that hormones influence anything, including political attitudes. Men's almost certainly do, too.* But trying to explain all that—something that took me three chapters to explain at the beginning of this book (and I still feel the need to explain again because it's so at odds with our intuitions about how we work)—isn't the sort of thing that fits neatly in a brief news article.

Research on topics like women's hormones or birth control is a political hot potato. And scientists know this. Very few people out there want to do research on topics that have the potential to yield results that can be misinterpreted as an anti-statement for women's rights. So much misinformation is out there about hormones, the brain, and how we all work

....

* We already know that they're influenced by their upper body strength, which is strongly linked to levels of testosterone.

that having thoughtful conversations about these highly charged topics is a very difficult thing to do, especially in the context of a newspaper or magazine article. This is a big deal to scientists because this is the primary way that our research results get communicated to the public.

This issue has been salient to me as I've been writing this book. I'm so aware of the possibility that this information could be misinterpreted as a message of fear or judgment. Or that I could say something that—taken out of context—could be used by someone with a political agenda to argue that access to the pill should be limited. And because these types of messages are so at odds with my intentions and beliefs, it has more than once given me second thoughts about whether to share this information or keep it to myself. Taking everything I say seriously means thinking critically about the one piece of medical technology that has singlehandedly done more for the advancement of women than any other device in history. But not taking this information seriously means allowing generations of women to make major decisions about their lives with their eyes closed.

A lot of people don't feel comfortable having to make the call on which of these is the lesser of two evils. For me, it wasn't an easy decision to make, either. I don't want the information I have given you to make you feel hopeless, afraid, or judged. And I certainly don't want someone to take anything I say out of context and try to use it to argue in favor of limiting women's access to hormonal contraceptives. But we have to have these conversations about potentially polarizing topics if we want to move women's health forward.

We live in a world in which women's hormones, sexuality, and fertility are politicized in ways that men's are not.* And this politicization makes it difficult to talk about nuanced research that looks critically at the pill. But not talking about these things hurts women. As women, we need to be advocates for having more, not fewer, conversations about how

....
* Which is total sexist bullsh**.

our bodies, brains, and hormones work. Although science needs to take more meaningful steps to earn our trust, we have to be more willing to listen when we hear things that might sound like something we don't want to hear. When women and science work together, we can usher in a new era of understanding of who we are, on the pill and off it. Without this sort of cooperation and trust, women lose.

SELF-DECEPTION AND THE BLAME GAME

Competition and politics have each contributed to our lack of knowledge about our bodies and who we become on the pill. However, these aren't the only forces acting against us. We have, in some ways, been our own worst enemies when it comes to thinking critically about the pill. And this is a situation that has been motivated by our desire to believe that the issue of birth control for women is solved.

Although most of us think that perception is fairly objective, this isn't actually how it works. There's way too much going on at any given moment for our brain to process everything at once, so it has to pick and choose what to pay attention to and what to ignore. And once our brain decides to notice something, it doesn't hold back on the use of creative license in interpreting what it has observed. Some of this picking, choosing, and interpreting goes on in a pretty straightforward way. For instance, if you walk into a room full of people, you are more likely to notice the people than the light fixtures or the grain of wood used on the floors.* Or, if you're on a budget, you're going to interpret the prices on a restaurant menu differently from someone who isn't.

....

* Unless you just bought new light fixtures or wood floors . . . or are in the market for them. Things that are top of mind—even when they're stupid or random—capture our attention, too. I almost rear-ended someone after buying new tires because I couldn't keep my eyes off a set of particularly good-looking Goodyear Ultra Grips that passed by in the lane next to me.

But other times, this picking and choosing is motivated by what the brain wants to believe. When we want something to be true, our brain will actively seek out and believe information that says that it is, regardless of the sketchiness of the source or the absurdity of the argument (truthiness, anyone?). Information that we don't want to be true, on the other hand, is ignored or dismissed, sometimes even in the face of mountains of evidence to the contrary (climate change denial, anyone?). This tendency for our brain to see the world as we want to see it (rather than how it is) is known as the confirmation bias, and the more motivated we are to believe something, the more exaggerated it becomes.

This is worth noting here because one thing that people are very motivated to believe is that birth control, as an issue facing women, is solved. Women, the men they have sex with, and the doctors who serve them all have a dog in the fight when it comes to thinking critically about the birth control pill. And the result is that we're all motivated to avoid thinking too deeply about whether birth control is actually a good idea for women. Women are motivated by their desire for safe, affordable, effective, and easy-to-use contraception. Men are motivated by pregnancy avoidance, too, but also by their desire to keep sex easy to come by and an intense hatred of condoms. Doctors are motivated by their desire to serve their patients and stay in business. None of us want to go back to living in a time when women weren't able to exercise all but complete control over their fertility. So the answer to this, for many of us (I am included in this group) has been to develop a blind spot when it comes to the pill, never questioning the wisdom of changing a woman's hormonal profile in the name of pregnancy prevention.

The pill has done so much to improve women's lives that entertaining the possibility it might do things to women's bodies that we don't want it to is simply not an option for a lot of us. The stakes are too high. Our brains use every trick in the book to make sure we perceive the world in a way that supports the view that the effects of the pill are limited to the ovaries, plus a small handful of other minor systems involved in generating so-called side effects. And this is true despite the fact that adhering to this belief, for some women, requires nothing short of a complete betrayal of their own experiences.

How many of us have trivialized our struggles with the necessarily non-targeted effects of hormonal contraception and told ourselves that *we* were the problem? Or how many of us told ourselves or were told by our doctors that we just need to take an additional pill—like an antidepressant or an anxiolytic—to offset the unpleasant way our birth control makes us feel? And how many of us did these things because we felt like there was no other good option?

The stakes are so high for women when it comes to the issue of being able to safely and effectively regulate fertility that many of us would rather turn the blame inward than question the wisdom of our birth control pills. And this self-blame has been reinforced by the medical establishment—an establishment that until very recently knew almost nothing about women and how our bodies work—in their routine dismissal or trivialization of women's concerns about the way they feel on the pill. Instead of thinking critically about the wisdom of the pill, we are taught to blame ourselves for any pain, discomfort, and sadness that we feel when we're on it.* And we've been willing to do this because we feel like we don't have any other good options. This sense has created a situation in which women never think to question the wisdom of the pill, and instead question the wisdom of their own bodies, thinking there must be something wrong with themselves because of their inability to handle how the pill makes them feel.

We need to stop blaming women for feeling bad on the birth control pill and start thinking critically about *why* they're feeling bad. The pill changes women's profile of sex hormones, which is a key part of who we are. So *of course* it changes how some of us feel. And this isn't a character

....

* Which, given the very small amount of research that has been done on women's bodies and women's health, is not surprising at all.

flaw. It's because the pill does all kinds of things in the body at once. And this is a big deal. We just haven't treated it as one until now.

Treating the pill as the big deal that it is will require a major course adjustment for all of us. We've all been far too cavalier about making changes to women's sex hormones. And if you need evidence of this, consider for a moment the differences in the way we treat birth control pills and anabolic steroids, those drugs favored by athletes who don't mind cheating to win. The primary ingredient in steroids is a synthetic version of the primary male sex hormone, testosterone. These synthetics work by stimulating testosterone receptors and getting cells to run their testosterone program. This causes the body to experience changes like increased muscle mass, skin breakouts, and the magnification of certain male-like behavioral traits (like bar fighting and wall punching).

Now, as you are probably well aware, anabolic steroids are illegal without a prescription. They are classified as a Schedule III controlled substance and—if you're caught with them—you're looking at a $1,000 fine and up to a year in prison. Steroids, because they stimulate hormone receptors, have a wide range of effects on men's bodies and brains. When taken over long periods of time, these changes can be bad for men's health. Given that men might want to take them anyway, steroids are illegal without a prescription, in an attempt to discourage steroid use in the service of public health.

Are you starting to sense the irony?

We worry about men using artificial sex hormones because of all the effects they have on the body. At the same time, women are routinely prescribed female sex hormones and kept on them for years at a time *despite* all the effects that they have on the body. We are willing to turn a blind eye to all the ways the pill can change women because we simply can't entertain going back to living in a world where women don't have control over their fertility.

And we shouldn't have to.

I do not think we should abandon the birth control pill. But we need to take our blinders off. The birth control pill changes women's sex hormones, which means that it changes who women are. And even though there isn't enough research for us to know all the *ways* that this is true, we know enough to know that it *is* true. And we know that the pill is influencing women's lives. It is time to stop being okay with whatever science happens to provide for us and time to ask for what we need. We need good, thoughtful science done on how we work and who we become on the pill. And we need to look for other ways for us to regulate our fertility so that we have more options. Most important, though, we need to stop blaming ourselves if we don't like the way that our birth control makes us feel. We are not the problem. Although thinking critically about the wisdom of the birth control pill may be inconvenient, it is a necessary first step in the direction of asking for something better.

CHAPTER 11: WHAT NOW?
A LETTER TO MY DAUGHTER

Should you be on the birth control pill? And if so, which one?

These are the questions that you have probably been waiting for me to answer. And as much as I'd love to be able to give you those answers, I can't. The right answers to these questions are deeply personal and can be determined only by a person who is an expert on your life. And that person is you.

To help you think through these questions, I am going to have a conversation with you about the pill that I plan to have with my own daughter (who is eleven as I write this) when she is ready to start thinking about her own contraceptive options. I hope that you find it useful as you consider how the pill might fit into your own life. I also hope that you use it as a means of starting meaningful conversations with your doctor, your partner, your friends, and your own daughters.

THE PILL IS A BIG DEAL

The science of who women become on the pill is young, which means that our understanding of the specific ways that the pill changes women will continue to evolve for years to come. However, one thing is certain despite the newness of the science and the tentativeness of the conclusions that can currently be drawn: Changing women's hormones changes women. And this is a big deal.

Although we don't yet know that the pill does, the research suggests that it probably has a hand in women's mate preferences, our sensitivity to smells, our relationship satisfaction, the functioning of our stress response, the activities of multiple neurotransmitter systems, the activities of multiple hormones, our moods, our persistence in difficult tasks, our ability to learn and remember, and our sex drive. And this is probably just the tip of the iceberg. Our sex hormones influence billions of cells throughout our bodies—including a huge number of them in the brain—meaning that the effects of the pill on who women are likely to echo throughout their bodies from head to toe. Although the benefits of pregnancy prevention may be sufficiently great to warrant these costs for some women, they won't be for others. And because your doctor isn't going to talk to you about the kinds of psychological and behavioral trade-offs women make on the pill (save for occasional discussions about the possibility of mood changes), you will need to consider them for yourself.

You are a different person on the birth control pill than you are when you're off the pill. And there's no bigger deal than this.

So, know what you're getting into and make your decision with your eyes wide open. For most women, these trade-offs make sense at some points in their life but not at others. Considering these trade-offs alongside your life goals when making a decision about the pill will help make sure that you can always be the version of yourself you most want to be.

TIMING MATTERS

A second thing to consider when thinking about the pill is your age. This is something that we haven't yet talked about, but is potentially really critical because our hormones—in addition to everything else they do—also play an essential role in how our brains are put together.

Up to this point, our discussion of sex hormones has focused on the types of fleeting effects that hormones have on adult bodies when present, but that go away once the hormone is removed. These are called activational effects, and they work in a now-you-see-it, now-you-don't fashion. Women go on the pill because of the activational effects of the pill's hormones on the HPG axis that keep you non-pregnant. And the reason that you have to take a new pill every day is that these effects go away once the hormones are metabolized and exit the body.

But hormones play a vital role in organizing how the body and brain are put together, too. These are called organizational effects, and they don't go away once the hormone is removed. In this role, the hormones actually influence how the body and brain are *built*, which means that the effects are pretty much permanent.

For example, a major reason that baby boys and girls come into the world with different brains and bodies is that baby boys produce high levels of the male hormone, testosterone, in utero. Exposure to prenatal testosterone directs the cells in their growing bodies to organize themselves in the ways that we recognize as being male. They tell the reproductive organ cells to build penises and testes, and tell the brain cells to organize themselves in a way that predicts earlier gross motor development but later language stills. In the absence of prenatal testosterone, all babies look and act just like little girls, even when they're not.

For example, "boys" with congenital androgen insensitivity syndrome—which is a rare disorder that makes male bodies unable to read testosterone signals—are completely indistinguishable from girls to the naked eye. Those who have this disorder, despite having a Y chromosome (which is the chromosomal calling card for being male), grow up looking like girls, acting like girls, and thinking like girls. Most girls and women who have this disorder (they overwhelmingly identify as female) don't even know that they have a disorder at all until they seek out medical advice for never getting a period or growing pubic hair. At that point, if the doctor takes an ultrasound, she'll discover that the young woman has no uterus or ovaries but two undescended testes instead. Later, a karyotype will reveal that the young woman is chromosomally male, despite being a female by all other measures.

Such is the organizational power of the sex hormones. They influence how our brains and bodies are put together.

The organizational influence of our sex hormones doesn't stop in utero or in childhood. Instead, they continue to play a huge role in calling the shots with all the sex-specific developmental changes that go on during puberty and adolescence. As you probably remember (despite trying desperately to forget), puberty and adolescence are periods of HUGE developmental change. And it's not only the visible parts of our bodies that change during this time. The brain changes, too. A lot. And your sex hormones are the head contractor in this super-important remodeling project. They play a key role in rolling out the brain's new adult blueprint.

Here is why the issue of where you are in development might matter with the pill. Although research hasn't yet confirmed or denied that the pill can influence brain development when taken during adolescence or early adulthood, the brain usually isn't done developing until we're in our early to mid-twenties. There is no magic number in terms of the perfect time to go on the pill and not have it affect your brain development (maybe after twenty-five?), but I would be cautious before age nineteen or twenty. After twenty, although the brain is still putting the final details on the frontal lobes, the benefits of pregnancy prevention may outweigh the benefits of leaving this process unperturbed. This is, of course, if you are sexually active. If you aren't having sex yet, I would say hold off as long as you can. Although there's a decent chance it won't make a difference either way, there isn't enough research for us to know whether this is true or not. It's usually better to be safe than sorry. And if you can be safe, not sorry, at a time when you aren't having sex with anyone anyway, that would seem to be the best way to go.

There are other reasons to consider nineteen or twenty as a minimum age for starting the pill. One has to do with the effects of the pill on depression and suicide risk, both of which are much higher for adolescent women (ages fifteen to nineteen) than women twenty and older. This tells me that the still-developing adolescent brain—in addition to the fact that it's still developing—might not be well equipped to deal with all the psychological changes that seem to be initiated by the pill. We don't yet know enough about why the adolescent brain is so sensitive to these changes, and until we do, caution is in order. This is especially true if you have a personal or family history of depression. Your mental health is too big of a deal to leave to chance. It seems like a good idea to consider alternative means of birth control if you are younger than twenty with a family history of mood disorders. No more women should lose their lives from their birth control pills, and the research suggests that taking them at the age of twenty or older is one way to significantly reduce the likelihood of the incredibly tragic outcome of suicide.

Finally, consider where you are in development, because the feedback loops that regulate your ovulatory cycle (the HPG axis from chapter 4) and your stress response (the HPA axis from chapter 7) are still figuring themselves out early in a woman's reproductive career. The sensitivity of these feedback loops is something that takes time to develop, and they adapt to each woman's unique hormonal profile. If a woman's level of this hormone or that hormone is relatively low, the receptors for this or that hormone will become increasingly sensitive to them. If her levels are relatively high, on the other hand, they learn to be less so. Going on the pill when these feedback loops are still figuring themselves out might change their sensitivity in ways that affect women's ability to regulate stress and reproductive hormones. Although we know almost nothing about whether this actually happens (or what it might mean if it does), this is another reason to be cautious with the pill early in your reproductive career.

I raise these concerns* not to alarm you, but to give you some things

....
* I have been asked whether—in light of these concerns—I think we should limit women's access to the pill if they are younger than twenty. My answer to this is an unmitigated

to consider. I started on the pill when I was eighteen. At the time, I didn't know anything about brains, hormones, development, or feedback loops of any sort. My doctor, if she had any concerns about these things, certainly didn't tell me about them. So I made my decision to go on the pill while my brain was still developing, without knowing what that might mean for me, my brain, or my HPG axis. Although I like to think that I would have made a different decision if I had all the information, I'm not sure that I would have. I was in a relationship and in college and was super-motivated to not be pregnant. So I may well have ignored my own advice. And you might find peace knowing that everything turned out okay for me with the choices I made. My HPG axis is relatively well behaved and my brain does what it should most of the time. Although there's no way of knowing how this would compare with who I would have become had I delayed taking the pill, I'm okay despite my early birth control pill use, and you probably would be, too. You have more information than I did, though, and I urge you to at least consider where you are in your development when choosing whether hormonal contraception is right for you.

Protecting yourself from unwanted pregnancy is huge and necessary. But we have more tools than ever before to allow us to do this with minimal hormonal disruption. And this is something that you should take seriously when your brain is still developing. We have at our disposal fertility-tracking apps (which are also an awesome way to learn about you and your cycle; I really like Flo), copper IUDs, condoms that suck less than condoms used to suck, the morning-after pill, spermicides, cervical caps, and sponges. If you are serious about avoiding pregnancy, you can do it. With the pill or without it. And you are now in a much better position than I was to make that decision knowing all that it entails.

....

"absolutely not." In some cases, being on the pill—even in the midst of brain development—is the best choice for a woman. And nobody is better equipped to make that choice than a woman herself.

INDIVID-YOU-LIZED MEDICINE

One of the things that we've talked about a lot in this book is the idea that pregnancy prevention is a big deal for women. And it's enough of a big deal that, for many women, the benefits of not getting pregnant are sufficiently huge to outweigh the costs. So, until science gives us a better way to avoid pregnancy, there's a good chance that you'll be on the pill at some point in your life.

And although the pill necessarily changes the version of yourself that the brain creates, this doesn't mean that you are going to become a case study in everything that I've described in these pages. Your own experiences on the pill will be intensely personal and unique to you. This means that for some women, portions of this book may read like an autobiography of their lives. For other women, though, it may be difficult to see themselves in the research I have presented and the women's stories I have told.

This is because all studies in science contain an element of what we call "error variance." *Error variance* is just a technical term for the data points that fall outside the typically observed range. These are the outliers, and all studies have them. It's possible that you might be one of them—a data point floating out in space away from the line that describes how the majority of people respond (see picture on the next page).

Data are what you get when you strip away all that is unique and meaningful about each of us and throw us into a giant mixing bowl with others who have been likewise stripped of their individuality and uniqueness. And a lot of times this tells us really useful information about the things we have in common with others who share our condition (pill versus no pill), but not always. The way that your body responds to any given pill will be influenced by a whole bunch of different things that are specific to you and won't always be captured in a research study. Sometimes (and maybe more often than not), you're going to be an outlier. This is why it's so important for you to know yourself and to become an expert on you

A PLOT DEPICTING STUFF THAT HAPPENS ON THE PILL

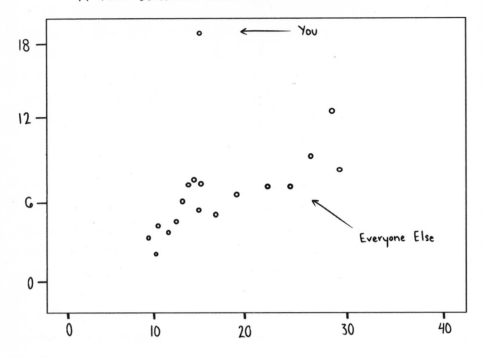

All studies have error variance. This means that when science finds that women experience XYZ on the pill, it might not describe your experiences at all.

and what works for you and what doesn't. And since individualized medicine isn't yet a thing, you'll need to work with the tools you've got to find the best birth control pill for you.

Here's what you need to ask yourself if you go on the pill:

- Do I feel like myself on the pill?

- Have my behaviors changed since going on the pill?

- Has my mood changed since going on the pill?

- Have my relationships (both sexual and nonsexual) changed since going on the pill?

- Has my performance at school or work changed since going on the pill?

- Have my interests changed since going on the pill?

- Have my motivations changed since going on the pill? Am I more or less motivated to do things that I used to like to do before going on it?

. . . AND THIS IS THE BIG ONE . . .

- How do I feel about all this?

Keeping a journal is, as I mentioned earlier, one of the best ways I can think of to chronicle these things for yourself. If possible, start the journal before you go on the pill. Make note of how you feel, what types of things interest you, and how your relationships are doing. This will give you a trail of bread crumbs back to yourself once you're on it. Have you changed? For better or worse? How do you feel about the trade-offs you're making?

As we've talked about, the brain has a pesky tendency to believe that whatever experiences it is currently encoding and creating are reality and that things have always been that way. This is especially true when the changes that go on are subtle or unfold slowly in the body, as they do on the pill. And this is the way it usually happens. For most women, the pill doesn't have a sledgehammer effect on how they feel or the types of things they want to do. It's not noticeable in the way that it's noticeable when you take an antidepressant or have a few drinks. This is why for me, and for many women I have talked to, the influence of the pill was no-ticeable only once we were off it.

Before I went on the pill, I was someone who craved experiences. I was really into music and food and traveling. I also loved exercising and spent a fair amount of time focusing on my appearance. Not in a super girly-girl kind of way (I clarify only because anyone who knows me would say, "Wait . . ."), but I loved shopping and doing creative things with my hair and makeup. I also (without entering TMIville) was quick to notice attractive men, and my interest in sex was . . . not lacking.

After spending some time on the pill, many of these things began to vanish from the radar screen. But there was no sledgehammer. I didn't wake up one day and suddenly not want to do anything that I'd wanted to do before. I probably would have noticed *that*. Instead, what happened was that over time, a lot of these things just fell by the wayside. I stopped exercising and shopping. I developed a casual indifference to men and sex. And unless I was in the car, I favored silence to music (which itself took a backseat to NPR). And as hard as I've tried to remember my internal narrative—what I was telling myself about why these things were happening—I don't remember needing to develop a particularly compelling rationale for any of it. I'm pretty sure that I just assumed that I was getting busier, more mature, and less easily distracted by distractors. What I do know for certain is that—at some point within the first year I was on the pill—I had stopped doing many of the things that I used to love. And my brain, doing what brains do, was able to explain away these changes in ways that were convincing enough to make itself believe.

And once I was off the pill, there wasn't a sledgehammer, either. I didn't suddenly notice that I was doing things differently. It didn't feel noteworthy that I'd started going back to the gym. Or that I'd gotten a Spotify account. Or that I was growing out my hair for the first time in a decade . . . I just felt like I wanted to do these things again, and not like they were the type of thing that required an explanation. It was only after these things had been going on for a few months—and they became noticeable patterns—that I was able to see that I was re-becoming the person I was before.

This is why journaling can be so useful. Keeping a journal will allow you to observe your emotional, motivational, and behavioral patterns so that you can note any changes. Do you have more happy days than sad ones once you are on the pill (or vice versa)? Do you go out with your friends more or less frequently than you used to? What about everything else? Make note of your patterns so that you can learn about who you are* on the pill and off it. This will help you recognize which version of yourself is most compatible with the person you'd like to be.

If you want to be on the pill, you can safely be on it. And you can probably find one that will work for you. There are close to one hundred different formulations out there, so if you aren't happy with the one that you're on, don't be shy about asking your doctor to let you try another one. The table in chapter 4 will help you learn what is in the pills you're taking so that you can make better guesses about what might work and what won't. You might also consider talking to any of your female relatives who have experience with the pill. Given that you share genes with them, there's a decent chance that their experiences will be similar to yours.

Above all, be patient with yourself.

Women are under so much pressure to be perfect at everything without having to ask for help. But we shouldn't be afraid to ask our doctors to help us troubleshoot until we find a pill we like, and we shouldn't be afraid to ask our partners to handle the birth control for a while when we're trying to get it all figured out. Take the time to find a mode of pregnancy protection that makes you feel like the person you want to be. And if you can't find something that you like immediately, don't let this cause you stress. With time, patience, and self-compassion, you will be able to find something that works for you.

....

* Which, I know, sounds a little stupid, but we don't actually have that much insider information on ourselves. Almost everything we know about ourselves is learned. We learn who we are by mentally observing our own thoughts and behaviors and seeing how we compare to others and how they respond to us. This is why the research finds that other people can guess how we're going to respond to things (e.g., a surprise party, a bad test grade) with almost as much accuracy as we can ourselves. And neither guess is that accurate most of the time. Most of us (and I certainly wouldn't consider myself above the fray here) don't have a detailed map of who we are.

TAKING A BREAK

For many women, the decision to be on the pill is one that's made early in life and then not revisited until they're ready to have children or they're thirty-five (which is the age at which doctors usually tell women that it's time to quit because of the increased risk of blood clots). And this means that there are a lot of women who are on the pill for ten or more years without pause or interruption. Although there are cases in which this might make sense (more on this in a minute), I don't know if it is always the best decision for all women.

I say this for a couple of reasons. The first is that we just don't know that much about the effects of long-term birth control pill use on the brain. Given that the pill changes not only what women's sex hormones do but also what everything else in the body does—including the activities of the GABAergic system, the activities of the HPA axis, and the activities of everything else—I think that we should be cautious about being on the pill continually for huge spans of time. This isn't anything to be alarmed about, but I do question the wisdom of doctors routinely allowing their patients to remain on the pill, uninterrupted, for more than a decade without knowing whether this causes any long-term psychological changes.

It's also no small matter that most women choose their careers and long-term romantic partners when they're in their twenties and thirties and have been on the pill for a long time. And the research suggests that it's at least a possibility that the version of you that is on the pill could build a life that does not want to be inhabited by the version of yourself that is not. I have spoken with several women who were on the pill for long spans of time (anywhere between seven and fifteen years) who are convinced that this is the story of their lives. After going off the pill, they found that their careers or husbands (chosen while on the pill) no longer fit. And, as you can imagine, this is a heartbreaking dilemma to be in. To feel like you have betrayed yourself by making choices that fit a version of yourself you no longer recognize. And to feel like you don't fit in the life that you worked so hard to build. You won't be on the pill forever. So, you might want to consider taking periodic breaks from the pill during the times in your life when you're making choices that will affect you for the rest of your life.

It might also be a good idea to take breaks so that you can keep one foot in what it feels like to be the non-pill version of yourself. One woman I spoke to while in the process of writing this book was on the pill continuously for fifteen years. Now that she is over thirty-five and has to go off it, she feels so uncomfortable in her own skin that she's started antidepressants. This won't necessarily be the case for everyone (and it could be the case that she was depressed all along and that the pill was helping her manage her depression), but this is something worth thinking about. If you get used to feeling like the version of yourself on the pill, it could decrease your ability to feel at home in your own body. And, although there's not yet any science out there supporting this idea or refuting it, it's at least worth considering as you plan your birth control strategy over time.

If you don't need the pill for a while, consider taking a break. There were multiple spans of time during my years on the pill when I wasn't having sex with anyone. I just stayed on it out of habit since I figured it wasn't hurting me at all. Looking back, I don't know if this was the best idea. I don't think that the pill has changed me in any irreversible way, but there's really no way of knowing whether that's true or not. There's just not enough research out there on what long-term pill use means for women's brains. Take a brain check and see where you're at and how you feel once you've been off it for a couple of months. If you prefer the way you feel off the pill, this might be an opportunity for you to consider a new means of pregnancy prevention or to find a new pill. And if you find that being off it makes you miserable, this tells you something, too. There's a lot of evidence supporting the idea that the pill can be helpful for women with certain types of hormonally triggered mood disorders (like PMDD). So if this describes you—and taking breaks from the pill makes you feel hopeless and sad—know that you can safely stay on it. Whatever you choose, you are going to be safe and okay. I hope that you're able to take heart in knowing that. Whatever feels best for you and your goals is the right choice, whether this means being on or off the pill.

If you do go off it, it probably won't change your life overnight. And for some women, it won't feel like it changes anything at all. Although the pill changes what all women's brains do, for some women, these changes aren't all that noticeable. For others, the changes are noticeable but not bothersome. Each woman's experiences are unique. If you feel the same on it as you do off it, be thankful that your body has been put together in a way that makes you less vulnerable to the whims of your hormonal environment. If you feel different when you're on the pill compared with how you feel when you're off it, you can now know with certainty that there are reasons you feel this way. A growing body of science is backing up what women have been telling their doctors for years. The pill changes us. For better and for worse.

SOME FINAL THOUGHTS

As I will say to my daughter, sweet June, a few years from now when it's time for this conversation, you are in a better position than ever to make yourself into the version of yourself that you most want to be. It may be that this is a version of yourself on the pill. It may be that this is the version of yourself off it. Regardless of what you choose, you can now make the decision with your eyes wide open.

If you choose to be on the pill, this is a decision you can safely make. And it's amazing to be alive during a time when we have this as an option. Because of the pill, women are now able to do things with our lives that our great-grandmothers wouldn't have dreamed possible. And as we continue to know more about how the pill changes women, you will be able to make this choice knowing full well the trade-offs that your choice entails.

But the issue of birth control for women is not solved. It's time for all of us to join together to ask science for some new choices and for more information about what happens to us with the choices we have. We shouldn't have to change who we are to protect ourselves from pregnancy, and we should know enough about how our own bodies work to recognize that this is exactly what we're doing when we go on the birth control pill.

This will require nothing less than a complete paradigm shift in how we view our brains, our hormones, and ourselves. And for some of us, it might require rethinking the pill. The first step on this path is for all of us to start having open, honest conversations with our mothers, daughters, sisters, girlfriends, doctors, and partners about who we are and who we become on the pill. Although the science is still new and these conversations are just getting started, let today be the day that you begin one of your own.

This might be TMI, but . . .

Acknowledgments

I owe a huge thank-you to my amazing family. My husband and my two kind, funny children have been so patient with me during this process. Thank you for helping me carve out enough time to get this thing written and for all your emotional support during the process. Thank you to my incredible parents for always believing in me (even during the times in my life when I was a risky gamble) and for lending me your house when I needed a quiet place to work on Sunday afternoons. Riley Turner is the amazingly talented artist who created the figures used to illustrate all the research results I presented in this book (and she was a high school student at the time she made them!). Thank you for lending me your talents, Riley. And thank you to the crowdsourced wisdom of Colleyville moms for helping me find her.

I couldn't have done any of this without the institutional support from TCU. Thank you especially hugely to Phil Hartman and Mauricio Papini for always being supportive of me and my various research-related endeavors. It is a huge pleasure to work in such a collegial and supportive environment. I would also like to thank all my colleagues and students. I learn so much from all of you, and you make my "work" fun. Big things happen at small schools.

I have been hugely fortunate to have my research—including some of the research presented in this work—funded by the National Science Foundation (BCS-1322573 and BCS-1551201). Basic research is the bedrock of major discoveries, and the NSF does an amazing job making new discoveries possible with very few resources. Thank you to the NSF for investing some of these resources in my lab's work and making the science I do possible.

I want to thank the following people for offering me feedback and assistance with various stages of this book: Athena Aktipis, Ann Beardsley, Hannah Bradshaw, David Buss, Kristina Durante, Jeffrey Gassen, Lori Hooper, Doug Kenrick, Summer Mengelkoch, Randi Proffitt Leyva, James Roney, and Misty Womack. I also need to give a huge shout-out to Tori Short, who has been nothing short of an angel sent from the heavens when it came to researching, fact-checking, and reference-generating (you're the best!). I am also hugely grateful to Gary Boehm, who is the only reason that I know anything at all about neuroscience and who has helped me at every stage of writing this book (including the parts where I just needed someone to tell me to work on something else instead). Thank you to everyone who has done the critical research that I talk about in this book. You are doing a huge service to women with your work, and I hope you'll forgive me if I've messed up any of the details or oversimplified things beyond what you consider to be in good taste. I look forward to continuing to learn from all the things you do. Thank you to all the amazing women who have shared with me their "This might be TMI, but . . ." birth control pill stories. I know that so many women will identify with your experiences.

Many friends, colleagues, and students have helped me in other ways—whether it has been in terms of research collaboration, teaching me new things, inspiration, or helping to fetch papers or other things that needed tending to in the process of writing this book (including, sometimes, nothing more than a well-timed glass of wine). In no particular order that's not alphabetical, I'd like to thank Fred Anapol, Ann Beardsley, Jim Beardsley, Max Butterfield, Jaime Cloud, Adam Cohen, Sean Conlan, Amy Coren, Danielle DelPriore, Josh Duntley, Kristina Durante, Judy Easton, Bruce Ellis, J. Patrick Gray, Greg Eickholt, James Eickholt, June Eickholt, Diana Fleischman, Oscar Galindo, Carrie Goetz, Kelly Goldsmith, Vladas Griskevicius, Chris Henry, Jim Hill, Joe Horn, Russell Jackson, Joonghwan Jeon, Tia Johnson, Maggie Kleiser, John Koechel, Barry Kuhle, Angie Lawrence, Norm Li, Charlie Lord, Brett Major, Nicole Matthews, Ellie Miller, Chiraag Mittal, Steve Neuberg, C. Sylas Nicolas, Carin Perilloux, Julia Peterman, Marjorie Prokosch, Kern Reeve, Christopher Rodeheffer, Alix Rudd, Eric Russell, Mike Ryan, Sarah Schad, Emily Stone, Morgan Tatsumi, Jennifer Wallace, Jordon White, Dean Williams, Erin Woolsey, the amazing women of Saddlebrook, and my high school English teacher, Tim Mocarski, for telling me that I need to "use my funny" when I write.

Finally, I owe a huge thank-you to my incredible agent, Lindsay Edgecombe, and my equally incredible editor, Caroline Sutton. I can't thank you all enough for your support and for sharing my vision for this book. Thank you, also, to all the folks at Avery and LGR who have worked behind the scenes to make all this possible. I am at a loss for words about how grateful I am to all of you for this incredible opportunity.

Thank you, thank you, thank you.

Notes

CHAPTER 1: WHAT IS A WOMAN?

15. **If even *one* of your ancestors:** Buss, D. M. (1994). *The evolution of desire*. New York: Basic Books.

17. **complications from pregnancy and childbirth continue to kill:** Alkema, L., Chou, D., Hogan, D., Zhang, S., Moller, A., Gemmill, A., . . . Say, L. (2016). Global, regional, and national levels and trends in maternal mortality between 1990 and 2015, with scenario-based projections to 2030: A systematic analysis by the UN Maternal Mortality Estimation Inter-Agency Group. *The Lancet, 387*(10017), 462-474. doi:10.1016/s0140-6736(15)00838-7.

17. **requiring women to secure an additional six hundred or so calories:** Subcommittee on Nutrition During Lactation, Committee on Nutritional Status During Pregnancy and Lactation, Food and Nutrition Board, Institute of Medicine, & National Academy of Sciences. (1991). Meeting maternal nutrient needs during lactation. *Nutrition during lactation* (pp. 213–235). Washington, D.C.: National Academies Press; Khan, S. L. (2004). Maternal nutrition during breastfeeding. *New Beginnings, 21*(2), 44–52.

19. **more likely to die from every recordable cause:** Hill, K., & Hurtado, A. M. (1996). *Aché life history: The ecology and demography of a foraging people*. New York: Aldine de Gruyter.

19. **in one of the most-talked-about experiments of its time:** Clark, R. D., & Hatfield, E. (1989). Gender differences in receptivity to sexual offers. *Journal of Psychology and Human Sexuality, 2*, 39–55.

22. **men who report feeling highly certain about being the biological fathers:** Anderson, K. G. (2006). How well does paternity confidence match actual paternity? *Current Anthropology, 47*(3), 513–520. doi:10.1086/504167.

22. **facial resemblance of children to each of their parents:** Alvergne, A., Faurie, C., & Raymond, M. (2010). Are parents' perceptions of offspring facial resemblance consistent with actual resemblance? Effects on parental investment. *Evolution and Human Behavior, 31*(1), 7–15.

23. **much of the research in my own lab:** Hill, S. E., Prokosch, M. L., & DelPriore, D. J. (2015). The impact of disease threat on women's desire for novel partners: Is variety the best medicine? *Journal of Personality and Social Psychology, 109*(2), 244–261;

DelPriore, D. J. & Hill, S. E. (2013). The effects of paternal disengagement on women's sexual decision-making: An experimental approach. *Journal of Personality and Social Psychology, 105*, 234–246.

26. **Nothing in biology makes sense except in the light of evolution:** Theodosius Dobzhansky (1973). *The American Biology Teacher, 35* (3), 25–129. www.jstor.org/stable/4444260.

28. **Menstrual symptoms cause more than one hundred million lost work hours:** Silberg, J. L., Martin, N. G., & Heath, A. C. (1987). Genetic and environmental factors in primary dysmenorrhea and its relationship to anxiety, depression, and neuroticism. *Behavior Genetics, 17*(4), 363–383. doi:10.1007/bf01068137.

31. **Approximately 32 percent of fertilized eggs:** Evers, J. L. (2002). Female subfertility. *The Lancet, 93*(9327), 151–159. doi:10.1016/s0140-6736(02)65865-9.

32. **additional 24 percent of fertilized eggs:** Gilbert, S. F. (2000). *Developmental biology*. Sunderland, MA: Sinauer Associates.

32. **half the fertilized eggs not making the cut:** Gold, R. B. (2005). The implications of defining when a woman is pregnant. *Guttmacher Report on Public Policy, 8*(2), 7–10; Cramer, D. W., & Wise, L. A. (2000). The epidemiology of recurrent pregnancy loss. *Seminars in Reproductive Medicine, 18*(4), 331–340; Wong, C. C., Loewke, K. E., Bossert, N. L., Behr, B., Jonge, C. J., Baer, T. M., & Pera, R. A. (2010). Non-invasive imaging of human embryos before embryonic genome activation predicts development to the blastocyst stage. *Nature Biotechnology, 28*(10), 1115–1121. doi:10.1038/nbt.1686; Schieve, L. A., Tatham, L., Peterson, H. B., Toner, J., & Jeng, G. (2003). Spontaneous abortion among pregnancies conceived using assisted reproductive technology in the United States. *Obstetrics and Gynecology, 101*(5, part 1), 959–967. doi: 10.1016/S0029-7844(03)00121-2.

CHAPTER 2: YOU ARE YOUR HORMONES

39. **The fish in question is the plainfin midshipman:** Lee, J. S., & Bass, A. H. (2006). Dimorphic male midshipman fish: Reduced sexual selection or sexual selection for reduced characters? *Behavioral Ecology, 17*(4), 670–675.

40. **because of the activities of their hormones:** Schlinger, B. A., Greco, C., & Bass, A. H. (1999). Aromatase activity in hindbrain vocal control region of a teleost fish: Divergence among males with alternative reproductive tactics. *Proceedings of the Royal Society of London B: Biological Sciences, 266*(1415), 131–136.

42. **women tend to feel hungrier, sleepier, and more relaxed:** Lovick, T. (2012). Estrous cycle and stress: Influence of progesterone on the female brain. *Brazilian Journal of Medical and Biological Research, 45*(4), 314–320. doi:10.1590/s0100-879x2012 007500044; Silva, A. F., Sousa, D. S., Medeiros, A. M., Macêdo, P. T., Leão, A. H.,

Ribeiro, A. M., . . . Silva, R. H. (2016). Sex and estrous cycle influence diazepam effects on anxiety and memory: Possible role of progesterone. *Progress in Neuro-Psychopharmacology and Biological Psychiatry, 70*, 68–76. doi:10.1016/j.pnpbp.2016.05.003; Li, S. H., & Graham, B. M. (2017). Why are women so vulnerable to anxiety, trauma-related and stress-related disorders? The potential role of sex hormones. *The Lancet Psychiatry, 4*(1), 73–82. doi:10.1016/s2215-0366(16)30358-3.

43. **"And it's terrifying."** This interview was printed with permission from *This American Life*. It was taken from episode 220, titled "Testosterone." Retrieved from https://www.thisamericanlife.org/220/testosterone

45. **testosterone changes in response to age:** Klinesmith, J., Kasser, T., & McAndrew, F. T. (2006). Guns, testosterone, and aggression. *Psychological Science, 17*(7), 568–571. doi:10.1111/j.1467-9280.2006.01745.x.

46. **highly dependent offspring have required this:** Raeburn, P. (2015). *Do fathers matter? What science is telling us about the parent we've overlooked.* New York: Scientific American/Farrar, Straus and Giroux; Alonso, D. L., & Ortiz-Rodríguez, I. M. (2017). Offspring mortality was a determinant factor in the evolution of paternal investment in humans: An evolutionary game approach. *Journal of Theoretical Biology, 419*, 44–51. doi:10.1016/j.jtbi.2017.01.043.

46. **attuned to cues of sexual interest:** Isidori, A. M., Giannetta, E., Gianfrilli, D., Greco, E. A., Bonifacio, V., Aversa, A., . . . Lenzi, A. (2005). Effects of testosterone on sexual function in men: Results of a meta-analysis. *Clinical Endocrinology, 63*, 381–394; Peters, M., Simmons, L. W., & Rhodes, G. (2008). Testosterone is associated with mating success but not attractiveness or masculinity in human males. *Animal Behaviour, 76*(2), 297–303. doi:10.1016/j.anbehav.2008.02.008.

46. **turn down the volume on testosterone production:** Burnham, T. C., Chapman, J. F., Gray, P. B., McIntyre, M. H., Lipson, S. F., & Ellison, P. T. (2003). Men in committed, romantic relationships have lower testosterone. *Hormones and Behavior, 44*(2), 119–122. doi:10.1016/s0018-506x(03)00125-9.

47. **fathers showed more than double the decline in testosterone:** Gettler, L. T., McDade, T. W., Feranil, A. B., & Kuzawa, C. W. (2011). Longitudinal evidence that fatherhood decreases testosterone in human males. *PNAS, 108*(39), 16194–16199. doi:10.1073/pnas.1105403108.

CHAPTER 3: YOU IN THE TIME OF FERTILITY

53. **marked by an increase in sexual desire:** Adams, D. B., Gold, A. R., & Burt, A. D. (1978). Rise in female-initiated sexual activity at ovulation and its suppression by oral contraceptives. *New England Journal of Medicine, 299*(21), 1145–1150. doi:10.1056/nejm197811232992101; Bullivant, S. B., Sellergren, S. A., Stern, K., Spencer, N. A., Jacob, S., Mennella, J. A., & McClintock, M. K. (2004). Women's sexual experience

during the menstrual cycle: Identification of the sexual phase by noninvasive measurement of luteinizing hormone. *Journal of Sex Research, 41*(1), 82–93. doi:10.1080/00224490409552216; Dennerstein, L., Gotts, G., Brown, J. B., Morse, C. A., Farley, T. M., & Pinol, A. (1994). The relationship between the menstrual cycle and female sexual interest in women with PMS complaints and volunteers. *Psychoneuroendocrinology, 19*(3), 293–304. doi:10.1016/0306-4530(94)90067-1; Diamond, L. M., & Wallen, K. (2010). Sexual minority women's sexual motivation around the time of ovulation. *Archives of Sexual Behavior, 40*(2), 237–246. doi:10.1007/s10508-010-9631-2; Matteo, S., & Rissman, E. F. (1984). Increased sexual activity during the midcycle portion of the human menstrual cycle. *Hormones and Behavior, 18*(3), 249–255. doi:10.1016/0018-506x(84)90014-x; Pillsworth, E. G., Haselton, M. G., & Buss, D. M. (2004). Ovulatory shifts in female sexual desire. *Journal of Sex Research, 41*(1), 55–65. doi:10.1080/00224490409552213; Stanislaw, H., & Rice, F. J. (1988). Correlation between sexual desire and menstrual cycle characteristics. *Archives of Sexual Behavior, 17*(6), 499–508. doi:10.1007/bf01542338; Wallen, K. (2001). Sex and context: Hormones and primate sexual motivation. *Hormones and Behavior, 40*(2), 339–357. doi:10.1006/hbeh.2001.1696; Wilcox, A., Baird, D. D., Dunson, D. B., McConnaughey, R. D., Kenser, J. S., & Weinberg, C. R. (2004). On the frequency of intercourse around ovulation: Evidence for biological influences. *Human Reproduction, 19*(7), 1539–1543. doi:10.1093/humrep/deh305; Regan, P. C. (1996). Rhythms of desire: The association between menstrual cycle phases and female sexual desire. *Canadian Journal of Human Sexuality, 5*, 145–156; Schreiner-Engel, P., Schiavi, R. C., Smith, H., & White, D. (1981). Sexual arousability and the menstrual cycle. *Psychosomatic Medicine, 43*(3), 199–214.

53. **driven by increasing levels of estrogen:** Roney, J. R., & Simmons, Z. L. (2013). Hormonal predictors of sexual motivation in natural menstrual cycles. *Hormones and Behavior, 63*(4), 636–645. doi:10.1016/j.yhbeh.2013.02.013.

53. **progesterone had the opposite effect:** Roney, J. R., & Simmons, Z. L. (2016). Within-cycle fluctuations in progesterone negatively predict changes in both in-pair and extra-pair desire among partnered women. *Hormones and Behavior, 81*, 45–52. doi:10.1016/j.yhbeh.2016.03.008.

53. **also found in lesbian women:** Diamond, L. M., & Wallen, K. (2010). Sexual minority women's sexual motivation around the time of ovulation. *Archives of Sexual Behavior, 40*(2), 237–246. doi:10.1007/s10508-010-9631-2.

53. **found in nonhuman primates:** Roney, J. R., & Gettler, L. T. (2015). The role of testosterone in human romantic relationships. *Current Opinion in Psychology, 1*, 81–86. doi:10.1016/j.copsyc.2014.11.003; Wallen, K., Winston, L. A., Gaventa, S., Davis-DaSilva, M., & Collins, D. C. (1984). Periovulatory changes in female sexual behavior and patterns of ovarian steroid secretion in group-living rhesus monkeys. *Hormones and Behavior, 18*(4), 431–450. doi:10.1016/0018-506x(84)90028-x; Kendrick, K. M., & Dixson, A. F. (1985). Luteinizing hormone releasing hormone

enhances proceptivity in a primate. *Neuroendocrinology, 41*(6), 449–453. doi:10.1159/000124218; Zehr, J. L., Maestripieri, D., & Wallen, K. (1998). Estradiol increases female sexual initiation independent of male responsiveness in rhesus monkeys. *Hormones and Behavior, 33*(2), 95–103. doi:10.1006/hbeh.1998.1440.

54. **study of sixty-eight partnered women:** Wilcox, A., Baird, D. D., Dunson, D. B., McConnaughey, R. D., Kenser, J. S., & Weinberg, C. R. (2004). On the frequency of intercourse around ovulation: Evidence for biological influences. *Human Reproduction, 19*(7), 1539–1543. doi:10.1093/humrep/deh305.

54. **effects emerge from changes in women's sexual motivations:** Regan, P. C. (1996). Rhythms of desire: The association between menstrual cycle phases and female sexual desire. *Canadian Journal of Human Sexuality, 5*, 145–156; Roney, J. R., & Gettler, L. T. (2015). The role of testosterone in human romantic relationships. *Current Opinion in Psychology, 1*, 81–86. doi:10.1016/j.copsyc.2014.11.003; Wallen, K. (2001). Sex and context: Hormones and primate sexual motivation. *Hormones and Behavior, 40*(2), 339–357. doi:10.1006/hbeh.2001.1696; Bullivant, S. B., Sellergren, S. A., Stern, K., Spencer, N. A., Jacob, S., Mennella, J. A., & McClintock, M. K. (2004). Women's sexual experience during the menstrual cycle: Identification of the sexual phase by noninvasive measurement of luteinizing hormone. *Journal of Sex Research, 41*(1), 82–93. doi:10.1080/00224490409552216; Van Goozen, S. H., Wiegant, V. M., Endert, E., Helmond, F. A., & Van de Poll, N. E. (1997). Psychoendocrinological assessment of the menstrual cycle: The relationship between hormones, sexuality, and mood. *Archives of Sexual Behavior, 26*(4), 359–382. doi:10.1023/A:1024587217927.

55. **research finds that women feel sexier:** Schwarz, S., & Hassebrauck, M. (2008). Self-perceived and observed variations in women's attractiveness throughout the menstrual cycle—a diary study. *Evolution and Human Behavior, 29*(4), 282–288. doi:10.1016/j.evolhumbehav.2008.02.003; Röder, S., Brewer, G., & Fink, B. (2009). Menstrual cycle shifts in women's self-perception and motivation: A daily report method. *Personality and Individual Differences, 47*(6), 616–619. doi:10.1016/j.paid.2009.05.019

55. **are more open to new experiences:** Durante, K. M., & Arsena, A. R. (2015). Playing the field: The effect of fertility on women's desire for variety. *Journal of Consumer Research, 41*(6), 1372–1391. doi:10.1086/679652.

55. **put more effort into their appearance:** Durante, K. M., Griskevicius, V., Hill, S. E., Perilloux, C., & Li, N. P. (2011). Ovulation, female competition, and product choice: Hormonal influences on consumer behavior. *Journal of Consumer Research, 37*(6), 921–934. doi:10.1086/656575; Mortezaie, M., Haselton, M. G., Bleske-Rechek, A., Pillsworth, E. G., & Frederick, D. A. (2007). Ovulatory shifts in ornamentation: Near ovulation, women dress to impress. *Hormones and Behavior, 51*(1), 40–45. doi:10.1037/e511092014-268; Röder, S., Brewer, G., & Fink, B. (2009). Menstrual cycle shifts in women's self-perception and motivation: A daily report

method. *Personality and Individual Differences, 47*(6), 616–619. doi:10.1016/j
.paid.2009.05.019.

55. **Women at high fertility also wear more makeup:** Guéguen, N. (2012). Makeup
and menstrual cycle: Near ovulation, women use more cosmetics. *Psychological Record,
62*(3), 541–548. doi:10.1007/bf03395819.

55. **wear sexier clothes:** Durante, K. M., Li, N. P., & Haselton, M. G. (2008).
Changes in women's choice of dress across the ovulatory cycle: Naturalistic and
laboratory task-based evidence. *Personality and Social Psychology Bulletin, 34*(11),
1451–1460. doi:10.1177/0146167208323103.

55. **buy sexier clothes:** Durante, K. M., Griskevicius, V., Hill, S. E., Perilloux, C., &
Li, N. P. (2011). Ovulation, female competition, and product choice: Hormonal
influences on consumer behavior. *Journal of Consumer Research, 37*(6), 921–934.
doi:10.1086/656575.

55. **wear more red:** Beall, A. T., & Tracy, J. L. (2013). Women are more likely to wear
red or pink at peak fertility. *Psychological Science, 24*(9), 1837–1841. doi:10.1177/
0956797613476045; Eisenbruch, A. B., Simmons, Z. L., & Roney, J. R. (2015). Lady
in red. *Psychological Science, 26*(8), 1332–1338. doi:10.1177/0956797615586403.

55. **appear particularly attractive and desirable to men:** Elliot, A. J., & Niesta, D.
(2008). Romantic red: Red enhances men's attraction to women. *Journal of Personality
and Social Psychology, 95*(5), 1150–1164. doi:10.1037/0022-3514.95.5.1150; Elliot, A. J.,
Tracy, J. L., Pazda, A. D., & Beall, A. T. (2013). Red enhances women's
attractiveness to men: First evidence suggesting universality. *Journal of Experimental
Social Psychology, 49*(1), 165–168. doi:10.1016/j.jesp.2012.07.017; Kayser, D. N., Elliot,
A. J., & Feltman, R. (2010). Red and romantic behavior in men viewing women.
European Journal of Social Psychology, 40(6), 901–908. doi:10.1002/ejsp.757; Pazda, A. D.,
Elliot, A. J., & Greitemeyer, T. (2012). Sexy red: Perceived sexual receptivity mediates
the red-attraction relation in men viewing woman. *Journal of Experimental Social
Psychology, 48*(3), 787–790. doi:10.1016/j.jesp.2011.12.009; Schwarz S., & Singer, M.
(2013). Romantic red revisited: Red enhances men's attraction to young, but not
menopausal women. *Journal of Experimental Social Psychology, 49*(1), 161–164.
doi:10.1016/j.jesp.2012.08.004.

58. **ovulatory-shift hypothesis:** Gangestad, S. W., & Thornhill, R. (1998).
Menstrual cycle variation in women's preferences for the scent of symmetrical men.
Proceedings of the Royal Society B: Biological Sciences, 265(1399), 927–933. doi:10.1098/
rspb.1998.0380; Gangestad, S. W., Thornhill, R., & Garver-Apgar, C. E. (2005).
Adaptations to ovulation. *Current Directions in Psychological Science, 14*(6), 312–316.
doi:10.1111/j.0963-7214.2005.00388.x.

58. **prefer the scent of men who are socially dominant and have symmetrical faces:**
Gangestad, S. W., & Thornhill, R. (1998). Menstrual cycle variation in women's

preferences for the scent of symmetrical men. *Proceedings of the Royal Society B: Biological Sciences, 265*(1399), 927–933. doi:10.1098/rspb.1998.0380; Havlicek, J., Roberts, S. C., & Flegr, J. (2005). Women's preference for dominant male odour: Effects of menstrual cycle and relationship status. *Biology Letters, 1*(3), 256–259. doi:10.1098/rsbl.2005.0332; Scheib, J. E., Gangestad, S. W., & Thornhill, R. (1999). Facial attractiveness, symmetry and cues of good genes. *Proceedings of the Royal Society B: Biological Sciences, 266*(1431), 1913–1917. doi:10.1098/rspb.1999.0866.

58. **prefer more masculine male faces:** Johnston, V. S., Hagel, R., Franklin, M., Fink, B., & Grammer, K. (2001). Male facial attractiveness: Evidence for hormone-mediated adaptive design. *Evolution and Human Behavior, 22*(4), 251–267. doi:10.1016/s1090-5138(01)00066-6; Penton-Voak, I. S., & Perrett, D. I. (2000). Female preference for male faces changes cyclically. *Evolution and Human Behavior, 21*(1), 39–48. doi:10.1016/s1090-5138(99)00033-1; Penton-Voak, I. S., Perrerr, D. I., Castles, D. L., Kobayashi, T., Burt, D. M., Murray, L. K., & Minamisawa, R. (1999). Menstrual cycle alters face preference. *Nature, 399*, 741–742. doi:10.1038/21557; Roney, J. R., & Simmons, Z. L. (2008). Women's estradiol predicts preference for facial cues of men's testosterone. *Hormones and Behavior, 53*(1), 14–19. doi:10.1016/j.yhbeh.2007.09.008; Roney, J. R., & Simmons, Z. L. (2008). Women's estradiol predicts preference for facial cues of men's testosterone. *Hormones and Behavior, 53*(1), 14–19. doi:10.1016/j.yhbeh.2007.09.008.

58. **deeper, more masculine male voices:** Feinberg, D. R., Debruine, L. M., Jones, B. C., & Little, A. C. (2008). Correlated preferences for men's facial and vocal masculinity. *Evolution and Human Behavior, 29*(4), 233–241. doi:10.1016/j.evolhumbehav.2007.12.008; Puts, D. A. (2006). Cyclic variation in women's preferences for masculine traits. *Human Nature, 17*(1), 114–127. doi:10.1007/s12110-006-1023-x.

59. **find socially dominant, confident men more attractive:** Gangestad, S. W., Simpson, J. A., Cousins, A. J., Garver-Apgar, C. E., & Christensen, P. N. (2004). Women's preferences for male behavioral displays change across the menstrual cycle. *Psychological Science, 15*(3), 203–207. doi:10.1111/j.0956-7976.2004.01503010.x; Lukaszewski, A. W., & Roney, J. R. (2009). Estimated hormones predict women's mate preferences for dominant personality traits. *Personality and Individual Differences, 47*(3), 191–196. doi:10.1016/j.paid.2009.02.019.

59. **Estrogen loves testosterone:** Gildersleeve, K., Haselton, M. G., & Fales, M. R. (2014). Supplemental material for do women's mate preferences change across the ovulatory cycle? A meta-analytic review. *Psychological Bulletin, 140*(5), 1205–1259. doi:10.1037/a0035438.

59. **higher marital satisfaction at high fertility:** Larson, C. M., Haselton, M. G., Gildersleeve, K. A., & Pillsworth, E. G. (2013). Changes in women's feelings about their romantic relationships across the ovulatory cycle. *Hormones and Behavior, 63*(1), 128–135. doi:10.1016/j.yhbeh.2012.10.005; Meltzer, A. L. (2017). Wives with

masculine husbands report increased marital satisfaction near peak fertility. *Evolutionary Behavioral Sciences, 11*(2), 161–172. doi:10.1037/ebs0000083.

59. **women's desire for sexy men at different times in their cycle:** Simpson, J., Cantu, S., Griskevicius, V., Weisberg, Y., Durante, K., & Beal, D. (2014). Fertile and selectively flirty: Women's behavior toward men changes across the ovulatory cycle. *Psychological Science, 25*(2), 431–438. doi:10.1037/e578192014-171.

60. **increase in female attention by decreasing their investment in their existing mate:** Hasegawa, M., Arai, E., Watanabe, M., & Nakamura, M. (2008). Methods for correcting plumage color fading in the barn swallow. *Ornithological Science, 7*(2), 117–122. doi:10.2326/1347-0558-7.2.117.

61. **exhibit less interest in babies and parenting:** Kuo, P. X., Saini, E. K., Thomason, E., Schultheiss, O. C., Gonzalez, R., & Volling, B. L. (2015). Individual variation in fathers' testosterone reactivity to infant distress predicts parenting behaviors with their 1-year-old infants. *Developmental Psychobiology, 58*(3), 303–314. doi:10.1002/dev.21370.

61. **continued interest in extra-pair sexual opportunities:** McIntyre, M., Gangestad, S. W., Gray, P. B., Chapman, J. F., Burnham, T. C., O'Rourke, M. T., & Thornhill, R. (2006). Romantic involvement often reduces men's testosterone levels—but not always: The moderating role of extrapair sexual interest. *Journal of Personality and Social Psychology, 91*(4), 642–651. doi:10.1037/0022-3514.91.4.642; Mazur, A., & Michalek, J. (1998). Marriage, divorce, and male testosterone. *Social Forces, 77*(1), 315. doi:10.2307/3006019.

61. **more relationship instability:** Booth, A., & Dabbs, J. M., Jr. (1993). Testosterone and men's marriages. *Social Forces, 72*(2), 463–477. doi:10.1093/sf/72.2.463; Gangestad, S. W., & Simpson, J. A. (2000). The evolution of human mating: Trade-offs and strategic pluralism. *Behavioral and Brain Sciences, 23*(4), 573–587. doi:10.1017/s0140525x0000337x; Gray, P. B., Parkin, J. C., & Samms-Vaughan, M. E. (2007). Hormonal correlates of paternal interactions: A hospital-based investigation in urban Jamaica. *PsycEXTRA Dataset, 52*(4), 499–507. doi:10.1037/e616352011-205; Roney, J. R., Hanson, K. N., Durante, K. M., & Maestripieri, D. (2006). Reading men's faces: Women's mate attractiveness judgments track men's testosterone and interest in infants. *Proceedings of the Royal Society B: Biological Sciences 273*(1598), 2169–2175. doi:10.1098/rspb.2006.3569; Anders, S. M., & Goldey, K. L. (2010). Testosterone and partnering are linked via relationship status for women and "relationship orientation" for men. *Hormones and Behavior, 58*(5), 820–826. doi:10.1016/j.yhbeh.2010.08.005.

63. **strong preference for sexy men:** Gangestad, S. W., Thornhill, R., & Garver-Apgar, C. E. (2005). Women's sexual interests across the ovulatory cycle depend on

primary partner developmental instability. *Proceedings of the Royal Society B: Biological Sciences, 272*(1576), 2023–2027. doi:10.1098/rspb.2005.3112.

63. **For example, in one study:** Rosen, M. L. & López, H. H. (2009). Menstrual cycle shifts in attentional bias for courtship language. *Evolution and Human Behavior, 30*(2), 131–140.

64. **greater number of extra-pair sexual fantasies:** Gangestad, S. W., Thornhill, R., & Garver-Apgar, C. E. (2005). Women's sexual interests across the ovulatory cycle depend on primary partner developmental instability. *Proceedings of the Royal Society B: Biological Sciences, 272*(1576), 2023–2027. doi:10.1098/rspb.2005.3112; Haselton, M. G., & Gangestad, S. W. (2006). Conditional expression of women's desires and men's mate guarding across the ovulatory cycle. *Hormones and Behavior, 49*(4), 509–518. doi:10.1016/j.yhbeh.2005.10.006.

64. **less willing to let their partners interact:** Krems, J., Neel, R., Neuberg, S. L., Puts, D. A., & Kenrick, D. (2016). Supplemental material for women selectively guard their (desirable) mates from ovulating women. *Journal of Personality and Social Psychology, 110*(4), 551–573. doi:10.1037/pspi0000044.supp; Hurst, A. C., Alquist, J. L., & Puts, D. A. (2017). Women's fertility status alters other women's jealousy and mate guarding. *Personality and Social Psychology Bulletin, 43*(2), 191–203. doi:10.1177/0146167216678859.

64. **ovulating women as being less trustworthy:** Hurst, A. C., Alquist, J. L., & Puts, D. A. (2017). Women's fertility status alters other women's jealousy and mate guarding. *Personality and Social Psychology Bulletin, 43*(2), 191–203. doi:10.1177/0146167216678859.

66. **silhouettes dancing and walking at high and low fertility:** Bernhard, F., Hugill, N., & Lange, B. P. (2012). Women's body movements are a potential cue to ovulation. *Personality and Individual Differences, 53*(6), 759–763. doi:10.1016/j.paid.2012.06.005.

67. **same women's faces taken at a non-fertile phase:** Roberts, S. C., Havlicek, J., Flegr, J., Hruskova, M., Little, A. C., Jones, B. C., . . . Petrie, M. (2004). Female facial attractiveness increases during the fertile phase of the menstrual cycle. *Proceedings of the Royal Society B: Biological Sciences, 271*(Suppl. 5). doi:10.1098/rsbl.2004.0174.

67. **Similar effects are found for vocal recordings:** Bryant, G. A., & Haselton, M. G. (2009). Vocal cues of ovulation in human females. *Biology Letters, 5*(1), 12–15. doi:10.1098/rsbl.2008.0507; Puts, D. A., Bailey, D. H., Cárdenas, R. A., Burriss, R. P., Welling, L. L., Wheatley, J. R., & Dawood, K. (2013). Women's attractiveness changes with estradiol and progesterone across the ovulatory cycle. *Hormones and Behavior, 63*(1), 13–19. doi:10.1016/j.yhbeh.2012.11.007.

67. **estrogen . . . changes how feminine and healthy women appear:** Smith, M. L., Perrett, D., Jones, B., Cornwell, R., Moore, F., Feinberg, D., . . . Hillier, S. G. (2006). Facial appearance is a cue to oestrogen levels in women. *Proceedings of the Royal Society B: Biological Sciences, 273*(1583), 135–140. doi:10.1098/rspb.2005.3296.

67. **less attractive at points in the cycle that are dominated by progesterone:** Puts, D. A., Bailey, D. H., Cárdenas, R. A., Burriss, R. P., Welling, L. L., Wheatley, J. R., & Dawood, K. (2013). Women's attractiveness changes with estradiol and progesterone across the ovulatory cycle. *Hormones and Behavior, 63*(1), 13–19. doi:10.1016/j.yhbeh.2012.11.007.

68. **women's natural body scents collected at high fertility:** Gildersleeve, K. A., Haselton, M. G., Larson, C. M., & Pillsworth, E. G. (2012). Body odor attractiveness as a cue of impending ovulation in women: Evidence from a study using hormone-confirmed ovulation. *Hormones and Behavior, 61*(2), 157–166. doi:10.1016/j.yhbeh.2011.11.005; Woodward, S. L., Thompson, M. E., & Gangestad, S. W. (2015). Women exposed to the scents of fertile-phase and luteal-phase women: Evaluative, competitive, and endocrine responses. *Adaptive Human Behavior and Physiology, 1*(4), 434–448. doi:10.1007/s40750-014-0019-8; Singh, D., & Bronstad, P. M. (2001). Female body odour is a potential cue to ovulation. *Proceedings of the Royal Society B: Biological Sciences, 268*(1469), 797–801. doi:10.1098/rspb.2001.1589; Havlicek, J., Dvorakova, R., Bartos, L., & Flegr, J. (2006). Non-advertized does not mean concealed: Body odour changes across the human menstrual cycle. *Ethology, 112*(1), 81–90. doi:10.1111/j.1439-0310.2006.01125.x.

68. **not observed for women on the pill:** Kuukasjarvi, S., Eriksson, C. P., Koskela, E., Mappes, T., Nissinen, K., & Rantala, M. J. (2004). Attractiveness of women's body odors over the menstrual cycle: The role of oral contraceptives and receiver sex. *Behavioral Ecology, 15*(4), 579–584. doi:10.1093/beheco/arh050.

68. **perceived as being less intense and more pleasant at high fertility:** Doty, R., Ford, M., Preti, G., & Huggins, G. (1975). Changes in the intensity and pleasantness of human vaginal odors during the menstrual cycle. *Science, 190*(4221), 1316–1318. doi:10.1126/science.1239080.

68. **men's testosterone increases after smelling T-shirts:** Miller, S. L., & Maner, J. K. (2010). Scent of a woman: Men's testosterone responses to olfactory ovulation cues. *Psychological Science, 21*(2), 276–283. doi:10.1177/0956797609357733.

68. **smelling scents collected from women's armpits and vulvas:** Cerda-Molina, A. L., Hernández-López, L., de la O, C. E., Chavira-Ramírez, R., & Mondragón-Ceballos, R. (2013). Changes in men's salivary testosterone and cortisol levels, and in sexual desire after smelling female axillary and vulvar scents. *Frontiers in Endocrinology, 4*, 159. http://doi.org/10.3389/fendo.2013.00159.

68. **Communicating fertility cues at this particular bodily junction:**
Maruthupandian, J., & Marimuthu, G. (2013). Cunnilingus apparently increases
duration of copulation in the Indian flying fox, Pteropus giganteus. *PLOS One, 8*(3).
doi:10.1371/journal.pone.0059743.

69. **engaged in more behavioral mimicry:** Miller, S. L., & Maner, J. K. (2011).
Ovulation as a male mating prime: Subtle signs of women's fertility influence men's
mating cognition and behavior. *Journal of Personality and Social Psychology, 100*(2),
295–308. doi:10.1037/a0020930.

71. **being aware of undesirable behavioral tendencies:** Ariely, D., & Wertenbroch,
K. (2002). Procrastination, deadlines, and performance: Self-control by
precommitment. *Psychological Science, 13*(3), 219–224. doi:10.1111/1467-9280.00441.

CHAPTER 4: HORMONES ON REPLAY

83. **Different generations of progestins:** Sitruk-Ware, R. (2006). New progestagens
for contraceptive use. *Human Reproduction Update, 12,* 169–178.

85. **masculinizing effects on the brain:** McFadden, D. (2000). Masculinizing effects
on otoacoustic emissions and auditory evoked potentials in women using oral
contraceptives. *Hearing Research, 142*(1–2), 23–33. doi:10.1016/s0378-
5955(00)00002-2.

85. **decreasing verbal fluency and increasing performance on mental rotation tasks:**
Griksiene, R., & Ruksenas, O. (2011). Effects of hormonal contraceptives on mental
rotation and verbal fluency. *Psychoneuroendocrinology, 36*(8), 1239–1248. doi:10.1016/j
.psyneuen.2011.03.001.

85. **make your fur turn black:** Asa, C. S., Porton, I. J., & Junge, R. (2007).
Reproductive cycles and contraception of black lemurs (*Eulemur macaco*) with depot
medroxyprogesterone acetate during the breeding season. *Zoo Biology, 26*(4), 289–298.
doi:10.1002/zoo.20136.

91. **the pill, per se, does not *cause* weight gain:** Rosenberg, M. (1998). Weight
change with oral contraceptive use and during the menstrual cycle. *Contraception,
58*(6), 345–349. doi:10.1016/s0010-7824(98)00127-9.

91. **estrogen surge that prompts ovulation predicts decreased food intake:** Roney,
J. R., & Simmons, Z. L. (2017). Ovarian hormone fluctuations predict within-cycle
shifts in women's food intake. *Hormones and Behavior, 90,* 8–14. doi:10.1016/j
.yhbeh.2017.01.009; Czaja, J. (1975). Ovarian hormones and food intake in female
guinea pigs and rhesus monkeys. *Hormones and Behavior, 6*(4), 329–349. doi:10.1016/
0018-506x(75)90003-3; Geary, N. (2004). The estrogenic inhibition of eating.
Neurobiology of Food and Fluid Intake Handbook of Behavioral Neurobiology, 14,
307–345. doi:10.1007/0-306-48643-1_12; Lissner, L., Stevens, J., Levitsky, D. A.,
Rasmussen, K. M., & Strupp, B. J. (1988). Variation in energy intake during the

menstrual cycle: Implications for food-intake research. *American Journal of Clinical Nutrition, 48*(4), 956–962. doi:10.1093/ajcn/48.4.956; Gong, E. J., Garrel, D., & Calloway, D. H. (1989). Menstrual cycle and voluntary food intake. *American Journal of Clinical Nutrition, 49*(2), 252–258. doi:10.1093/ajcn/49.2.252; Lyons, P. M., Truswell, A. S., Mira, M., Vizzard, J., & Abraham, S. F. (1989). Reduction of food intake in the ovulatory phase of the menstrual cycle. *American Journal of Clinical Nutrition, 49*(6), 1164–1168. doi:10.1093/ajcn/49.6.1164; Buffenstein, R. (1995). Food intake and the menstrual cycle: A retrospective analysis, with implications for appetite research. *Physiology and Behavior, 58*(6), 1067–1077. doi:10.1016/0031-9384(95)02003-9; Asarian, L., & Geary, N. (2006). Modulation of appetite by gonadal steroid hormones. *Philosophical Transactions of the Royal Society B: Biological Sciences, 361*(1471), 1251–1263. doi:10.1098/rstb.2006.1860.

91. **hunger and food intake are at their lowest:** Roney, J. R., & Simmons, Z. L. (2017). Ovarian hormone fluctuations predict within-cycle shifts in women's food intake. *Hormones and Behavior, 90*, 8–14. doi:10.1016/j.yhbeh.2017.01.009.

91. **food intake is highest when progesterone peaks:** Asarian, L., & Geary, N. (2006). Modulation of appetite by gonadal steroid hormones. *Philosophical Transactions of the Royal Society of London. Series B, Biological Sciences, 361*(1471), 1251–1263. doi:10.1098/rstb.2006.1860.

92. **have the highest ratio of progestin to estrogen:** Berenson, A. B., & Rahman, M. (2009). Changes in weight, total fat, percent body fat, and central-to-peripheral fat ratio associated with injectable and oral contraceptive use. *American Journal of Obstetrics and Gynecology, 200*(3), 329.e1–329.e8. doi:10.1016/j.ajog.2008.12.052

92. **shows no link between pill taking and weight gain:** Rosenberg, M. (1998). Weight change with oral contraceptive use and during the menstrual cycle. *Contraception, 58*(6), 345–349. doi:10.1016/s0010-7824(98)00127-9.

CHAPTER 5: SEXY IS IN THE EYE OF THE PILL TAKER

101. **promotes the health of any resulting children:** Brown, J. L. (1997). A theory of mate choice based on heterozygosity. *Behavioral Ecology, 8*(1), 60–65. doi:10.1093/beheco/8.1.60; Garver-Apgar, C. E., Gangestad, S. W., Thornhill, R., Miller, R. D., & Olp, J. J. (2006). Major histocompatibility complex alleles, sexual responsivity, and unfaithfulness in romantic couples. *Psychological Science, 17*(10), 830–835.

102. **exhibit an unwavering preference for men with *less* masculine faces and voices:** Putz, D. A., Gaulin, S. J., Sporter, R. J., & McBurney, D. H. (2004). Sex hormones and finger length. *Evolution and Human Behavior, 25*(3), 182–199. doi:10.1016/j.evolhumbehav.2004.03.005; Jones, B., Little, A., Boothroyd, L., Debruine, L., Feinberg, D., Smith, M. L., . . . Perrett, D. (2005). Commitment to relationships and preferences for femininity and apparent health in faces are strongest

on days of the menstrual cycle when progesterone level is high. *Hormones and Behavior, 48*(3), 283–290. doi:10.1016/j.yhbeh.2005.03.010; Feinberg, D.R., Jones, B. C., Law Smith, M. J., Moore, F. R., DeBruine, L. M., Cornwell, R. E., Hillier, S. G., & Perrett, D. I. (2006). Menstrual cycle, trait estrogen level, and masculinity preferences in the human voice. *Hormones and Behavior, 49*(2), 215–222. 10.1016/j .yhbeh.2005.07.004.

103. **women's ideal male faces became significantly less masculine:** Little, A. C., Burriss, R. P., Petrie, M., Jones, B. C., & Roberts, S. C. (2013). Oral contraceptive use in women changes preferences for male facial masculinity and is associated with partner facial masculinity. *Psychoneuroendocrinology, 38*(9), 1777–1785. doi:10.1016/j .psyneuen.2013.02.014

104. **survey of relationship quality:** Roberts, S. C., Klapilova, K., Little, A. C., Burriss, R. P., Jones, B. C., Debruine, L. M., . . . Havlicek, J. (2011). Relationship satisfaction and outcome in women who meet their partner while using oral contraception. *Proceedings of the Royal Society B: Biological Sciences, 279*(1732), 1430–1436. doi:10.1098/rspb.2011.1647.

107. **less activity in the reward centers of the brain:** Montoya, E. R., & Bos, P. A. (2017). How oral contraceptives impact social-emotional behavior and brain function. *Trends in Cognitive Sciences, 21*(2), 125–136. doi:10.1016/j.tics.2016.11.005.

107. **more activity in these centers when looking at money:** Bonenberger, M., Groschwitz, R. C., Kumpfmueller, D., Groen, G., Plener, P. L., & Abler, B. (2013). It's all about money. *NeuroReport, 24*(17), 951–955. doi:10.1097/ wnr.0000000000000024.

109. **data collected from two samples of married couples:** Russell, V. M., McNulty, J. K., Baker, L. R., & Meltzer, A. L. (2014). The association between discontinuing hormonal contraceptives and wives' marital satisfaction depends on husbands' facial attractiveness. *Proceedings of the National Academy of Sciences, 111*(48), 17081–17086. doi:10.1073/pnas.1414784111.

111. **differences between women's facial preferences or relationship satisfaction:** Jones, B. C., Hahn, A. C., Fisher, C. I., Wang, H., Kandrik, M., Han, C., . . . Debruine, L. M. (2018). No compelling evidence that preferences for facial masculinity track changes in women's hormonal status. *Psychological Science, 29*(6), 996–1005. doi:10.1101/136549; Jern, P., Kärnä, A., Hujanen, J., Erlin, T., Gunst, A., Rautaheimo, H., . . . Zietsch, B. P. (2018). A high-powered replication study finds no effect of starting or stopping hormonal contraceptive use on relationship quality. *Evolution and Human Behavior, 39*(4), 373–379. doi:10.1016/j.evolhumbehav .2018.02.008.

112. **blunt women's sensory acuity:** Caruso, S. (2001). A prospective study evidencing rhinomanometric and olfactometric outcomes in women taking oral contraceptives. *Human Reproduction, 16*(11), 2288–2294. doi:10.1093/humrep/

16.11.2288; Caruso, S., Maiolino, L., Rugolo, S., Intelisano, G., Farina, M., Cocuzza, S., & Serra, A. (2003). Auditory brainstem response in premenopausal women taking oral contraceptives. *Human Reproduction, 18*(1), 85–89. doi:10.1093/humrep/deg003; Snihur, A., & Hampson, E. (2012). Oral contraceptive use in women is associated with defeminization of otoacoustic emission patterns. *Neuroscience, 210*, 258–265. doi:10.1016/j.neuroscience.2012.02.006.

112. **women's sensitivity to six different scents:** Renfro, K. J., & Hoffmann, H. (2013). The relationship between oral contraceptive use and sensitivity to olfactory stimuli. *Hormones and Behavior, 63*(3), 491–496. doi:10.1016/j.yhbeh.2013.01.001.

117. **health of the children born to couples who met on the pill:** Birnbaum, S., Ein-Dor, T., & Birnbaum, G. E. (2016). Can contraceptive pill affect future offspring's health? The implications of using hormonal birth control for human evolution. *Evolutionary Psychological Science, 3*(2), 89–96. doi:10.1007/s40806-016-0074-4.

CHAPTER 6: SEX ON DRUGS

125. **This pattern is observed:** Wallwiener, C. W., Wallwiener, L-M., Seeger, H., Mück, A. O., Bitzer, J., & Wallwiener, M. (2010). Prevalence of sexual dysfunction and impact of contraception in female German medical students. *Journal of Sexual Medicine, 7*(6), 2139–2148. doi:10.1111/j.1743-6109.2010.01742.x; Wallwiener, C. W., Wallwiener, L-M., Seeger, H., Schönfisch, B., Mueck, A. O., Bitzer, J., . . . Wallwiener, M. (2015). Are hormonal components of oral contraceptives associated with impaired female sexual function? A questionnaire-based online survey of medical students in Germany, Austria, and Switzerland. *Archives of Gynecology and Obstetrics, 292*(4), 883–890. doi:10.1007/s00404-015-3726-x.

125. **changes in individual women's sexual functioning:** Caruso, S., Agnello, C., Intelisano, G., Farina, M., Mari, L. D., & Cianci, A. (2004). Sexual behavior of women taking low-dose oral contraceptive containing 15µg ethinylestradiol /60µg gestodene. *Contraception, 69*(3), 237–240. doi:10.1016/j.contraception .2003.11.001.

125. **whether the pill had an impact on women's interest in sex:** Rupp, H. A., & Wallen, K. (2007). Sex differences in viewing sexual stimuli: An eye-tracking study in men and women. *Hormones and Behavior, 51*(4), 524–533. doi:10.1016/j .yhbeh.2007.01.008.

128. **spend a little extra effort on their appearance:** Durante, K. M., Griskevicius, V., Hill, S. E., Perilloux, C., & Li, N. P. (2011). Ovulation, female competition, and product choice: Hormonal influences on consumer behavior. *Journal of Consumer Research, 37*(6), 921–934. doi:10.1086/656575; Hill, S. E., Rodeheffer, C. D., Griskevicius, V., Durante, K., & White, A. E. (2012). Boosting beauty in an economic decline: Mating, spending, and the lipstick effect. *Journal of Personality and*

Social Psychology, 103(2), 275–291. doi:10.1037/a0028657; Schmitt, D. P., & Buss, D. M. (1996). Strategic self-promotion and competitor derogation: Sex and context effects on the perceived effectiveness of mate attraction tactics. *Journal of Personality and Social Psychology, 70*(6), 1185–1204. doi:10.1037//0022-3514.70.6.1185.

128. **as wll as dieting, exercising, and visiting tanning beds:** Hill, S. E. & Durante, K. M. (2011). Courtship, Competition, and the Pursuit of Attractiveness: Mating Goals Facilitate Health-related Risk-Taking and Strategic Risk Suppression in Women. *Personality and Social Psychology Bulletin, 37,* 383–394. doi: 10.1177/0146167210395603.

128. **Take music, for instance:** Miller, G. F. (2000). Evolution of human music through sexual selection. In N. L. Wallin, B. Merker, & S. Brown (Eds.), *The origins of music* (pp. 329–360). Cambridge, MA: MIT Press.

132. **T plays an important role in women's sexual function:** Wåhlin-Jacobsen, S., Kristensen, E., Pedersen, A. T., Laessøe, N. C., Cohen, A. S., Hougaard, D. M., & . . . Giraldi, A. (2017). Androgens and psychosocial factors related to sexual dysfunctions in premenopausal women. *Journal of Sexual Medicine, 14*(3), 366–379. doi:10.1016/j .jsxm.2016.12.237; Vale, F. C., Coimvra, B. B., Lopes, G. P., & Geber, S. (2017). Sexual dysfunction in premenopausal women could be related to hormonal profile. *Gynecological Endocrinology, 33*(2), 145–147. doi:10.1080/09513590.2016.1226793.

132. **the pill can cause women's levels of free T to steeply decline:** Zimmerman, Y., Eijkemans, M. J., Bennink, H. J., Blankenstein, M. A., & Fauser, B. C. (2013). The effect of combined oral contraception on testosterone levels in healthy women: A systematic review and meta-analysis. *Human Reproduction Update, 20*(1), 76–105. doi:10.1093/humupd/dmt038; Fern, M., Rose, D. P., & Fern, E. B. (1978). Effect of oral contraceptives on plasma androgenic steroids and their precursors. *Obstetrics and Gynecology, 51*(5), 541–544. doi:10.1097/00006250-197805000-00005; Aden, U., Jung-Hoffmann, C., & Kuhl, H. (1998). A randomized cross-over study on various hormonal parameters of two triphasic oral contraceptives. *Contraception, 58*(2), 75–81. doi:10.1016/s0010-7824(98)00071-7; Wiegratz, I., Kutschera, E., Lee, J., Moore, C., Mellinger, U., Winkler, U., & Kuhl, H. (2003). Effect of four different oral contraceptives on various sex hormones and serum-binding globulins. *Contraception, 67*(1), 25–32. doi:10.1016/s0010-7824(02)00436-5; Ågren, U. M., Anttila, M., Mäenpää-Liukko, K., Rantala, M., Rautiainen, H., Sommer, W. F., & Mommers, E. (2011). Effects of a monophasic combined oral contraceptive containing nomegestrol acetate and 17β-oestradiol in comparison to one containing levonorgestrel and ethinylestradiol on markers of endocrine function. *European Journal of Contraception and Reproductive Health Care, 16*(6), 458–467. doi:10.3109/13625187.2011.614363.

132. **61 percent lower than naturally cycling women:** Zimmerman, Y., Eijkemans, M. J., Bennink, H. J., Blankenstein, M. A., & Fauser, B. C. (2013). The effect of combined oral contraception on testosterone levels in healthy women: A systematic

review and meta-analysis. *Human Reproduction Update, 20*(1), 76–105; Vange, N. V., Blankenstein, M., Kloosterboer, H., Haspels, A., & Thijssen, J. (1990). Effects of seven low-dose combined oral contraceptives on sex hormone binding globulin, corticosteroid binding globulin, total and free testosterone. *Contraception, 41*(4), 345–352. doi:10.1016/0010-7824(90)90034-s; Coenen, C., Thomas, C., Borm, G., Hollanders, J., & Rolland, R. (1996). Changes in androgens during treatment with four low-dose contraceptives. *Contraception, 53*(3), 171–176. doi:10.1016/0010-7824(96)00006-6; Greco, T., Graham, C. A., Bancroft, J., Tanner, A., & Doll, H. A. (2007). The effects of oral contraceptives on androgen levels and their relevance to premenstrual mood and sexual interest: A comparison of two triphasic formulations containing norgestimate and either 35 or 25µg of ethinyl estradiol. *Contraception, 76*(1), 8–17. doi:10.1016/j.contraception.2007.04.002.

132. **for a couple of different reasons:** Aden, U., Jung-Hoffmann, C., & Kuhl, H. (1998). A randomized cross-over study on various hormonal parameters of two triphasic oral contraceptives. *Contraception, 58*(2), 75–81. doi:10.1016/s0010-7824(98)00071-7; Alexander, G. (1990). Testosterone and sexual behavior in oral contraceptive users and nonusers: A prospective study. *Hormones and Behavior, 24*(3), 388–402. doi:10.1016/0018-506x(90)90017-r; Wiegratz, I., Jung-Hoffmann, C., & Kuhl, H. (1995). Effect of two oral contraceptives containing ethinylestradiol and gestodene or norgestimate upon androgen parameters and serum binding proteins. *Contraception, 51*(6), 341–346. doi:10.1016/0010-7824(95)00098-u; Coenen, C., Thomas, C., Borm, G., Hollanders, J., & Rolland, R. (1996). Changes in androgens during treatment with four low-dose contraceptives. *Contraception, 53*(3), 171–176. doi:10.1016/0010-7824(96)00006-6; Thorneycroft, I. H., Stanczyk, F. Z., Bradshaw, K. D., Ballagh, S. A., Nichols, M., & Weber, M. E. (1999). Effect of low-dose oral contraceptives on androgenic markers and acne. *Contraception, 60*(5), 255–262. doi:10.1016/s0010-7824(99)00093-1; Edwards, D. A., & Oneal, J. L. (2009). Oral contraceptives decrease saliva testosterone but do not affect the rise in testosterone associated with athletic competition. *Hormones and Behavior, 56*(2), 195–198. doi:10.1016/j.yhbeh.2009.01.008.

132. **causes your ovaries and adrenal glands to produce less T:** Fern, M., Rose, D. P., & Fern, E. B. (1978). Effect of oral contraceptives on plasma androgenic steroids and their precursors. *Obstetrics and Gynecology, 51*(5), 541–544. doi:10.1097/00006250-197805000-00005; Madden, J. D., Milewich, L., Parker, C., Carr, B. R., Boyar, R. M., & Macdonald, P. C. (1978). The effect of oral contraceptive treatment on the serum concentration of dehydroisoandrosterone sulfate. *American Journal of Obstetrics and Gynecology, 132*(4), 380–384. doi:10.1016/0002-9378(78)90771-8; Carlström, K., Karlsson, R., & Schoultz, B. V. (2002). Diurnal rhythm and effects of oral contraceptives on serum dehydroepiandrosterone sulfate (DHEAS) are related to alterations in serum albumin rather than to changes in adrenocortical steroid secretion. *Scandinavian Journal of Clinical and Laboratory Investigation, 62*(5), 361–368. doi:10.1080/00365510260296519; Speroff, L., & Fritz, M. A. (2005). *Clinical gynecologic*

endocrinology and infertility. Philadelphia: Lippincott Williams & Wilkins; Davison, S., & Bell, R. (2006). Androgen physiology. *Seminars in Reproductive Medicine, 24*(2), 71–77. doi:10.1055/s-2006-939565; Kuhl, H., Gahn, G., Romberg, G., März, W., & Taubert, H. (1985). A randomized cross-over comparison of two low-dose oral contraceptives upon hormonal and metabolic parameters: I. Effects upon sexual hormone levels. *Contraception, 31*(6), 583–593. doi:10.1016/0010-7824(85)90058-7; Jung-Hoffmann, C., Heidt, F., & Kuhl, H. (1988). Effect of two oral contraceptives containing 30 µg ethinylestradiol and 75µg gestodene or 150µg desogestrel upon various hormonal parameters. *Contraception, 38*(6), 593–603. doi:10.1016/0010-7824(88)90044-3; Aden, U., Jung-Hoffmann, C., & Kuhl, H. (1998). A randomized cross-over study on various hormonal parameters of two triphasic oral contraceptives. *Contraception, 58*(2), 75–81. doi:10.1016/s0010-7824(98)00071-7.

133. **increase levels of sex-hormone-binding globulin:** Zimmerman, Y., Eijkemans, M. J., Bennink, H. J., Blankenstein, M. A., & Fauser, B. C. (2013). The effect of combined oral contraception on testosterone levels in healthy women: A systematic review and meta-analysis. *Human Reproduction Update, 20*(1), 76–105. doi:10.1093/humupd/dmt038; Wiegratz, I., Jung-Hoffmann, C., & Kuhl, H. (1995). Effect of two oral contraceptives containing ethinylestradiol and gestodene or norgestimate upon androgen parameters and serum-binding proteins. *Contraception, 51*(6), 341–346. doi:10.1016/0010-7824(95)00098-u; Coenen, C., Thomas, C., Borm, G., Hollanders, J., & Rolland, R. (1996). Changes in androgens during treatment with four low-dose contraceptives. *Contraception, 53*(3), 171–176. doi:10.1016/0010-7824(96)00006-6.

133. **binds to T and makes it inactive:** Bancroft, J., Sherwin, B. B., Alexander, G. M., Davidson, D. W., & Walker, A. (1991). Oral contraceptives, androgens, and the sexuality of young women: II. The role of androgens. *Archives of Sexual Behavior, 20*(2), 121–135. doi:10.1007/bf01541939; Zimmerman, Y., Eijkemans, M. J., Bennink, H. J., Blankenstein, M. A., & Fauser, B. C. (2013). The effect of combined oral contraception on testosterone levels in healthy women: A systematic review and meta-analysis. *Human Reproduction Update, 20*(1), 76–105.

133. **women's T response to each of the different movie clips:** López, H. H., Hay, A. C., & Conklin, P. H. (2009). Attractive men induce testosterone and cortisol release in women. *Hormones and Behavior, 56*(1), 84–92. doi:10.1016/j.yhbeh.2009.03.004.

133. **women's T *decreased* in response to sexual scenarios:** Goldey, K. L., & Anders, S. M. (2011). Sexy thoughts: Effects of sexual cognitions on testosterone, cortisol, and arousal in women. *Hormones and Behavior, 59*(5), 754–764. doi:10.1016/j.yhbeh.2010.12.005.

133–34. **diminished vaginal lubrication and an increased risk of pain during sex:** Davis, S. R., Guay, A. T., Shifren, J. L., & Mazer, N. A. (2004). Endocrine aspects of female sexual dysfunction. *Journal of Sexual Medicine, 1*(1), 82–86.

134. **may continue to remain elevated in women:** Panzer, C., Wise, S., Fantini, G., Kang, D., Munarriz, R., Guay, A., & Goldstein, I. (2006). Impact of oral contraceptives on sex-hormone-binding globulin and androgen levels: A retrospective study in women with sexual dysfunction. *Journal of Sexual Medicine, 3*(1), 104–113.

134–35. **separates your partner from every other man in the world:** Behnia, B., Heinrichs, M., Bergmann, W., Jung, S., Germann, J., Schedlowski, M., . . . Kruger, T. H. (2014). Differential effects of intranasal oxytocin on sexual experiences and partner interactions in couples. *Hormones and Behavior, 65*(3), 308–318. doi:10.1016/j .yhbeh.2014.01.009.

135. **they don't see their partners any differently:** Scheele, D., Plota, J., Stoffel-Wagner, B., Maier, W., & Hurlemann, R. (2016). Hormonal contraceptives suppress oxytocin-induced brain reward responses to the partner's face. *Social Cognitive and Affective Neuroscience, 11*(5), 767–774. doi:10.1093/scan/nsv157.

136. **decreased concentrations of allopregnanolone in the brain:** Santoru, F., Berretti, R., Locci, A., Porcu, P., & Concas, A. (2014). Decreased allopregnanolone induced by hormonal contraceptives is associated with a reduction in social behavior and sexual motivation in female rats. *Psychopharmacology, 231*(17), 3351–3364. doi:10.1007/s00213-014-3539-9; Porcu, P., Mostallino, M. C., Sogliano, C., Santoru, F., Berretti, R., & Concas, A. (2012). Long-term administration with levonorgestrel decreases allopregnanolone levels and alters GABAA receptor subunit expression and anxiety-like behavior. *Pharmacology Biochemistry and Behavior, 102*(2), 366–372. doi:10.1016/j.pbb.2012.05.011.

136. **increased sexual functioning and satisfaction:** Caruso, S., Agnello, C., Intelisano, G., Farina, M., Mari, L. D., Sparacino, L., & Cianci, A. (2005). Prospective study on sexual behavior of women using 30μg ethinylestradiol and 3mg drospirenone oral contraceptive. *Contraception, 72*(1), 19–23. doi:10.1016/j .contraception.2005.02.002; Caruso, S., Sareri, M. I., Agnello, C., Romano, M., Presti, L. L., Malandrino, C., & Cianci, A. (2011). Conventional vs. extended-cycle oral contraceptives on the quality of sexual life: Comparison between two regimens containing 3mg drospirenone and 20μg ethinyl estradiol. *Journal of Sexual Medicine, 8*(5), 1478–1485. doi:10.1111/j.1743-6109.2011.02208.x.

137. **mid-cycle sexiness boost:** Alvergne, A., & Lummaa, V. (2010). Does the contraceptive pill alter mate choice in humans? *Trends in Ecology and Evolution, 25*(3), 171–179. doi:10.1016/j.tree.2009.08.003.

138. **pill-taking women don't get this monthly sexiness spike:** Kuukasjarvi, S. (2004). Attractiveness of women's body odors over the menstrual cycle: The role of oral contraceptives and receiver sex. *Behavioral Ecology, 15*(4), 579–584. doi:10.1093/ beheco/arh050; Miller, G., Tybur, J. M., & Jordan, B. D. (2007). Ovulatory cycle effects on tip earnings by lap dancers: Economic evidence for human estrus? *Evolution*

and Human Behavior, 28(6), 375–381. doi:10.1016/j.evolhumbehav.2007.06.002; Alvergne, A., & Lummaa, V. (2010). Does the contraceptive pill alter mate choice in humans? *Trends in Ecology and Evolution, 25*(3), 171–179. doi:10.1016/j.tree.2009.08.003.

138. **decreases the number of spontancons mounting attempts they receive:** Baum, M. J., Everitt, B. J., Herbert, J., & Keverne. E. B. (1977). Hormonal basis of proceptivity and receptivity in female primates. *Archives of Sexual Behavior, 6*(4), 353–353. doi:10.1007/bf01541207; Baum, M. J. (1983). Hormonal modulation of sexuality in female primates. *BioScience, 33*(9), 578–582. doi:10.2307/1309209; Dahl, Dahl, J. F., Nadler, R. D., & Collins, D. C. (1991). Monitoring the ovarian cycles of Pan troglodytes and P. paniscus: A comparative approach. *American Journal of Primatology, 24*(3–4), 195–209. doi:10.1002/ajp.1350240306.

138. **egregious reduction in sexual interest:** Shively, C. A., Manuck, S. B., Kaplan, J. R., & Koritnik, D. R. (1990). Oral contraceptive administration, interfemale relationships, and sexual behavior in Macaca fascicularis. *Archives of Sexual Behavior, 19*(2), 101–117. doi:10.1007/bf01542226.

139. **women's level of commitment to their partners and the mate-guarding behaviors of men:** French, J. E., Meltzer, A. L., & Maner, J. K. (2017). Men's perceived partner commitment and mate guarding: The moderating role of partner's hormonal contraceptive use. *Evolutionary Behavioral Sciences, 11*(2), 173–186. http://dx.doi.org/10.1037/ebs0000087.

140. **might decrease mate-guarding behaviors:** Haselton, M. G., & Gangestad, S. W. (2006). Conditional expression of women's desires and men's mate guarding across the ovulatory cycle. *Hormones and Behavior, 49*(4), 509–518. doi:10.1016/j.yhbeh.2005.10.006.

141. **hormonal contraceptive shot containing a first-generation progestin:** Crawford, J. C., Boulet, M., & Drea, C. M. (2010). Smelling wrong: Hormonal contraception in lemurs alters critical female odour cues. *Proceedings of the Royal Society B: Biological Sciences, 278*(1702), 122–130. doi:10.1098/rspb.2010.1203.

141. **scent cues provide others with information about identity:** Penn, D. J., Oberzaucher, E., Grammer, K., Fischer, G., Soini, H. A., Wiesler, D., . . . Brereton, R. G. (2006). Individual and gender fingerprints in human body odour. *Journal of the Royal Society Interface, 4*(13), 331–340. doi:10.1098/rsif.2006.0182; Weisfeld, G. E., Czilli, T., Phillips, K. A., Gall, J. A., & Lichtman, C. M. (2003). Possible olfaction-based mechanisms in human kin recognition and inbreeding avoidance. *Journal of Experimental Child Psychology, 85*(3), 279–295. doi:10.1016/s0022-0965(03)00061-4; Roberts, S. C., Gosling, L. M., Spector, T. D., Miller, P., Penn, D. J., & Petrie, M. (2005). Body odor similarity in noncohabiting twins. *Chemical Senses, 30*(8), 651–656. doi:10.1093/chemse/bji058.

141. **genetic quality:** Rikowski, A., & Grammer, K. (1999). Human body odour, symmetry and attractiveness. *Proceedings of the Royal Society B: Biological Sciences, 266*(1422), 869–874. doi:10.1098/rspb.1999.0717; Thornhill, R., & Gangestad, S. W. (1999). The scent of symmetry a human sex pheromone that signals fitness? *Evolution and Human Behavior, 20*(3), 175–201. doi:10.1016/s1090-5138(99)00005-7; Havlicek, J., & Lenochova, P. (2006). The effect of meat consumption on body odor attractiveness. *Chemical Senses, 31*(8), 747–752. doi:10.1093/chemse/bjl017.

141. **fertility status:** Singh, D., & Bronstad, P. M. (2001). Female body odour is a potential cue to ovulation. *Proceedings of the Royal Society B: Biological Sciences, 268*(1469), 797–801. doi:10.1098/rspb.2001.1589; Kuukasjarvi, S. (2004). Attractiveness of women's body odors over the menstrual cycle: The role of oral contraceptives and receiver sex. *Behavioral Ecology, 15*(4), 579–584. doi:10.1093/beheco/arh050.

CHAPTER 7: THE CURIOUS CASE OF THE MISSING CORTISOL

145. **methodological footnote in a research presentation:** Ellis, B. J., Oldehinkel, A. J., & Nederhof, E. (2016). The adaptive calibration model of stress responsivity: An empirical test in the Tracking Adolescents Individual Lives Survey study. *Development and Psychopathology, 29*(03), 1001–1021. doi:10.1017/s0954579416000985.

145. **cortisol surge is so characteristic of the stress response:** Foley, P., & Kirschbaum, C. (2010). Human hypothalamus–pituitary–adrenal axis responses to acute psychosocial stress in laboratory settings. *Neuroscience and Biobehavioral Reviews, 35*(1), 91–96. doi:10.1016/j.neubiorev.2010.01.010.

146. **Trier Social Stress Test:** Kirschbaum, C., Pirke, K., & Hellhammer, D. H. (1993). The "Trier Social Stress Test"—a tool for investigating psychobiological stress responses in a laboratory setting. *Neuropsychobiology, 28*(1–2), 76–81. doi:10.1159/000119004.

146. **two- or threefold increase in salivary cortisol levels:** Dickerson, S. S., & Kemeny, M. E. (2004). Acute stressors and cortisol responses: A theoretical integration and synthesis of laboratory research. *Psychological Bulletin, 130*(3), 355–391. doi:10.1037/0033-2909.130.3.355; Kudielka, B. M., Hellhammer, D. H., & Kirschbaum, C. (2007). Ten years of research with the Trier Social Stress Test— revisited. In *Social Neuroscience: Integrating Biological and Psychological Explanations of Social Behavior* (pp. 56–83). New York: Guilford Press.

148. **powerful elicitors of stress:** Roney, J. R. (in preparation). Cortisol increases in response to sexual attraction; Flinn, M. V., Nepomnaschy, P. A., Muehlenbein, M. P., & Ponzi, D. (2011). Evolutionary functions of early social modulation of hypothalamic-pituitary-adrenal axis development in humans. *Neuroscience and Biobehavioral Reviews, 35*(7), 1611–1629. doi:10.1016/j.neubiorev.2011.01.005.

149. **stress response seems to remain completely intact in pill-taking women:** Kirschbaum, C., Platte, P., Pirke, K., & Hellhammer, D. (1996). Adrenocortical activation following stressful exercise: Further evidence for attenuated free cortisol responses in women using oral contraceptives. *Stress and Health, 12*(3), 137–143. doi:10.1002/(SICI)1099-1700(199607)12:3<137::AID-SMI685>3.0.CO;2-C.

149. **Women on the pill *feel* just as stressed out:** Bouma, E. M., Riese, H., Ormel, J., Verhulst, F. C., & Oldehinkel, A. J. (2009). Adolescents' cortisol responses to awakening and social stress: Effects of gender, menstrual phase and oral contraceptives. The TRAILS study. *Psychoneuroendocrinology, 34*(6), 884–893. doi:10.1016/j.psyneuen.2009.01.003.

152. **redistributing energy that was being used for fueling growth:** Sapolsky, R. M. (2004). *Why zebras don't get ulcers.* New York: Henry Holt and Co.

152. **cortisol promotes perceptual vigilance:** Quervain, D. D., Schwabe, L., & Roozendaal, B. (2016). Stress, glucocorticoids and memory: Implications for treating fear-related disorders. *Nature Reviews Neuroscience, 18*(1), 7–19. doi:10.1038/nrn.2016.155; Strelzyk, F., Hermes, M., Naumann, E., Oitzl, M., Walter, C., Busch, H., . . . Schachinger, H. (2012). Tune it down to live it up? Rapid, nongenomic effects of cortisol on the human brain. *Journal of Neuroscience, 32*(2), 616–625. doi:10.1523/jneurosci.2384-11.2012.

152. **revs up the neural processes involved in learning and memory:** Lupien, S., & McEwen, B. (1997). The acute effects of corticosteroids on cognition: Integration of animal and human model studies. *Brain Research Reviews, 24*(1), 1–27. doi:10.1016/s0165-0173(97)00004-0; McEwen, B. S., & Wingfield, J. C. (2003). The concept of allostasis in biology and biomedicine. *Hormones and Behavior, 43*(1), 2–15. doi:10.1016/s0018-506x(02)00024-7; Seeman, T. E., Singer, B. H., Rowe, J. W., Horwitz, R. I., & McEwen, B. S. (1997). Price of adaptation: Allostatic load and its health consequences. *Archives of Internal Medicine, 157*(19), 2259. doi:10.1001/archinte.1997.00440400111013; Weymar, M., Löw, A., Öhman, A., & Hamm, A. O. (2011). The face is more than its parts: Brain dynamics of enhanced spatial attention to schematic threat. *NeuroImage, 58*(3), 946–954. doi:10.1016/j.neuroimage.2011.06.061; Yuen, E. Y., Liu, W., Karatsoreos, I. N., Feng, J., McEwen, B. S., & Yan, Z. (2009). Acute stress enhances glutamatergic transmission in prefrontal cortex and facilitates working memory. *Proceedings of the National Academy of Sciences, 106*(33), 14075–14079. doi:10.1073/pnas.0906791106.

152. ***chronic* activation of the HPA axis wreaks havoc in the body:** Rauch, S. L., Shin, L. M., Whalen, P. J., & Pitman, R. K. (1998). Neuroimaging and the neuroanatomy of posttraumatic stress disorder. *CNS Spectrums, 3*(2), 30–41; Rauch, S. L., Shin, L. M., & Phelps, E. A. (2006). Neurocircuitry models of posttraumatic stress disorder and extinction: Human neuroimaging research—Past, present, and future. *Biological Psychiatry, 60*(4), 376–382. doi:10.1016/j.biopsych.2006.06.004;

Veer, I. M., Oei, N. L., van Buchem, M. A., Spinhoven, P., Elzinga, B. M., & Rombouts, S. B. (2015). Evidence for smaller right amygdala volumes in posttraumatic stress disorder following childhood trauma. *Psychiatry Research: Neuroimaging, 233*(3), 436–442. doi:10.1016/j.pscychresns.2015.07.016.

153. **pill-taking women lacking an HPA-axis response to stress:** Kirschbaum, C., Platte, P., Pirke, K., & Hellhammer, D. (1996). Adrenocortical activation following stressful exercise: Further evidence for attenuated free cortisol responses in women using oral contraceptives. *Stress and Health, 12*(3), 137–143. doi:10.1002/(SICI)1099-1700(199607)12:3<137::AID-SMI685>3.0.CO;2-C; Roche, D. J., King, A. C., Cohoon, A. J., & Lovallo, W. R. (2013). Hormonal contraceptive use diminishes salivary cortisol response to psychosocial stress and naltrexone in healthy women. *Pharmacology Biochemistry and Behavior, 109*, 84–90. doi:10.1016/j.pbb.2013.05.007; Bonen, A., Haynes, F. W., & Graham, T. E. (1991). Substrate and hormonal responses to exercise in women using oral contraceptives. *Journal of Applied Physiology, 70*(5), 1917–1927. doi:10.1152/jappl.1991.70.5.1917; Kirschbaum, C., Pirke, K., & Hellhammer, D. H. (1995). Preliminary evidence for reduced cortisol responsivity to psychological stress in women using oral contraceptive medication. *Psychoneuroendocrinology, 20*(5), 509–514. doi:10.1016/0306-4530(94)00078-o; Meulenberg, P., Ross, H., Swinkels, L., & Benraad, T. (1987). The effect of oral contraceptives on plasma-free and salivary cortisol and cortisone. *Clinica Chimica Acta, 165*(2–3), 379–385. doi:10.1016/0009-8981(87)90183-5; Meulenberg, P., & Hofman, J. (1990). The effect of oral contraceptive use and pregnancy on the daily rhythm of cortisol and cortisone. *Clinica Chimica Acta, 190*(3), 211–221. doi:10.1016/0009-8981(90)90175-r; Crewther, B. T., Hamilton, D., Casto, K., Kilduff, L. P., & Cook, C. J. (2015). Effects of oral contraceptive use on the salivary testosterone and cortisol responses to training sessions and competitions in elite women athletes. *Physiology and Behavior, 147*, 84–90. doi:10.1016/j.physbeh.2015.04.017.

153. **women's cortisol release in response to the TSST:** Kirschbaum, C., Pirke, K., & Hellhammer, D. H. (1995). Preliminary evidence for reduced cortisol responsivity to psychological stress in women using oral contraceptive medication. *Psychoneuroendocrinology, 20*(5), 509–514. doi:10.1016/0306-4530(94)00078-o.

155. **cortisol actually *decreased* in response to stress:** Bouma, E. M., Riese, H., Ormel, J., Verhulst, F. C., & Oldehinkel, A. J. (2009). Adolescents' cortisol responses to awakening and social stress: Effects of gender, menstrual phase and oral contraceptives. The TRAILS study. *Psychoneuroendocrinology, 34*(6), 884–893. doi:10.1016/j.psyneuen.2009.01.003.

155. **HPA-axis response to the stress-inducing drug naltrexone:** Roche, D. J., King, A. C., Cohoon, A. J., & Lovallo, W. R. (2013). Hormonal contraceptive use diminishes salivary cortisol response to psychosocial stress and naltrexone in healthy

women. *Pharmacology Biochemistry and Behavior, 109*, 84–90. doi:10.1016/j
.pbb.2013.05.007.

155. **or to strenuous exercise:** Bonen, A., Haynes, F. W., & Graham, T. E. (1991).
Substrate and hormonal responses to exercise in women using oral contraceptives.
Journal of Applied Physiology, 70(5), 1917–1927. doi:10.1152/jappl.1991.70.5.1917.

155. **cortisol response to this stress was a mere shadow:** Kirschbaum, C., Platte, P.,
Pirke, K., & Hellhammer, D. (1996). Adrenocortical activation following stressful
exercise: Further evidence for attenuated free cortisol responses in women using oral
contraceptives. *Stress and Health, 12*(3), 137–143. doi:10.1002/(SICI)1099-
1700(199607)12:3<137::AID-SMI685>3.0.CO;2-C.

155. **their morning cortisol peak is lower:** Pruessner, J. C., Hellhammer, D. H., &
Kirschbaum, C. (1999). Burnout, perceived stress, and cortisol responses to
awakening. *Psychosomatic Medicine, 61*(2), 197–204. doi:10.1097/00006842-
199903000-00012.

155. **their daily cortisol curve is flatter:** Meulenberg, P., Ross, H., Swinkels, L., &
Benraad, T. (1987). The effect of oral contraceptives on plasma-free and salivary
cortisol and cortisone. *Clinica Chimica Acta, 165*(2–3), 379–385. doi:10.1016/0009-
8981(87)90183-5; Meulenberg, P., & Hofman, J. (1990). The effect of oral
contraceptive use and pregnancy on the daily rhythm of cortisol and cortisone. *Clinica
Chimica Acta, 190*(3), 211–221. doi:10.1016/0009-8981(90)90175-r; Roche, D. J.,
King, A. C., Cohoon, A. J., & Lovallo, W. R. (2013). Hormonal contraceptive use
diminishes salivary cortisol response to psychosocial stress and naltrexone in healthy
women. *Pharmacology Biochemistry and Behavior, 109*, 84–90. doi:10.1016/j
.pbb.2013.05.007.

155. **less able to regulate cortisol that is administered to them in the lab:** Gaffey, A.
E., Wirth, M. M., Hoks, R. M., Jahn, A. L., & Abercrombie, H. C. (2014).
Circulating cortisol levels after exogenous cortisol administration are higher in
women using hormonal contraceptives: Data from two preliminary studies. *Stress,
17*(4), 314–320. doi:10.3109/10253890.2014.919447.

155. **continue to exhibit differences in HPA-axis function:** Mordecai, K. L., Rubin,
L. H., Eatough, E., Sundermann, E., Drogos, L., Savarese, A., & Maki, P. M.
(2016). Cortisol reactivity and emotional memory after psychosocial stress in oral
contraceptive users. *Journal of Neuroscience Research, 95*(1–2), 126–135. doi:10.1002/
jnr.23904.

156. **Pill-taking women *do* have higher levels of CBG:** Simunková, K., Stárka, L.,
Hill, M., Kríz, L., Hampl, R., & Vondra, K. (2008). Comparison of total and salivary
cortisol in a low-dose ACTH (Synacthen) test: Influence of three-month oral
contraceptives administration to healthy women. *Physiological Research, 57*, S193–S199.

156. **170ish percent more:** Wiegratz, I., Jung-Hoffmann, C., & Kuhl, H. (1995). Effect of two oral contraceptives containing ethinylestradiol and gestodene or norgestimate upon androgen parameters and serum binding proteins. *Contraception, 51*(6), 341–346. doi:10.1016/0010-7824(95)00098-u.

156. **CBG plays a role in blunting pill-taking women's stress response:** Roche, D. J., King, A. C., Cohoon, A. J., & Lovallo, W. R. (2013). Hormonal contraceptive use diminishes salivary cortisol response to psychosocial stress and naltrexone in healthy women. *Pharmacology Biochemistry and Behavior, 109*, 84–90. doi:10.1016/j.pbb.2013.05.007.

157. **Their daily cortisol rhythms are also blunted:** Kirschbaum, C., Platte, P., Pirke, K., & Hellhammer, D. (1996). Adrenocortical activation following stressful exercise: Further evidence for attenuated free cortisol responses in women using oral contraceptives. *Stress and Health, 12*(3), 137–143. doi:10.1002/(SICI)1099-1700(199607)12:3<137::AID-SMI685>3.0.CO;2-C; Roche, D. J., King, A. C., Cohoon, A. J., & Lovallo, W. R. (2013). Hormonal contraceptive use diminishes salivary cortisol response to psychosocial stress and naltrexone in healthy women. *Pharmacology Biochemistry and Behavior, 109*, 84–90. doi:10.1016/j.pbb.2013.05.007; Bonen, A., Haynes, F. W., & Graham, T. E. (1991). Substrate and hormonal responses to exercise in women using oral contraceptives. *Journal of Applied Physiology, 70*(5), 1917–1927. doi:10.1152/jappl.1991.70.5.1917; Kirschbaum, C., Pirke, K., & Hellhammer, D. H. (1995). Preliminary evidence for reduced cortisol responsivity to psychological stress in women using oral contraceptive medication. *Psychoneuroendocrinology, 20*(5), 509–514. doi:10.1016/0306-4530(94)00078-o; Meulenberg, P., Ross, H., Swinkels, L., & Benraad, T. (1987). The effect of oral contraceptives on plasma-free and salivary cortisol and cortisone. *Clinica Chimica Acta, 165*(2-3), 379–385. doi:10.1016/0009-8981(87)90183-5; Meulenberg, P., & Hofman, J. (1990). The effect of oral contraceptive use and pregnancy on the daily rhythm of cortisol and cortisone. *Clinica Chimica Acta, 190*(3), 211–221. doi:10.1016/0009-8981(90)90175-r; Crewther, B. T., Hamilton, D., Casto, K., Kilduff, L. P., & Cook, C. J. (2015). Effects of oral contraceptive use on the salivary testosterone and cortisol responses to training sessions and competitions in elite women athletes. *Physiology and Behavior, 147*, 84–90. doi:10.1016/j.physbeh.2015.04.017.

157. **their levels of total cortisol . . . are *higher*:** Hertel, J., König, J., Homuth, G., Auwera, S. V., Wittfeld, K., Pietzner, M., . . . Grabe, H. J. (2017). Evidence for stress-like alterations in the HPA-axis in women taking oral contraceptives. *Scientific Reports, 7*(1), 1–14. doi:10.1038/s41598-017-13927-7.

157. **Pill-taking women's levels of CBG . . . are significantly higher:** Simunková, K., Stárka, L., Hill, M., Kríz, L., Hampl, R., & Vondra, K. (2008). Comparison of total and salivary cortisol in a low-dose ACTH (Synacthen) test: Influence of three-month oral

contraceptives administration to healthy women. *Physiological Research, 57*, S193–S199; Wiegratz, I., Jung-Hoffmann, C., & Kuhl, H. (1995). Effect of two oral contraceptives containing ethinylestradiol and gestodene or norgestimate upon androgen parameters and serum binding proteins. *Contraception, 51*(6), 341–346. doi:10.1016/0010-7824(95)00098-u.

157. **their ACTH response is blunted:** Jacobs, A. J., Odom, M. J., Word, R. A., & Carr, B. R. (1989). Effect of oral contraceptives on adrenocorticotropin and growth hormone secretion following CRH and GHRH administration. *Contraception, 40*(6), 691–699. doi:10.1016/0010-7824(89)90072-3.

157. **their subsequently measured levels of free cortisol are lower:** Kirschbaum, C., Kudielka, B. M., Gaab, J., Schommer, N. C., & Hellhammer, D. H. (1999). Impact of gender, menstrual cycle phase, and oral contraceptives on the activity of the hypothalamus-pituitary-adrenal axis. *Psychosomatic Medicine, 61*(2), 154–162. doi:10.1097/00006842-199903000-00006.

157. **their ability to manage excess cortisol is already maxed out:** Gaffey, A. E., Wirth, M. M., Hoks, R. M., Jahn, A. L., & Abercrombie, H. C. (2014). Circulating cortisol levels after exogenous cortisol administration are higher in women using hormonal contraceptives: Data from two preliminary studies. *Stress, 17*(4), 314–320. doi:10.3109/10253890.2014.919447.

158. **The adrenal glands are releasing less cortisol:** Kirschbaum, C., Kudielka, B. M., Gaab, J., Schommer, N. C., & Hellhammer, D. H. (1999). Impact of gender, menstrual cycle phase, and oral contraceptives on the activity of the hypothalamus-pituitary-adrenal axis. *Psychosomatic Medicine, 61*(2), 154–162. doi:10.1097/00006842-199903000-00006.

158. **The pituitary gland is releasing less ACTH:** Jacobs, A. J., Odom, M. J., Word, R. A., & Carr, B. R. (1989). Effect of oral contraceptives on adrenocorticotropin and growth hormone secretion following CRH and GHRH administration. *Contraception, 40*(6), 691–699. doi:10.1016/0010-7824(89)90072-3.

158. **the liver is releasing tons of CBG:** Simunková, K., Stárka, L., Hill, M., Kríz, L., Hampl, R., & Vondra, K. (2008). Comparison of total and salivary cortisol in a low-dose ACTH (Synacthen) test: Influence of three-month oral contraceptives administration to healthy women. *Physiological Research, 57*, S193–S199.

158. **similar to that of someone who has experienced chronic stress:** Hertel, J., König, J., Homuth, G., Auwera, S. V., Wittfeld, K., Pietzner, M., . . . Grabe, H. J. (2017). Evidence for stress-like alterations in the HPA-axis in women taking oral contraceptives. *Scientific Reports, 7*(1), 1–14. doi:10.1038/s41598-017-13927-7.

158. **four well-established biological markers of chronic stress exposure:** Hertel, J., König, J., Homuth, G., Auwera, S. V., Wittfeld, K., Pietzner, M., . . . Grabe, H. J.

(2017). Evidence for stress-like alterations in the HPA-axis in women taking oral contraceptives. *Scientific Reports, 7*(1), 1–14. doi:10.1038/s41598-017-13927-7.

158. **chronic stress predicts having a smaller hippocampus:** Conrad, C. D. (2008). Chronic stress-induced hippocampal vulnerability: The glucocorticoid vulnerability hypothesis. *Reviews in the Neurosciences, 19*(6). doi:10.1515/revneuro.2008.19.6.395; Magarinos, A. M., Verdugo, J. M., & McEwen, B. S. (1997). Chronic stress alters synaptic terminal structure in hippocampus. *Proceedings of the National Academy of Sciences, 94*(25), 14002–14008. doi:10.1073/pnas.94.25.14002.

158. **attempted silencing of genes that get turned on by cortisol:** Klengel, T., Mehta, D., Anacker, C., Rex-Haffner, M., Pruessner, J. C., Pariante, C. M., . . . Binder, E. B. (2013). Allele-specific FKBP5 DNA demethylation mediates gene–childhood trauma interactions. *Nature Neuroscience, 16*, 33–41. doi:10.1038/nn.3275.

159. **They exhibited *all four* of them:** Hertel, J., König, J., Homuth, G., Auwera, S. V., Wittfeld, K., Pietzner, M., . . . Grabe, H. J. (2017). Evidence for stress-like alterations in the HPA-axis in women taking oral contraceptives. *Scientific Reports, 7*(1), 1–14. doi:10.1038/s41598-017-13927-7.

160. **can cause structural and functional changes in areas of the brain:** Conrad, C. D. (2010). A critical review of chronic stress effects on spatial learning and memory. *Progress in Neuro-Psychopharmacology and Biological Psychiatry, 34*(5), 742–755. doi:10.1016/j.pnpbp.2009.11.003; Joëls, M., Karst, H., Krugers, H. J., & Lucassen, P. J. (2007). Chronic stress: Implications for neuronal morphology, function and neurogenesis. *Frontiers in Neuroendocrinology, 28(2–3)*, 72–96. doi:10.1016/j .yfrne.2007.04.001; Mirescu, C., & Gould, E. (2006). Stress and adult neurogenesis. *Hippocampus, 16*(3), 233–238. doi:10.1002/hipo.20155; Vyas, A., Mitra, R., Shankaranarayana Rao, B. S., & Chattarji, S. (2002). Chronic stress induces contrasting patterns of dendritic remodeling in hippocampal and amygdaloid neurons. *Journal of Neuroscience, 22*(15), 6810–6818. doi:10.1523/JNEUROSCI.22-15-06810.2002.

160. **links hippocampal damage to learning and memory problems:** Anand, K. S., & Dhikav, V. (2012). Hippocampus in health and disease: An overview. *Annals of Indian Academy of Neurology, 15*(4), 239–246. http://doi.org/10.4103/0972-2327.104323.

160. **pill-taking women have lower hippocampal volume:** Hertel, J., König, J., Homuth, G., Auwera, S. V., Wittfeld, K., Pietzner, M., . . . Grabe, H. J. (2017). Evidence for stress-like alterations in the HPA-axis in women taking oral contraceptives. *Scientific Reports, 7*(1), 1–14. doi:10.1038/s41598-017-13927-7; Gingnell, M., Engman, J., Frick, A., Moby, L., Wikström, J., Fredrikson, M., & Sundström-Poromaa, I. (2013). Oral contraceptive use changes brain activity and mood in women with previous negative affect on the pill: A double-blinded, placebo-controlled randomized trial of a levonorgestrel-containing combined oral contraceptive. *Psychoneuroendocrinology, 38*(7), 1133–1144. doi:10.1016/j .psyneuen.2012.11.006; Petersen, N., & Cahill, L. (2015). Amygdala reactivity to

negative stimuli is influenced by oral contraceptive use. *Social Cognitive and Affective Neuroscience, 10*(9), 1266–1272. doi:10.1093/scan/nsv010.

160. **a hallmark of Alzheimer's disease is hippocampal shrinkage:** West, M., Coleman, P., Flood, D., & Troncoso, J. (1994). Differences in the pattern of hippocampal neuronal loss in normal ageing and Alzheimer's disease. *The Lancet, 344*(8925), 769–772. doi:10.1016/s0140-6736(94)92338-8.

160. **links hippocampal shrinkage to more everyday cognitive and emotional problems:** Kempermann, G., Krebs, J., & Fabel, K. (2008). The contribution of failing adult hippocampal neurogenesis to psychiatric disorders. *Current Opinion in Psychiatry, 21*(3), 290–295. doi:10.1097/yco.0b013e3282fad375; Lagace, D. C., Donovan, M. H., Decarolis, N. A., Farnbauch, L. A., Malhotra, S., Berton, O., . . . Eisch, A. J. (2010). Adult hippocampal neurogenesis is functionally important for stress-induced social avoidance. *Proceedings of the National Academy of Sciences of the United States of America, 107*(9), 4436–4441. doi:10.1073/pnas.0910072107; Pittenger, C., & Duman, R. S. (2008). Stress, depression and neuroplasticity: A convergence of mechanisms. *Neuropsychopharmacology, 33*(1), 88–109. doi:10.1038/sj.npp.1301574.

161. **pill-taking women performed worse than naturally cycling women:** Bradshaw, H. K. & Hill, S.E. (working paper). Oral contraceptive use predicts decreased performance on cognitively taxing tasks.

161. **other parts of the brain that are impacted by the pill:** Grams, A. E., Gempt, J., Stahl, A., & Förschler, A. (2010). Female pituitary size in relation to age and hormonal factors. *Neuroendocrinology, 92*(2), 128–132. doi:10.1159/000314196; Pletzer, B., Kronbichler, M., Aichhorn, M., Bergmann, J., Ladurner, G., & Kerschbaum, H. H. (2010). Menstrual cycle and hormonal contraceptive use modulate human brain structure. *Brain Research, 1348*, 55–62. doi:10.1016/j .brainres.2010.06.019; Pletzer, B., Kronbichler, M., & Kerschbaum, H. (2015). Differential effects of androgenic and anti-androgenic progestins on fusiform and frontal gray matter volume and face recognition performance. *Brain Research, 1596*, 108–115. doi:10.1016/j.brainres.2014.11.025; Petersen, N., & Cahill, L. (2015). Amygdala reactivity to negative stimuli is influenced by oral contraceptive use. *Social Cognitive and Affective Neuroscience, 10*(9), 1266–1272. doi:10.1093/scan/nsv010.

161. **onset of depressive symptoms:** Macmaster, F. P., & Kusumakar, V. (2004). Hippocampal volume in early onset depression. *BMC Medicine, 2.* doi:10.1186/1741-7015-2-2.

161. **increase the risk of glucose intolerance:** McCurley, J. L., Mills, P. J., Roesch, S. C., Carnethon, M., Giacinto, R. E., Isasi, C. R., . . . Gallo, L. C. (2015). Chronic stress, inflammation, and glucose regulation in U.S. Hispanics from the HCHS/SOL Sociocultural Ancillary Study. *Psychophysiology, 52*(8), 1071–1079. http://doi .org/10.1111/psyp.12430.

161. **weight gain:** Aschbacher, K., Kornfeld, S., Picard, M., Puterman, E., Havel, P. J., Stanhope, K., Lustig, R. H., & Epel, E. (2014). Chronic stress increases vulnerability to diet-related abdominal fat, oxidative stress, and metabolic risk, *Psychoneuroendocrinology, 46*, 14–22. doi:10.1016/j.psyneuen.2014.04.003.

161. **coronary heart disease:** Castelli, W. P. (1986). The triglyceride issue: A view from Framingham. *American Heart Journal, 112*(2), 432–437.

162. **pill-taking and naturally cycling women listen to a short narrated story:** Nielsen, S. E., Ahmed, I., & Cahill, L. (2014). Postlearning stress differentially affects memory for emotional gist and detail in naturally cycling women and women on hormonal contraceptives. *Behavioral Neuroscience, 128*(4), 482–493. doi:10.1037/a0036687.

163. **known to elicit a strong cortisol surge in healthy adults:** Roney, J. R. (in preparation). Cortisol increases in response to sexual attraction.

166. **contributes to a host of nasty outcomes:** Maes, M., Galecki, P., Chang, Y. S., & Berk, M. (2011). A review on the oxidative and nitrosative stress (O&NS) pathways in major depression and their possible contribution to the (neuro)degenerative processes in that illness. *Progress in Neuro-Psychopharmacology and Biological Psychiatry, 35*(3), 676–692. doi:10.1016/j.pnpbp.2010.05.004; Zunszain, P. A., Anacker, C., Cattaneo, A., Carvalho, L. A., & Pariante, C. M. (2011). Glucocorticoids, cytokines and brain abnormalities in depression. *Progress in Neuro-Psychopharmacology and Biological Psychiatry, 35*(3), 722–729. doi:10.1016/j.pnpbp.2010.04.011.

166. **increase the risk of developing cancer, Alzheimer's, and diseases of autoimmunity:** Tsigos, C., & Chrousos, G. P. (2002). Hypothalamic–pituitary–adrenal axis, neuroendocrine factors and stress. *Journal of Psychosomatic Research, 53*(4), 865–871. doi:10.1016/S0022-3999(02)00429-4; Fries, E., Hesse, J., Hellhammer, J., & Hellhammer, D. H. (2005). A new view on hypocortisolism. *Psychoneuroendocrinology, 30*(10), 1010–1016. doi:10.1016/j.psyneuen.2005.04.006.

166. **key player in this process is cortisol:** Hannibal, K. E., & Bishop, M. D. (2014). Chronic stress, cortisol dysfunction, and pain: A psychoneuroendocrine rationale for stress management in pain rehabilitation. *Physical Therapy, 94*(12), 1816–1825. doi:10.2522/ptj.20130597.

167. **promote dysregulation in the body's inflammatory response:** Tsigos, C., & Chrousos, G. P. (2002). Hypothalamic–pituitary–adrenal axis, neuroendocrine factors and stress. *Journal of Psychosomatic Research, 53*(4), 865–871. doi:10.1016/S0022-3999(02)00429-4; Fries, E., Hesse, J., Hellhammer, J., & Hellhammer, D. H. (2005). A new view on hypocortisolism. *Psychoneuroendocrinology, 30*(10), 1010–1016. doi:10.1016/j.psyneuen.2005.04.006.

167. **contribute to misbehavior on the part of the immune system:** Sørensen, C. J., Pedersen, O. B., Petersen, M. S., Sørensen, E., Kotzé, S., Thørner, L. W., . . .

Erikstrup, C. (2014). Combined oral contraception and obesity are strong predictors of low-grade inflammation in healthy individuals: Results from the Danish Blood Donor Study (DBDS). *PLOS One, 9*(2). doi:10.1371/journal.pone.0088196.

167. **linked to the development of multiple forms of autoimmunity:** Williams, W. V. (2017). Hormonal contraception and the development of autoimmunity: A review of the literature. *Linacre Quarterly, 84*(3), 275–295. doi:10.1080/00243639.2017.1360065.

167. **78 percent of people suffering from autoimmune diseases are women:** Fairweather, D., Frisancho-Kiss, S., & Rose, N. R. (2008). Sex differences in autoimmune disease from a pathological perspective. *American Journal of Pathology, 173*(3), 600–609. http://doi.org/10.2353/ajpath.2008.071008.

CHAPTER 8: WHAT THE FUNK?

174. **intolerable side effects:** Sanders, S. A., Graham, C. A., Bass, J. L., & Bancroft, J. (2001). A prospective study of the effects of oral contraceptives on sexuality and well-being and their relationship to discontinuation. *Contraception, 64*(1), 51–58. doi:10.1016/s0010-7824(01)00218-9.

174. **unpleasant changes in mood:** Gingnell, M., Engman, J., Frick, A., Moby, L., Wikström, J., Fredrikson, M., & Sundström-Poromaa, I. (2013). Oral contraceptive use changes brain activity and mood in women with previous negative affect on the pill: A double-blinded, placebo-controlled randomized trial of a levonorgestrel-containing combined oral contraceptive. *Psychoneuroendocrinology, 38*(7), 1133–1144. doi:10.1016/j.psyneuen.2012.11.006; Sanders, S. A., Graham, C. A., Bass, J. L., & Bancroft, J. (2001). A prospective study of the effects of oral contraceptives on sexuality and well-being and their relationship to discontinuation. *Contraception, 64*(1), 51-58. doi:10.1016/s0010-7824(01)00218-9; Rosenberg, M. J., & Waugh, M. S. (1998). Oral contraceptive discontinuation: A prospective evaluation of frequency and reasons. *American Journal of Obstetrics and Gynecology, 179*(3), 577–582. doi:10.1016/s0002-9378(98)70047-x; Jarva, J. A., & Oinonen, K. A. (2007). Do oral contraceptives act as mood stabilizers? Evidence of positive affect stabilization. *Archives of Women's Mental Health, 10*(5), 225–234. doi:10.1007/s00737-007-0197-5.

174. **Denmark is also home to a number of nationwide registers:** Thygesen, L. C., Daasnes, C., Thaulow, I., & Brønnum-Hansen, H. (2011). Introduction to Danish (nationwide) registers on health and social issues: Structure, access, legislation, and archiving. *Scandinavian Journal of Public Health, 39*(Suppl. 7), 12–16. doi:10.1177/1403494811399956.

175. **patterns of health and social behavior in a *whole population of people*:** Thygesen, L. C., Daasnes, C., Thaulow, I., & Brønnum-Hansen, H. (2011). Introduction to Danish (nationwide) registers on health and social issues: Structure, access,

legislation, and archiving. *Scandinavian Journal of Public Health, 39*(Suppl. 7), 12–16. doi:10.1177/1403494811399956.

175. **prescription and mental health records of these women:** Skovlund, C. W., Mørch, L. S., Kessing, L. V., & Lidegaard, Ø. (2016). Association of hormonal contraception with depression. *JAMA Psychiatry, 73*(11), 1154–1162. doi:10.1001/jamapsychiatry.2016.2387.

178. **can increase some women's risk of depression:** Toffol, E., Heikinheimo, O., Koponen, P., Luoto, R., & Partonen, T. (2011). Hormonal contraception and mental health: Results of a population-based study. *Human Reproduction, 26*(11), 3085–3093. doi:10.1093/humrep/der269; Gingnell, M., Engman, J., Frick, A., Moby, L., Wikström, J., Fredrikson, M., & Sundström-Poromaa, I. (2013). Oral contraceptive use changes brain activity and mood in women with previous negative affect on the pill: A double-blinded, placebo-controlled randomized trial of a levonorgestrel-containing combined oral contraceptive. *Psychoneuroendocrinology, 38*(7), 1133–1144. doi:10.1016/j.psyneuen.2012.11.006.

179. **might also increase women's risk of suicide:** Skovlund, C. W., Mørch, L. S., Kessing, L. V., Lange, T., & Lidegaard, Ø. (2018). Association of hormonal contraception with suicide attempts and suicides. *American Journal of Psychiatry, 175*(4), 336–342. doi:10.1176/appi.ajp.2017.17060616.

181. **known contributor to mental health problems:** Burke, H., Davis, M. C., Otte, C., & Mohr, D. C. (2005). Depression and cortisol responses to psychosocial stress: A meta-analysis. *Psychoneuroendocrinology, 30*, 846–856; Burke, H. M., Fernald, L. C., Gertler, P. J., & Adler, N. E. (2005). Depressive symptoms are associated with blunted cortisol stress response in very low income women. *Psychosomatic Medicine, 67*(6), 211–216.

181. **key player in the development of anxiety and depression:** Ayer, L., Greaves-Lord, K., Althoff, R. R., Hudziak, J. J., Dieleman, G. C., Verhulst, F. C., & Ende, J. V. (2013). Blunted HPA axis response to stress is related to a persistent dysregulation profile in youth. *Biological Psychology, 93*(3), 343–351. doi:10.1016/j.biopsycho.2013.04.002; Aihara, M., Ida, I., Yuuki, N., Oshima, A., Kumano, H., Takahashi, K., . . . Mikuni, M. (2007). HPA axis dysfunction in unmedicated major depressive disorder and its normalization by pharmacotherapy correlates with alteration of neural activity in prefrontal cortex and limbic/paralimbic regions. *Psychiatry Research: Neuroimaging, 155*(3), 245–256. doi:10.1016/j.pscychresns.2006.11.002; Varghese, F. P., & Brown, E. S. (2001). The hypothalamic-pituitary-adrenal axis in major depressive disorder. *Primary Care Companion to the Journal of Clinical Psychiatry, 3*(4), 151–155. doi:10.4088/pcc.v03n0401.

183. **gets released when doing things like meditation and yoga:** Krishnakumar, D., Hamblin, M. R., & Lakshmanan, S. (2015). Meditation and yoga can modulate brain

mechanisms that affect behavior and anxiety: A modern scientific perspective. *Ancient Science, 2*(1), 13. doi:10.14259/as.v2i1.171.

183. **has the effect of kick-starting action by your GABA receptors:** Morrell, M. J. (1999). Epilepsy in women: The science of why it is special. *Neurology, 53*(4), S42–S48; Majewska, M. D. (1987). Steroids and brain activity: Essential dialogue between body and mind. *Biochemical Pharmacology, 36,* 3781–3788.

184. **may have lower levels of these naturally occurring sedatives:** Follesa, P., Porcu, P., Sogliano, C., Cinus, M., Biggio, F., Mancuso, L., . . . Concas, A. (2002). Changes in GABAA receptor γ2 subunit gene expression induced by long-term administration of oral contraceptives in rats. *Neuropharmacology, 42*(3), 325–336. doi:10.1016/ s0028-3908(01)00187-3; Rapkin, A. J., Biggio, G., & Concas, A. (2006). Oral contraceptives and neuroactive steroids. *Pharmacology Biochemistry and Behavior, 84*(4), 628–634. doi:10.1016/j.pbb.2006.06.008.

184. **levels of progesterone's calming derivative, allopregnanolone:** Follesa, P., Porcu, P., Sogliano, C., Cinus, M., Biggio, F., Mancuso, L., . . . Concas, A. (2002). Changes in GABAA receptor γ2 subunit gene expression induced by long-term administration of oral contraceptives in rats. *Neuropharmacology, 42*(3), 325–336. doi:10.1016/s0028-3908(01)00187-3.

184. **blood levels of allopregnanolone were significantly lower:** Paoletti, A. M., Lello, S., Fratta, S., Orrù, M., Ranuzzi, F., Sogliano, C., . . . Melis, G. B. (2004). Psychological effect of the oral contraceptive formulation containing 3 mg of drospirenone plus 30 μg of ethinyl estradiol. *Fertility and Sterility, 81*(3), 645–651. doi:10.1016/j.fertnstert.2003.08.030; Rapkin, A. J., Biggio, G., & Concas, A. (2006). Oral contraceptives and neuroactive steroids. *Pharmacology Biochemistry and Behavior, 84*(4), 628–634. doi:10.1016/j.pbb.2006.06.00.

184. **the brain is usually harder hit than the peripheral blood:** Follesa, P., Porcu, P., Sogliano, C., Cinus, M., Biggio, F., Mancuso, L., . . . Concas, A. (2002). Changes in GABAA receptor γ2 subunit gene expression induced by long-term administration of oral contraceptives in rats. *Neuropharmacology, 42*(3), 325–336. doi:10.1016/s0028-3908(01)00187-3.

185. **mental-health-related issues, including panic disorder:** Hasler, G., Veen, J. W., Geraci, M., Shen, J., Pine, D., & Drevets, W. C. (2009). Prefrontal cortical gamma-aminobutyric acid levels in panic disorder determined by proton magnetic resonance spectroscopy. *Biological Psychiatry, 65*(3), 273–275. doi:10.1016/j .biopsych.2008.06.023.

185. **depression:** Brambilla, P., Perez, J., Barale, F., Schettini, G., & Soares, J. C. (2003). GABAergic dysfunction in mood disorders. *Molecular Psychiatry, 8*(8), 715–715. doi:10.1038/sj.mp.4001395.

185. **bipolar disorder:** Petty, F., & Sherman, A. (1984). Plasma GABA levels in psychiatric illness. *Journal of Affective Disorders, 6*(2), 131–138. doi:10.1016/0165-0327(84)90018-1; Petty, F., Kramer, G. L., Dunnam, D., & Rush, A. J. (1990). Plasma GABA in mood disorders. *Psychopharmacology Bulletin, 26*(2), 157–161; Petty, F., Kramer, G. L., Fulton, M., Moeller, F. G., & Rush, A. J. (1993). Low plasma GABA is a trait-like marker for bipolar illness. *Neuropsychopharmacology, 9*(2), 125–132. doi:10.1038/npp.1993.51.

185. **mood-related symptomology of PMS:** Halbreich, U., Petty, F., Yonkers, K., Kramer, G. L., Rush, A. J., & Bibi, K. W. (1996). Low plasma gamma-aminobutyric acid levels during the late luteal phase of women with premenstrual dysphoric disorder. *American Journal of Psychiatry, 153*(5), 718–720. doi:10.1176/ajp.153.5.718.

185. **can also increase a person's risk of alcohol dependence:** Petty, F., Fulton, M., Moeller, F. G., Kramer, G., Wilson, L., Fraser K. . . . (1993). Plasma gamma-aminobutyric acid (GABA) is low in alcoholics. *Psychopharmacology Bulletin, 29,* 277–281.

185. **Women have one of the fastest-growing rates of alcohol-use disorders:** Grant, B. F., Chou, S. P., Saha, T. D., . . . Hasi, D. S. (2017). Prevalence of 12-month alcohol use, high-risk drinking, and *DSM-IV* Alcohol use disorder in the United States, 2001-2002 to 2012-2013: Results from the National Epidemiologic Survey on Alcohol and Related Conditions. *JAMA Psychiatry, 74*(9): 911–923. doi:10.1001/jamapsychiatry.2017.2161.

186. **estrogen makes rewarding things feel even more rewarding:** Becker, J. B., Robinson, T. E., & Lorenz, K. A. (1982). Sex difference and estrous cycle variations in amphetamine-elicited rotational behavior. *European Journal of Pharmacology, 80*(1), 65–72. doi:10.1016/0014-2999(82)90178-9; Castner, S. A., Xiao, L., & Becker, J. B. (1993). Sex differences in striatal dopamine: In vivo microdialysis and behavioral studies. *Brain Research, 610*(1), 127–134. doi:10.1016/0006-8993(93)91225-h; Hu, M., & Becker, J. B. (2003). Effects of sex and estrogen on behavioral sensitization to cocaine in rats. *Journal of Neuroscience, 23*(2), 693–699. doi:10.1523/jneurosci.23-02-00693.2003; Lynch, W. J., Roth, M. E., Mickelberg, J. L., & Carroll, M. E. (2001). Role of estrogen in the acquisition of intravenously self-administered cocaine in female rats. *Pharmacology Biochemistry and Behavior, 68*(4), 641–646. doi:10.1016/s0091-3057(01)00455-5; Hu, M., Crombag, H. S., Robinson, T. E., & Becker, J. B. (2003). Biological basis of sex differences in the propensity to self-administer cocaine. *Neuropsychopharmacology, 29*(1), 81–85. doi:10.1038/sj.npp.1300301.

186. **progesterone attenuates these effects:** Evans, S. M., & Foltin, R. W. (2006). Exogenous progesterone attenuates the subjective effects of smoked cocaine in women, but not in men. *Neuropsychopharmacology, 31*(3), 659–674. doi:10.1038/sj.npp.1300887.

186. **dampening reward processing in the brain:** Skovlund, C. W., Mørch, L. S., Kessing, L. V., & Lidegaard, Ø. (2016). Association of hormonal contraception with depression. *JAMA Psychiatry, 73*(11), 1154–1162. doi:10.1001/jamapsychiatry.2016.2387.

186. **this makes us feel depressed:** Pizzagalli, D. A. (2014). Depression, stress, and anhedonia: Toward a synthesis and integrated model. *Annual Review of Clinical Psychology, 10,* 393–423. http://doi.org/10.1146/annurev-clinpsy-050212-185606.

186. **blunted positive emotional response to happy things:** Jarva, J. A., & Oinonen, K. A. (2007). Do oral contraceptives act as mood stabilizers? Evidence of positive affect stabilization. *Archives of Women's Mental Health, 10*(5), 225–234. doi:10.1007/s00737-007-0197-5.

186. **don't experience activity in the reward centers of their brains:** Scheele, D., Plota, J., Stoffel-Wagner, B., Maier, W., & Hurlemann, R. (2016). Hormonal contraceptives suppress oxytocin-induced brain reward responses to the partner's face. *Social Cognitive and Affective Neuroscience, 11*(5), 767–774. doi:10.1093/scan/nsv157.

187. **seem to be protected from most of the negative mood problems:** Hamstra, D. A., Kloet, E. R., Tollenaar, M., Verkuil, B., Manai, M., Putman, P., & Does, W. V. (2016). Mineralocorticoid receptor haplotype moderates the effects of oral contraceptives and menstrual cycle on emotional information processing. *Journal of Psychopharmacology, 30*(10), 1054–1061. doi:10.1177/0269881116647504.

187. **history of depression or mental illness:** Desoto, M., Geary, D. C., Hoard, M. K., Sheldon, M. S., & Cooper, L. (2003). Estrogen fluctuations, oral contraceptives and borderline personality. *Psychoneuroendocrinology, 28*(6), 751–766. doi:10.1016/s0306-4530(02)00068-9; Oinonen, K. A., & Mazmanian, D. (2002). To what extent do oral contraceptives influence mood and affect? *Journal of Affective Disorders, 70*(3), 229–240. doi:10.1016/s0165-0327(01)00356-1; Kutner, S. J., & Brown, W. L. (1972). History of depression as a risk factor for depression with oral contraceptives and discontinuance. *Journal of Nervous and Mental Disease, 155*(3), 163–169. doi:10.1097/00005053-197209000-00002.

187. **can stabilize mood in certain women with mental illness:** Rasgon, N., Bauer, M., Glenn, T., Elman, S., & Whybrow, P. C. (2003). Menstrual cycle related mood changes in women with bipolar disorder. *Bipolar Disorders, 5*(1), 48–52. doi:10.1034/j.1399-5618.2003.00010.x.

188. **personal or family history of mood-related side effects on the birth control pill:** Gingnell, M., Engman, J., Frick, A., Moby, L., Wikström, J., Fredrikson, M., & Sundström-Poromaa, I. (2013). Oral contraceptive use changes brain activity and mood in women with previous negative affect on the pill: A double-blinded, placebo-controlled randomized trial of a levonorgestrel-containing combined oral

contraceptive. *Psychoneuroendocrinology, 38*(7), 1133–1144. doi:10.1016/j.psyneuen.2012.11.006.

188. **taking progestin-only pills:** Svendal, G., Berk, M., Pasco, J. A., Jacka, F. N., Lund, A., & Williams, L. J. (2012). The use of hormonal contraceptive agents and mood disorders in women. *Journal of Affective Disorders, 140*(1), 92–96. doi:10.1016/j.jad.2012.03.030; Skovlund, C. W., Mørch, L. S., Kessing, L. V., & Lidegaard, Ø. (2016). Association of hormonal contraception with depression. *JAMA Psychiatry, 73*(11), 1154–1162. doi:10.1001/jamapsychiatry.2016.2387; Toffol, E., Heikinheimo, O., Koponen, P., Luoto, R., & Partonen, T. (2011). Hormonal contraception and mental health: Results of a population-based study. *Human Reproduction, 26*(11), 3085–3093. doi:10.1093/humrep/der269.

188. **using a non-oral product:** Skovlund, C. W., Mørch, L. S., Kessing, L. V., & Lidegaard, Ø. (2016). Association of hormonal contraception with depression. *JAMA Psychiatry, 73*(11), 1154–1162. doi:10.1001/jamapsychiatry.2016.2387.

188. **taking multi-phasic pills:** Bäckström, T., Hansson-Malmström, Y., Lindhe, B., Cavalli-Björkman, B., & Nordenström, S. (1992). Oral contraceptives in premenstrual syndrome: A randomized comparison of triphasic and monophasic preparations. *Contraception, 46*(3), 253–268. doi:10.1016/0010-7824(92)90006-f; Bancroft, J., Sanders, D., Warner, P., & Loudon, N. (1987). The effects of oral contraceptives on mood and sexuality: A comparison of triphasic and combined preparations. *Journal of Psychosomatic Obstetrics and Gynecology, 7*(1), 1–8. doi:10.3109/01674828709019585.

188. **You are nineteen or younger:** Skovlund, C. W., Mørch, L. S., Kessing, L. V., & Lidegaard, Ø. (2016). Association of hormonal contraception with depression. *JAMA Psychiatry, 73*(11), 1154–1162. doi:10.1001/jamapsychiatry.2016.2387.

188–89. **women's quality-of-life scores . . . were significantly higher:** Ernst, U., Baumgartner, L., Bauer, U., & Janssen, G. (2002). Improvement of quality of life in women using a low-dose desogestrel-containing contraceptive: Results of an observational clinical evaluation. *European Journal of Contraception and Reproductive Health Care, 7*(4), 238–243. doi:10.1080/ejc.7.4.238.243.

189. **pills containing the fourth-generation progestin drospirenone:** Poromaa, I. S., & Segebladh, B. (2012). Adverse mood symptoms with oral contraceptives. *Acta Obstetricia et Gynecologica Scandinavica, 91*(4), 420–427. doi:10.1111/j.1600--0412.2011.01333.x; Freeman, E. W., Kroll, R., Rapkin, A., Pearlstein, T., Brown, C., Parsey, K., . . . Foegh, M. (2001). Evaluation of a unique oral contraceptive in the treatment of premenstrual dysphoric disorder. *Journal of Women's Health and Gender-Based Medicine, 10*(6), 561–569. doi:10.1089/15246090152543148; Parsey, K. S., & Pong, A. (2000). An open-label, multicenter study to evaluate Yasmin, a low-dose combination oral contraceptive containing drospirenone, a new progestogen. *Contraception, 61*(2), 105–111. doi:10.1016/s0010-7824(00)00083-4; Sillem, M.,

Schneidereit, R., Heithecker, R., & Mueck, A. O. (2009). Use of an oral contraceptive containing drospirenone in an extended regimen. *European Journal of Contraception and Reproductive Health Care, 8*(3), 162–169. doi:10.1080/ejc.8.3.162.169; Apter, D., Borsos, A., Baumgärtner, W., Melis, G. B., Vexiau-Robert, D., Colligs-Hakert, A., . . . Kelly, S. (2003). Effect of an oral contraceptive containing drospirenone and ethinylestradiol on general well-being and fluid-related symptoms. *European Journal of Contraception and Reproductive Health Care, 8*(1), 37–51. doi:10.1080/713604397.

189. **third-generation progestin gestondene:** Deijen, J., Duyn, K., Jansen, W., & Klitsie, J. (1992). Use of a monophasic, low-dose oral contraceptive in relation to mental functioning. *Contraception, 46*(4), 359–367. doi:10.1016/0010-7824(92)90098-e.

189. **pills may improve mood and decrease irritability:** Schultz-Zehden, B., & Boschitsch, E. (2006). User experience with an oral contraceptive containing ethinylestradiol 30μg30 and drospirenone 3mg (Yasmin®) in clinical practice. *Treatments in Endocrinology, 5*(4), 251–256. doi:10.2165/00024677-200605040-00006; Short, M. (2009). User satisfaction with the combined oral contraceptive drospirenone 3 mg/ethinylestradiol 20 μg (Yasminelle®) in clinical practice. *Clinical Drug Investigation, 29*(3), 153–159. doi:10.2165/00044011-200929030-00002.

189. **mood-stabilizing benefits to women who have severe PMS:** Cheslack-Postava, K., Keyes, K. M., Lowe, S. R., & Koenen, K. C. (2015). Oral contraceptive use and psychiatric disorders in a nationally representative sample of women. *Archives of Women's Mental Health, 18*(1), 103–111. doi:10.1007/s00737-014-0453-4; Lopez, L., Kaptein, A., & Helmerhorst, F. (2012). Oral contraceptives containing drospirenone for premenstrual syndrome. *Cochrane Database of Systematic Reviews*. doi:10.1002/14651858.cd006586.

189. **be more at risk for negative mood changes on the pill:** Oinonen, K. A., & Mazmanian, D. (2002). To what extent do oral contraceptives influence mood and affect? *Journal of Affective Disorders, 70*(3), 229–240. doi:10.1016/s0165-0327(01)00356-1.

189. **pill can be a godsend for women who have PMS:** Apter, D., Borsos, A., Baumgärtner, W., Melis, G. B., Vexiau-Robert, D., Colligs-Hakert, A., . . . Kelly, S. (2003). Effect of an oral contraceptive containing drospirenone and ethinylestradiol on general well-being and fluid-related symptoms. *European Journal of Contraception and Reproductive Health Care, 8*(1), 37–51. doi:10.1080/713604397; Chiou, C., Trussell, J., Reyes, E., Knight, K., Wallace, J., Udani, J., . . . Borenstein, J. (2003). Economic analysis of contraceptives for women. *Contraception, 68*(1), 3–10. doi:10.1016/s0010-7824(03)00078-7; Freeman, E. W., Rickels, K., Sondheimer, S. J., & Polansky, M. (2001). Concurrent use of oral contraceptives with antidepressants for

premenstrual syndromes. *Journal of Clinical Psychopharmacology, 21*(5), 540–542. doi:10.1097/00004714-200110000-00018; Schultz-Zehden, B., & Boschitsch, E. (2006). User experience with an oral contraceptive containing ethinylestradiol 30μg 30and drospirenone 3mg (Yasmin®) in clinical practice. *Treatments in Endocrinology, 5*(4), 251–256. doi:10.2165/00024677-200605040-00006; Short, M. (2009). User satisfaction with the combined oral contraceptive drospirenone 3 mg/ethinylestradiol 20 μg (Yasminelle®) in clinical practice. *Clinical Drug Investigation, 29*(3), 153–159. doi:10.2165/00044011-200929030-00002.

189. **can even alleviate symptoms of premenstrual dysphoric disorder:** Lopez, L., Kaptein, A., & Helmerhorst, F. (2012). Oral contraceptives containing drospirenone for premenstrual syndrome. *Cochrane Database of Systematic Reviews.* doi:10.1002/14651858.cd006586. Cheslack-Postava, K., Keyes, K. M., Lowe, S. R., & Koenen, K. C. (2015). Oral contraceptive use and psychiatric disorders in a nationally representative sample of women. *Archives of Women's Mental Health, 18*(1), 103–111. doi:10.1007/s00737-014-0453-4.

189. **abnormal physiological responses to changing levels of hormones:** Kurshan, N., & Epperson, C. N. (2006). Oral contraceptives and mood in women with and without premenstrual dysphoria: A theoretical model. *Archives of Women's Mental Health, 9*(1), 1–14. doi:10.1007/s00737-005-0102-z; Genazzani, A. R., Stomati, M., Morittu, A., Bernardi, F., Monteleone, P., Casarosa, E., . . . Luisi, M. (2000). Progesterone, progestagens and the central nervous system. *Human Reproduction, 15*(Suppl. 1), 14–27. doi:10.1093/humrep/15.suppl_1.14; Rapkin, A., Morgan, M., Goldman, L., Brann, D., Simone, D., & Mahesh, V. (1997). Progesterone metabolite allopregnanolone in women with premenstrual syndrome. *Obstetrics and Gynecology, 90*(5), 709–714. doi:10.1016/s0029-7844(97)00417-1; Sundström, I., Andersson, A., Nyberg, S., Ashbrook, D., Purdy, R. H., & Bäckström, T. (1998). Patients with premenstrual syndrome have a different sensitivity to a neuroactive steroid during the menstrual cycle compared to control subjects. *Neuroendocrinology, 67*(2), 126–138. doi:10.1159/000054307.

189. **The pill irons out all the hormonal fluctuations:** Abraham, S., Luscombe, G., & Soo, I. (2003). Oral contraception and cyclic changes in premenstrual and menstrual experiences. *Journal of Psychosomatic Obstetrics and Gynecology, 24*(3), 185–193. doi:10.3109/01674820309039672; Bäckström, T., Hansson-Malmström, Y., Lindhe, B., Cavalli-Björkman, B., & Nordenström, S. (1992). Oral contraceptives in premenstrual syndrome: A randomized comparison of triphasic and monophasic preparations. *Contraception, 46*(3), 253–268. doi:10.1016/0010-7824(92)90006-f; Svendal, G., Berk, M., Pasco, J. A., Jacka, F. N., Lund, A., & Williams, L. J. (2012). The use of hormonal contraceptive agents and mood disorders in women. *Journal of Affective Disorders, 140*(1), 92–96. doi:10.1016/j.jad.2012.03.030; Oinonen, K. A., & Mazmanian, D. (2002). To what extent do oral contraceptives influence mood and affect? *Journal of Affective Disorders, 70*(3), 229–240. doi:10.1016/s0165-0327(01)00356-1.

CHAPTER 9: THE LAW OF UNINTENDED CONSEQUENCES

196. **changes how our digestive system works:** Khalili, H., Granath, F., Smedby, K. E., Ekbom, A., Neovius, M., Chan, A. T., & Olen, O. (2016). Association between long-term oral contraceptive use and risk of Crohn's disease complications in a nationwide study. *Gastroenterology, 150*(7), 1561–1567.e1. http://doi.org/10.1053/j .gastro.2016.02.041; Khalili, H., Higuchi, L. M., Ananthakrishnan, A. N., Richter, J. M., Feskanich, D., Fuchs, C. C., & Chan, A. T. (2013). Oral contraceptives, reproductive factors and risk of inflammatory bowel disease. *Gut, 62*(8), 1153–1159. http://doi.org/10.1136/gutjnl-2012-302362.

196. **what our microbiomes look like:** Falony, G., Joossens, M., Vieira-Silva, S., Wang, J., Darzi, Y., Faust, K., . . . Raes, J. (2016). Population-level analysis of gut microbiome variation. *Science, 352*(6285), 560–564. doi:10.1126/science.aad3503.

196. **how our immune system functions:** Fichorova, R. N., Chen, P., Morrison, C. S., Doncel, G. F., Mendonca, K., Kwok, C., . . . Mauck, C. (2015). The contribution of cervicovaginal infections to the immunomodulatory effects of hormonal contraception. *mBio, 6*(5). doi:10.1128/mbio.00221-15.

196. **what our other endocrine organs do:** Kudielka, B., Buske-Kirschbaum, A., Hellhammer, D., & Kirschbaum, C. (2004). HPA axis responses to laboratory psychosocial stress in healthy elderly adults, younger adults, and children: Impact of age and gender. *Psychoneuroendocrinology, 29*(1), 83–98. doi:10.1016/s0306-4530(02)00146-4.

196. **how our metabolism operates:** Wiegratz, I., Lee, J., Kutschera, E., Bauer, H., Hayn, C. V., Moore, C., . . . Kuhl, H. (2002). Effect of dienogest-containing oral contraceptives on lipid metabolism. *Contraception, 65*(3), 223–229. doi:10.1016/s0010-7824(01)00310-9.

197. **more than 56 percent of college students on U.S. campuses were women:** U.S. Department of Education, National Center for Education Statistics, National Center for Education Statistics, Higher Education General Information Survey, & Institute of Education Sciences. (2017). Table 303.70: Total undergraduate fall enrollment in degree-granting postsecondary institutions, by attendance status, sex of student, and control and level of institution: Selected years, 1970 through 2026. In U.S. Department of Education, National Center for Education Statistics (Ed.), *Digest of Education Statistics* (2017 ed.). Retrieved from https://nces.ed.gov/programs/digest /d16/tables/dt16_303.70.asp

197. **37.5 percent of women between the ages of twenty-five and thirty-four had a college degree:** U.S. Census Bureau. (2016). Educational attainment in the United States: 2015. Retrieved from https://www.census.gov/content/dam/Census/library /publications/2016/demo/p20-578.pdf

198. **only about 10 percent of women aged twenty-six to twenty-eight had completed a college degree:** U.S. Census Bureau. (2017). Percentage of the U.S. population who have completed four years of college or more from 1940 to 2017, by gender. Retrieved from https://www.statista.com/statistics/184272/educational-attainment-of-college-diploma-or-higher-by-gender/

199. **when the pill became legally available to single women:** Figure interpreted from research presented in Goldin, C., & Katz, L. (2000). The power of the pill: Oral contraceptives and women's career and marriage decisions. *Journal of Political Economy, 110*(4), 730–770. doi:10.3386/w7527.

200. **huge surge in the number of female applicants:** Goldin, C., & Katz, L. (2000). The power of the pill: oral contraceptives and women's career and marriage decisions. *Journal of Political Economy, 110*(4), 730–770. doi:10.3386/w7527.

200. **Women responded to the freedom granted to them by the pill:** Aud, S., KewalRamani, A., and Frohlich, L. (2011). America's youth: Transitions to adulthood (NCES 2012-026). U.S. Department of Education, National Center for Education Statistics. Washington, D.C.: U.S. Government Printing Office.

202. **dictate the conditions that need to be met for sex to occur:** Baumeister, R. F., & Vohs, K. D. (2004). Sexual economics: Sex as female resource for social exchange in heterosexual interactions. *Personality and Social Psychology Review, 8*(4), 339–363. doi:10.1207/s15327957pspr0804_2.

203. **women are now having more sex:** Regnerus, M. (2017). *Cheap sex: The transformation of men, marriage, and monogamy.* New York: Oxford University Press.

204. **may have the opposite effect on men:** Aud, S., KewalRamani, A., and Frohlich, L. (2011). America's youth: Transitions to adulthood (NCES 2012–026). U.S. Department of Education, National Center for Education Statistics. Washington, D.C.: U.S. Government Printing Office.

204. **Men who believed that women's standards were high outperformed:** Schad, S. E., Henderson, M., Snell, E. G., Proffitt Leyva, R. P., & Hill, S. E. (January 2017). Understanding the growing achievement gap between the sexes: The power of mating on persistence and motivation. Poster presented at the annual meeting of the Society for Personality and Social Psychology, San Antonio, Texas.

205. **the majority of college students were men:** Freeman, C. E. 2004. *Trends in the educational equity of girls and women.* Washington, D.C.: National Center for Education Statistics.

205. **that number dropped to 44 percent:** U.S. Department of Education, National Center for Education Statistics, National Center for Education Statistics, Higher Education General Information Survey, & Institute of Education Sciences. (2017). Table 303.70: Total undergraduate fall enrollment in degree-granting postsecondary

institutions, by attendance status, sex of student, and control and level of institution: Selected years, 1970 through 2026. In U.S. Department of Education, National Center for Education Statistics (Ed.), *Digest of Education Statistics* (2017 ed.). Retrieved from https://nces.ed.gov/programs/digest/d16/tables/dt16_303.70.asp

205. **Women are also staying in college longer:** Bae, Y., Choy, S., Geddes, C., Sable, J., & Snyder, T. (2000). *Trends in educational equity of girls and women.* Washington, D.C.: National Center for Education Statistics.

205. **Men also have a higher unemployment rate:** Bureau of Labor Statistics, U.S. Department of Labor, & the *Economics Daily* (2013). July unemployment rates: adult men, 7.0 percent; adult women, 6.5 percent; teens, 23.7 percent. In Bureau of Labor Statistics, *Economics Daily* (2013 ed.). Retrieved from https://www.bls.gov/opub/ted/2013/ted_20130806.htm.

206. **When men are able to gain access to women:** Regnerus, M. (2017). *Cheap sex: The transformation of men, marriage, and monogamy.* New York: Oxford University Press; Baumeister, R. F., & Vohs, K. D. (2004). Sexual Economics: Sex as Female Resource for Social Exchange in Heterosexual Interactions. *Personality and Social Psychology Review, 8*(4), 339–363. https://doi.org/10.1207/s15327957pspr0804_2.

206. **men will do whatever is required in order to obtain sex:** Baumeister, R. F., & Vohs, K. D. (2012). Sexual economics, culture, men, and modern sexual trends. *Society, 49*(6), 521. doi:10.1007/s12115-012-9596-y.

207. **72 percent of all adults eighteen and older had already taken the plunge:** Pew research center analysis of decennial census (1960–2000) and American Community Survey data (2008, 2010), IPUMS.

208. **people aren't getting married until they're around twenty-seven:** U.S. Census Bureau. (2016). Table MS-2: Estimated median age at first marriage, by sex: 1890 to the present. Retrieved from https://www.census.gov/data/tables/time-series/demo/families/marital.html

208. **only about half of those who are eighteen or older have made the choice:** Pew research center analysis of 1960–2000 decennial census (2006–2015), American Community Surveys, IPUMS, and U.S. Census Bureau's 2016 American Community Survey 1-Year estimates.

208. **has bifurcated the mating market into two distinct marketplaces:** Reichert, T. (2010). Bitter pill. *First Things: A Monthly Journal of Religion and Public Life, 203,* 25–34.

209. **As chronicled in Rebecca Traister's:** Traister, R. (2018). *All the single ladies: Unmarried women and the rise of an independent nation.* New York: Simon & Schuster.

209. **a choice that a growing number of women are making:** U.S. Census Bureau. (2017). Profile America Facts for Features: Unmarried and Single Americans Week.

Retrieved from https://www.census.gov/content/dam/Census/newsroom/facts-for
-features/2017/cb17-ff16.pdf

209. **single women outnumber married women:** Traister, R. (2018). *All the single ladies: Unmarried women and the rise of an independent nation.* New York: Simon & Schuster.

209. **adults under thirty-four who have never been married is up to 46 percent:** Mather, M. and Lavery, D. (2010) In U.S., proportion married at lowest recorded levels. *Population Reference Bureau.* Retrieved from https://www.prb.org /usmarriagedecline/

209–10. **right around the time when we finally have our sh** together at thirty-five:** U.S. Census Bureau. (2016). Table MS-2: Estimated median age at first marriage, by sex: 1890 to the present. Retrieved from https://www.census.gov/data/tables/ time-series/demo/families/marital.html

210. **majority of women in the United States still wait until after marriage to have kids:** Martin, J. A., Hamilton, B. E., Osterman, M. K., Driscoll, A. K., & Drake, P. (2018). Births: Final data for 2016. *National Vital Statistics Reports: From the Centers for Disease Control and Prevention, National Center for Health Statistics, National Vital Statistics System, 67*(1), 1–55.

210. **there are now more women in their thirties having babies:** Stobbe, M. (2017, May). Correction: US births and deaths story. Retrieved from https://www.apnews .com/cfed1e4019b545c19589c5a372257735?utm_campaign=SocialFlow&utm_source =Twitter&utm_medium=AP

210. **infertility-treatment business has quadrupled in the past twenty-five years:** Marketdata Enterprises. (2013, November). *U.S. fertility clinics and infertility services market worth $3.5 billion. recession is not a factor* [Press release]. Retrieved from https:// www.marketdataenterprises.com/wp-content/uploads/2014/01/Fertility Clinics PR 2013.pdf

211. **some debate in the literature about the reliability of these effects:** Havlíček, J., & Roberts, S. C. (2009). MHC-correlated mate choice in humans: A review. *Psychoneuroendocrinology, 34*(4), 497–512. doi:10.1016/j.psyneuen.2008.10.007.

211. **prefer the scent of men whose immune genes are dissimilar to their own:** Wedekind, C., Seebeck, T., Bettens, F., & Paepke, A. J. (1995). MHC-dependent mate preferences in humans. *Proceedings of the Royal Society B: Biological Sciences, 260*(1359), 245–249. doi:10.1098/rspb.1995.0087; Ober, C., Weitkamp, L. R., Cox, N., Dytch, H., Kostyu, D., & Elias, S. (1997). HLA and mate choice in humans. *American Journal of Human Genetics, 61*(3), 497–504. doi:10.1086/515511; Winternitz, J., Abbate, J. L., Huchard, E., Havlíček, J., & Garamszegi, L. Z. (2017). Patterns of MHC-dependent mate selection in humans and nonhuman primates: a meta-analysis. *Molecular Ecology, 26*(2), 668–688. doi:10.1111/mec.13920.

211. **don't seem to pick up on these scent-based cues:** Roberts, S. C., Gosling, L. M., Carter, V., & Petrie, M. (2008). MHC-correlated odour preferences in humans and the use of oral contraceptives. *Proceedings of the Royal Society B: Biological Sciences, 275*(1652), 2715–2722. doi:10.1098/rspb.2008.0825; Wedekind, C., Seebeck, T., Bettens, F., & Paepke, A. J. (1995). MHC-dependent mate preferences in humans. *Proceedings of the Royal Society B: Biological Sciences, 260*(1359), 245–249. doi:10.1098/rspb.1995.0087.

211. **choose men with *non*-complementary immune genes:** Roberts, S. C., Gosling, L. M., Carter, V., & Petrie, M. (2008). MHC-correlated odour preferences in humans and the use of oral contraceptives. *Proceedings of the Royal Society B: Biological Sciences, 275*(1652), 2715–2722. doi:10.1098/rspb.2008.0825.

211. **higher-than-average levels of genetic similarity in immune genes:** Komlos, L., Zamir, R., Joshua, H., & Halbrecht, I. (1977). Common HLA antigens in couples with repeated abortions. *Clinical Immunology and Immunopathology, 7*(3), 330–335. doi:10.1016/0090-1229(77)90066-6; Reznikoff-Etievant, M. F. (1988). Abortions of immunologic origin. *Reproduction, Nutrition, Development, 28*(6B), 1615–1627.

212. **pattern is also observed in nonhuman primates:** Schwensow, N., Eberle, M., & Sommer, S. (2008). Compatibility counts: MHC-associated mate choice in a wild promiscuous primate. *Proceedings of the Royal Society B: Biological Sciences, 275*(1634), 555–564. doi:10.1098/rspb.2007.1433.

CHAPTER 10: WHY DIDN'T I KNOW THIS ALREADY?

214. **story of gender in the United States and around the rest of the world:** Dusenbery, M. (2018, March). Medicine has a sexism problem, and it's making sick women sicker. Retrieved from https://www.huffingtonpost.com/entry/opinion-dusenbery-medical-sexism-research_us_5a9e01c4e4b0a0ba4ad72a3c

215. **research that was done in a sample that was 80 percent male:** Nieuwenhoven, L., & Klinge, I. (2010). Scientific excellence in applying sex- and gender-sensitive methods in biomedical and health research. *Journal of Women's Health, 19*(2), 313–321. doi:10.1089/jwh.2008.1156.

215. **it makes it harder for women's bodies to stop bleeding:** Howard, J. (2014). *Brigham and Women's Hospital Summer 2014.* Boston: Brigham Health.

215. **women make up only 19 percent of the participants in clinical trials:** Curno, M. J., Rossi, S., Hodges-Mameletzis, I., Johnston, R., Price, M. A., & Heidari, S. (2016). A systematic review of the inclusion (or exclusion) of women in HIV research. *JAIDS Journal of Acquired Immune Deficiency Syndromes, 71*(2), 181–188. doi:10.1097/qai.0000000000000842.

215. **eight out of ten prescription drugs (80 percent) were withdrawn from the U.S. market:** Simon, V. (2005). Wanted: Women in clinical trials. *Science, 308*(5728), 1517–1517. doi:10.1126/science.1115616.

217. **less than a quarter of these jobs are the kinds of research positions:** National Science Foundation, National Science Board, National Center for Science and Engineering Statistics. (2016). Science and Engineering Indicators 2016. Retrieved from https://www.nsf.gov/statistics/2016/nsb20161/#/report

220. **biomedical research using females as participants has to account for cycle phase:** Anthony, M., & Berg, M. J. (2002). Biologic and molecular mechanisms for sex differences in pharmacokinetics, pharmacodynamics and pharmacogenetics: Part I. *Journal of Women's Health and Gender-Based Medicine, 11*(7), 601-615. doi:10.1089/152460902760360559.

220. **can easily triple the amount of time and money it takes to answer a research question:** Brown, C., & Lloyd, K. (2001). Qualitative methods in psychiatric research. *Advances in Psychiatric Treatment, 7*(5), 350–356. doi:10.1192/apt.7.5.350.

220. **relationship between immune function and decision-making in women and men:** Gassen, J., . . . Boehm, G. W., & Hill, S. E. (under review). Inflammation predicts decision-making characterized by impulsivity, present focus, and an inability to delay gratification.

222. **included data** *only* **on men:** Rossman, I. (1986). Normal human aging: The Baltimore Longitudinal Study of Aging. *JAMA, 255*(7), 960. doi:10.1001/jama.1986.03370070114046.

223. **including preclinical research:** Shah, K., McCormack, C. E., & Bradbury, N. A. (2014). Do you know the sex of your cells? *American Journal of Physiology: Cell Physiology, 306*(1),C3–18. doi: 10.1152/ajpcell.00281.2013.

224. **the overwhelming majority of this research has been done using only male animals:** Beery, A. K., & Zucker, I. (2011). Sex bias in neuroscience and biomedical research. *Neuroscience and Biobehavioral Reviews, 35*(3), 565–572. doi:10.1016/j.neubiorev.2010.07.002.

225. **will no longer fund clinical trials involving humans that do not include women:** Schiebinger, L., Leopold, S. S., & Miller, V. M. (2016). Editorial policies for sex and gender analysis. *The Lancet, 388*(10062), 2841–2842. doi:10.1016/s0140-6736(16)32392-3.

225. **NIH has new policies to increase the inclusion of female animals:** Clayton, J. A., & Collins, F. S. (2014). Policy: NIH to balance sex in cell and animal studies. *Nature, 509*(7500), 282–283. doi:10.1038/509282a.

225. **research journals still don't require researchers to use females:** Gahagan, J., Gray, K., & Whynacht, A. (2015). Sex and gender matter in health research:

Addressing health inequities in health research reporting. *International Journal for Equity in Health, 14*(1), 12. doi:10.1186/s12939-015-0144-4.

233. **Schedule III controlled substance:** Hirby, J. (n.d.). Why are steroids illegal? Retrieved from https://thelawdictionary.org/article/why-are-steroids-illegal/

CHAPTER 11: WHAT NOW? A LETTER TO MY DAUGHTER

238. **The brain changes, too:** Blakemore, S., Burnett, S., & Dahl, R. E. (2010). The role of puberty in the developing adolescent brain. *Human Brain Mapping, 31*(6), 926–933. doi:10.1002/hbm.21052.

238. **your sex hormones are the head contractor:** Cahill, L. (2006). Why sex matters for neuroscience. *Nature Reviews Neuroscience, 7*(6), 477–484. doi:10.1038/nrn1909; Shirtcliff, E. A., Dahl, R. E., & Pollak, S. D. (2009). Pubertal development: Correspondence between hormonal and physical development. *Child Development, 80*(2), 327–337. doi:10.1111/j.1467-8624.2009.01263; Sisk, C. L., & Foster, D. L. (2004). The neural basis of puberty and adolescence. *Nature Neuroscience, 7*(10), 1040–1047. doi:10.1038/nn1326.

238. **brain usually isn't done developing until we're in our early to mid-twenties:** Johnson, S. B., Blum, R. W., & Giedd, J. N. (2009). Adolescent maturity and the brain: The promise and pitfalls of neuroscience research in adolescent health policy. *Journal of Adolescent Health, 45*(3), 216–221. http://doi.org/10.1016/j.jadohealth.2009.05.016.

239. **the age of twenty or older is one way to significantly reduce the likelihood:** Skovlund, C. W., Mørch, L. S., Kessing, L. V., Lange, T., & Lidegaard, Ø. (2018). Association of hormonal contraception with suicide attempts and suicides. *American Journal of Psychiatry, 175*(4), 336–342. doi:10.1176/appi.ajp.2017.17060616.

Index

Italic *n* indicates footnote

baboons, 65

bad boys, 59–60

Baumeister, Roy, 206, 206*n*

beautification effort, 128–29

behavior(s)

  flirting, 59–60, 63–64, 137

  hormones and, 6, 49, 55–56, 81,
    90–91

  mate guarding, 139–40, 140*n*

  risk-taking, 23, 23*n*

  sexual, 23, 23*n*, 44–45, 53–56, 136

  as testosterone markers, 101–2

  weight gain and, 90–92

benzodiazepines, 183

binge-eating disorder, 173

birth control, politics of, 228–29

birth control pill(s)

  achievement gap and, 196–201

  allopregnanolone and, 136

  brain fog and, 161

  continued effects of, 155–56

  courtship cues and, 129–30

  critical thinking about, 230–34

  decision to use, 235–49

  depression and, 169, 173

  effects of, 10, 236

  facilitating sex, 121

  first-generation, 82, 84, 141

  fourth-generation, 83–85, 133*n*,
    136, 189

  helping mood disorders, 247–48

  how you feel on, 247–48

  interdependent systems and, 195–96

  marital satisfaction and, 109

  masculinizing effects of, 81, 84

  meta-issues with, 10

  mimicking late cycle phase, 78

  minimum age for starting, 238–39,
    238*n*–39*n*

  mood and, 170–74

  partner selection and, 102–4, 117–19

  psychotic episodes and, 86

  reducing sex drive, 123, 125, 132

  second-generation, 78, 82–85, 133*n*

  side effects of, 88–90

  social and economic impacts of, 212

  taking breaks from, 246–47

  testosterone and, 133–34

  third-generation, 83–85, 133*n*, 188–89

  trying different varieties of, 84–86, 171,
    190–91, 245

  weight gain and, 89–92, 161

  See also hormonal contraceptives

black lemur, 84

blame, 230–34

bloating, 189

blood

  cortisol in, 152, 152*n*

  lipids in, 88, 158, 161

  sugars in, 153*n*, 161

blood clots, 88, 246

bonding

  oxytocin and, 134–35

  pair, 46, 55

Bradshaw, Hannah, 161

brain

  allopregnanolone in, 136

  attention and, 230–31

  cortisol and, 149–51

  developing, 238–39

  estrogen and, 115–16

  evolution of, 24–25

  hormone receptors in, 42

  in HPG axis, 75–76

mind and, 34–35
 reward center in, 134–35, 185–86
brain fog, 161
brain-volume loss, 159
bulimia, 173

casual sex, 18–19, 23, 23*n*, 61
cats, 65
CBGs. *See* corticosteroid-binding
 globulins
cell lines, 8, 8*n*, 223*n*
cell surface markers, 101–2, 101*n*
cervical caps, 240
Cheap Sex (Regnerus), 206*n*
cheating, 62–63
childbearing, delay of, 118, 210
childbirth, 32
child care, 46–47
children
 genetic benefits for, 57
 health problems in, 117–18
 paternal investment in, 61
chimpanzees, 123*n*, 138–39
chronic stress, 158–59. *See also* stress
circadian rhythm, 155
cocaine, 186*n*
college education, 196–201, 205
commitment, 60
conception, 50–51, 50*n*, 53, 60,
 78
conception (follicular) phase, 50–51, 78,
 92, 103
condoms, 240
congenital androgen insensitivity
 syndrome, 237–38
consequentiality, 123
copper IUDs, 177–78, 240

coronary heart disease, 161
corpus luteum, 50
corticosteroid-binding globulins (CBGs),
 153, 156–58
corticotropin-releasing hormone (CRH),
 149–51, 153, 157–58
cortisol
 daily rhythm of, 155
 elevating fat and sugar levels, 161
 the pill and, 146–47, 156–58
 process of releasing, 149–51
 sexual attraction and, 163
 See also stress response
cortisol signaling, 153, 158–60
courtship, 19, 129–30. *See also* partner
 selection
crazy feeling, 170*n*, 171–73
creativity, 129
CRH. *See* corticotropin-releasing
 hormone
cues
 in courtship, 128–29
 of fertility status, 67–70
 of high genetic quality, 61, 116
 scents as, 58, 67–70, 111–13,
 141–44, 211
 that children resemble parents, 22–23
cycle phases
 conception, 50–51, 78, 91, 103
 coordination of, 75–76
 dividing cycle into 2 to 4 phases, 222*n*
 follicular (Day 1), 50–51, 78, 91, 103
 food intake by, 90–91
 luteal (Days 20–22), 49, 92, 102,
 112–13, 189
 mid-cycle, 101–2, 137
 ovulation in, 78

in ovulatory cycle, 50–51

reward processing and, 185–86

as 17-beta estradiol, 41*n*

sexual desire and, 53–56, 65

synthetic, 79, 83–84

types of, 41*n*

See also pre-ovulatory estrogen surge

estrone, 41*n*

ethinyl estradiol (EE), 80, 82, 85, 133*n*, 136, 176–77, 184, 188

etonogestrel, 96, 177

evolution

of men's brains, 17, 202

of women's brains, 17

women viewed in light of, 23–26

See also natural selection

evolutionary benefits, 56–57, 62

evolutionary fitness, 56–57, 62

excitatory neurotransmitters, 182

exercise, HPA-axis response to, 155

faces

of children resembling parents, 22–23

erotica and, 125–26

of fertile women, 67, 103

masculine, 58–60, 102–4

men looking at, 125–26

of partners, 103–4, 134–35

responses to, 135*n*

symmetrical, 57–58, 61, 101

family history

of alcoholism, 185

of depression, 135, 187–88, 239

of mood disorders, 188, 239

fatigue, 189

feedback loops, 77–78, 239

female cell lines, 8, 8*n*, 223*n*

feminists and feminism

hormones and, 44–48

women's biology and, 25–26

fertility

concealed status of, 65–70

control over, 226–27, 232–34

politicization of, 227–30

sensory acuity and, 116, 116*n*

sex in time of, 52–56

status of rivals', 64

See also high fertility; low fertility

fertility-tracking apps, 240

fertilization, 27, 53, 78

fertilized egg, 29–31, 29*n*, 50–51

fight-or-flight response, 149

financial security, 105, 107–8, 120, 209

first-generation pills, 82, 84, 141

fish with three genders, 39–40

fitness benefits, 56–57, 62

flirting, 59–60, 63–64, 137

follicles, 50, 50*n*, 77

follicle-stimulating hormone (FSH), 76–77, 78–79

follicular (conception) phase, 50–51, 78, 91, 103

food intake, 90–91

fourth-generation pills, 83–85, 133*n*, 136, 189

free T, 132–33. *See also* testosterone

FSH. *See* follicle-stimulating hormone

GABA. *See* gamma-aminobutyric acid (GABA)

GABAergic system, 184–85, 184*n*, 246

HPG. *See* hypothalamic-
pituitary-gonadal axis
human chorionic gonadotropin (hCG),
31–32
hypothalamic-pituitary-adrenal (HPA) axis
chronic activation of, 152–53
coordinating ovulatory cycles, 75–76
exercise response and, 155
feedback loops in, 77–78
mood and, 155–59, 181–82
Pacific salmon and, 152n
pill-taking women and, 153–56
primary hormones of, 151
signaling of, 149–50
hypothalamic-pituitary-gonadal
(HPG) axis
components of, 75–78
development of, 239–40
preventing cascade of, 82, 84, 237
hypothalamus, 76–77, 76n, 149–51, 153
hysteria, 226

The Immortal Life of Henrietta Lacks
(Skloot), 8n
immune system
attacking embryo, 220
partner compatability and, 101–2,
101n–2n, 211–12
implantation, 29–31, 29n, 50–51. *See also*
embryo
implantation (luteal) phase, 49, 91, 102,
112–13, 189
Indian flying fox (*Pteropus giganteus*), 69
indirect fitness benefits, 57, 62
infertility, 209–13
infertility-treatment business, 210
inflammation, 166–67

inhibitory neurotransmitters, 182
interdependence
of all people, 212–13
in nature, 195–96
IUDs, 177–78, 240

jealousy, 139–40
journal, 190–91, 243–45

karyotype, 237–38
Keith Richards effect, 129

labial secretions, 141–43
lactation, costs of, 17
learning
cortisol and, 152
estrogen and, 115
hippocampal shrinkage and, 160–61
lemurs, 84, 141–43
lesbians, 11, 53
levonorgestrel (LNG), 79, 93–97,
176–77, 184
LH. *See* luteinizing hormone
life history theory, 106n–7n
liver, 13, 158
LNG. *See* levonorgestrel
long-term partner, 61
low commitment, 139–40
low fertility
appearance and, 55
desirability at, 66–67
desire at, 60
political views at, 227
scents at, 67–69
low sexual desire
in men, 124n
on the pill, 125

low sexual desire *(cont.)*

   relationship challenges and, 124, 124*n*–25*n*

   sexual lockdown and, 123

luteal (implantation) phase, 50, 91, 102, 112–13, 189

luteinizing hormone (LH), 76–78

major histocompatibility complex (MHC), 101*n*–2*n*

male cell lines, 8, 8*n*, 223*n*

mammals, 27

marital satisfaction, 55, 59, 109–10, 120

markers for good genes, 57–64, 101, 111–12. *See also* traits

marriage, 107–8, 207–9

masculinity

   facial, 58–60, 102–4

   preference for, 57–61

   scent of, 58, 112–13

   traits of, 58–60

masculinizing effects of progestin, 84

mate guarding, 139–40, 140*n*

mate selection. *See* partner selection

mating effort, 129–30, 138–39

mating market, 208

The Mating Mind (Miller), 127*n*

meaning, HPS-axis activity and, 165–66

medroxyprogesterone acetate (MPA), 93, 141, 143

memory

   cortisol and, 152

   estrogen and, 115

   forming long-term, 182

   hippocampal shrinkage and, 160–61

   HPA-axis activity and, 165–66

   pill taking and, 162–63

   stress and, 152, 160–62, 165–66, 182

men

   achievement gap and, 196–201

   adaptive challenges of, 24

   anabolic steroids and, 233

   attractiveness of, 101–2, 110

   evolutionary win for, 124–25

   low investment in reproduction of, 16

   with masculine faces, 58–60, 102–4

   mating psychology of, 17–19

   as motivation for women, 201–2

   motivations of, 231

   parenting psychology of, 22–23

   paternity uncertainty and, 21–22

   as research subjects, 218–19

   scent of, 58, 112–13

   sexual novelty and, 208

   sexual opportunism of, 18–21

   sexy, 57–63, 102, 107*n*

   testosterone and, 42–44

   women's scents and, 67–69

menstrual cycle. *See* ovulatory cycle

menstrual period. *See* period

menstruation

   costs of, 27–28, 28*n*

   initiation of, 31–32

MHC. *See* major histocompatibility complex

mid-cycle, 101–2, 137. *See also* cycle phases

Miller, Geoffrey, 65–67, 127*n*

mineralocorticoid receptor, 187, 187*n*

miscarriages, 211–12

monkeys, pill-taking, 138–39

Traister, Rebecca, 209

traits

    favoring reproduction, 15–16, 55*n*, 114

    of high genetic quality, 111–12, 116, 129

    inheriting, 24–25

    masculine, 58–60

    of women, 17

    See also markers for good genes

Trier Social Stress Test (TSST), 146, 153–54

triglycerides, 152*n*, 161–62

TSST. *See* Trier Social Stress Test

vagina, 55*n*

vaginal ring, 88, 177–78

vaginal secretions, 68

vigilance, cortisol and, 152

visual acuity, 116, 116*n*

visual stimulus, 125–26

Vohs, Kathleen, 206, 206*n*

voices of fertile women, 67

vulva, 68, 68*n*

weight gain, 91–92, 161

Why Zebras Don't Get Ulcers (Sapolsky), 152*n*

women

    achievement gap and, 196–201

    appearance-enhancement of, 55–56, 128

    atractiveness of, 127–28, 137–41

    autoimmune diseases and, 166–67

    biology of, 9–10, 25–26, 33–36

    dual-mating strategy and, 63–64

    feminism and, 25–26, 44–48

    gap in knowledge about, 214–16

    heterosexual cisgender, 11

    as "hormonal," 48, 226

    hysteria in, 226

    investment in children of, 21

    as irrational, 226

    lesbian women, 11, 53

    mating psychology of, 11, 17–21, 63

    motivating men, 201–2, 202*n*

    opportunities for reproduction of, 18

    ovulating women, 64

    parenting psychology of, 22–23

    prescription drugs and, 215

    psychology of, 24, 227–28

    remaining single, 209

    research studies and, 8–9, 214–26

    sexual risk-taking in, 23, 23*n*

    suicide and, 179–81

    young women, 188

    See also naturally cycling women; pill-taking women

women's rights, 228–29

Y chromosome, 237